One America in the 21st Century

One America
in the 21st Century

The Report of President Bill Clinton's Initiative on Race

Edited and with an Introduction by Steven F. Lawson

Foreword by John Hope Franklin

YALE UNIVERSITY PRESS • NEW HAVEN AND LONDON

Printed in the United States of America by Victor Graphics, Inc., Baltimore, Maryland.

Library of Congress Control Number: 2008927902
ISBN-13: 978-0-300-11669-4
ISBN-10: 0-300-11669-1

A catalogue record for this book is available from the British Library.

This paper meets the requirements of ANSI/NISO Z39.48-1992
(Permanence of Paper).

10 9 8 7 6 5 4 3 2 1

To Virginia Foster Durr and Robert W. Saunders,
who fought for racial justice in the twentieth century
and helped shape my conceptions
of the civil rights movement

CONTENTS

FOREWORD

John Hope Franklin

When President Clinton invited me in 1997 to chair a commission to study the problem of race in America, to conduct a dialogue on race, and to make recommendations for next steps, I accepted the challenge with pleasure. Surely the American people could talk about one of the country's oldest problems with the maturity and objectivity that it deserved. For a year and a half the seven members of the board—three women and four men, including three whites, two African Americans, one Asian American, and one Mexican American—joined in the effort to carry out the president's mandate. We would not have much time to prepare for what lay ahead. The first salvo—two days after the announcement of the board's creation—came in the form of an attack by Republican House Speaker Newt Gingrich and anti–affirmative action activist Ward Connerly in the *New York Times,* insisting that we were not qualified, and that, in any case, no such study as the president proposed was necessary. We had not met officially and would not meet for another month. Thus, even before we met we knew that our task would be a formidable one.

After the president informed the press of the creation of the advisory board, we joined him on Air Force One and flew to the West Coast, where he would announce our appointment the following day in a commencement address at the University of California at San Diego. In his address to the graduating class and the overflow crowd he spoke of the present and future as truly "the golden moment for America. . . . Our economy is the healthiest in a generation and the strongest in the world. Our culture, our science, our technology promise unimagined advances and exciting new careers. Our social problems, from crime to poverty, are finally bending to our efforts." But the problem of race persists, the president concluded sadly. "Now is the time we should learn together, talk together, and act together to build one America. . . . To succeed we must deal with the realities and perceptions affecting all racial groups in America. . . . Over the coming year I want to lead the American people in a great and unprecedented conversation about race." For a while the president did just that, traveling across the country as we held monthly meetings, town hall meetings, and the like. In Washington, he and Vice President Gore accepted our invitation to attend a regular public meeting. When the president did attend such meetings and participate in the discussion, the press incorrectly reported that he did so to put his advisory board back on track because it was floundering excessively and obviously needed guidance.

Opposition to the advisory board mounted, with several newspapers and other media outlets accusing it of bias. Such accusations were not only inac-

curate but patently unfair. I had hoped that President Clinton would address
the matter, since anything I would say would be regarded as self-serving. Not
only did the president remain silent, but, almost a decade later, in his own au-
tobiography of almost a thousand pages, the discussion of the President's Advisory Board on Race is confined to a statement that he appointed such a
board. There is not one word regarding the work of the board or of the national atmosphere of disdain or the adverse criticism under which it labored
throughout its life. Some defend the president by saying that he was preoccupied with many matters, and that assertion is undoubtedly true—a principal
reason why I attempted to conduct the work of the board without calling on
him each time we confronted a problem.

Some even claim that the Monica Lewinsky affair so preoccupied the attention of the president that he had little time for the affairs of state. I do not
share that conclusion. I was with the president numerous times while the
general public was completely absorbed with the scandal, but the president
seemed as composed as usual and unimpressed with matters with which the
general public was preoccupied. Perhaps he could have attempted to cover up
the mistakes he had made by diverting attention to his preoccupation with
the problem of race in America. If so, his inattention to the President's Advisory Board and his greater focus on other affairs of state seem to indicate
quite clearly what his priorities were. Few things could have given him a favorable place in history as achieving a significant contribution to the solution
of the problem of race in America.

The current campaign for the 2008 presidency is also instructive. The former
president's frenetic efforts to secure the presidency for the former first lady
have driven him to engage in activities that tend to dislodge him from his position as "the first Black president," a title some admirers had bestowed on
him. Because he has raised the race issue more than once in his wife's campaign against Senator Barack Obama for the Democratic presidential nomination, one is inclined to remark on the dissimilarity between his remarks in
1997 and 1998 and those of 2007 and 2008.

The report that the President's Advisory Board issued a decade ago is more
relevant today than it was then. Senator Obama's Philadelphia speech on race
in March 2008 was remarkable and path-breaking because it dealt with race in
a forceful, straightforward, insightful way. It is a clear example of how race
can be dealt with. It is a model that we can all emulate if we care to join in a
sincere effort to make race a powerful force for improvement, instead of allowing it to be a factor of reaction and resistance to change.

Preface

The documents that follow provide for the first time in published form the advisory board report of President Bill Clinton's initiative on race: "One America in the 21st Century: Forging a New Future." In addition to the text of the report, this volume includes selections from the report's appendix as well as President's Clinton's speech that launched the initiative on June 14, 1997, in San Diego. The work of the president's advisory board, headed by the distinguished historian John Hope Franklin, revealed that moving into the twenty-first century the United States faced many of the same racial problems from the past. However, the panel made it very clear that the racial composition of the country was rapidly changing and bringing a fresh set of challenges. Americans can no longer look at race simply in terms of black and white. As predicted in the report and confirmed a decade later, African Americans no longer constitute the nation's leading racial minority; Hispanic Americans have replaced them in that position. Although, as explained in the editor's introduction to the report, for various reasons the findings and recommendations of the report were virtually ignored at the time, they still have much relevance today.

Students, politicians, policymakers, and concerned citizens will benefit from reading this clearly written and amply documented report. To make it more valuable for classroom use, the report is accompanied by a timeline of events, placing the formation of the presidential advisory body in its historical context. Also, this edition includes explanatory notes from the editor to put the report in context, followed by a series of questions to stimulate further discussion about the work of the commission and the issues raised in the report. This volume, then, helps fulfill one of the key recommendations of the report calling for a continued dialogue about race.

In preparing this volume for publication I want to thank Chris Rogers, the Executive Editor of History and Current Events at Yale University Press, for suggesting the project and then seeing it through despite some unexpected complications. My students at Rutgers University, Sara Rzeszutek and Cheryl Citera, provided valuable research assistance.

Introduction

One America in the 21st Century: The Report of President Bill Clinton's Initiative on Race

In 1903, when the African-American scholar-activist W. E. B. DuBois wrote that "the color line" would be the predominant issue of the twentieth century, he had no way of knowing that race would continue to vex American society into the next century.[1] Four hundred years of, first, slavery, and then Jim Crow ensured that racial inequalities remained embedded in political, economic, social, and cultural institutions even after the successes of the civil rights movement in the 1960s. Despite triumphs in Congress and the courts, which extended principles of democracy and equality long ago promised in the Constitution, for a large portion of African Americans still trapped in poverty, legal equality proved inadequate without the economic means to secure a good education, get a well-paying job, afford comfortable housing, acquire adequate health care, and obtain fair treatment within the criminal justice system.

These shortcomings should come as no surprise. National commissions conducted detailed examinations of the obstacles to racial egalitarianism in the 1940s, 1960s, and 1990s. In each case, U.S. presidents who came under pressure to find solutions to racial discrimination set up fact-finding committees to offer recommendations. Presidents Harry S. Truman, Lyndon B. Johnson, and William Jefferson Clinton followed this strategy, which might accomplish one of two things. First, the president could build an agenda and rally public opinion behind it. Or, in a different vein, the chief executive might use the commission for cover to buy time and delay action until either the issue passed or he had the political capital to move ahead. In either circumstance, presidents staffed commissions with members inclined to produce moderate proposals and take the heat off of the White House while the group deliberated and reached consensus. Each attempt at presidential intervention reflected the strength or weakness of the civil rights movement. For Truman and Johnson the establishment of a presidential commission stimulated demands for reform; in Clinton's case the committee's work fizzled in the absence of strong institutional pressure from within and concerted pressure from outside the government for racial equality.

President Truman's Committee on Civil Rights

Harry S. Truman's Committee on Civil Rights, formed in 1946, provides the classic example of a presidential initiative on race. The committee emerged out of the historical context of World War II and the Cold War. In fighting Hitler's brand of Aryan white supremacy abroad, the United States provided African Americans with ideological ammunition to challenge white supremacy at home. Many black veterans who fought in the racially segregated military returned to the South expecting to reclaim their political rights and open doors to equal opportunity. By the late 1940s, when the United States had replaced Nazi Fascism with Soviet Communism as the chief enemy of the "free world," African Americans possessed additional leverage to press their demands for first-class citizenship. In propaganda battles with the Soviets on the international stage, the United States could ill afford to mouth democratic principles against Communist tyranny while blacks faced persecution in the South. Furthermore, World War II prompted an exodus of tens of thousands of blacks to the North in search of jobs and freedom. Although their aspirations generally went unfulfilled, Southern migrants gained access to the ballot for the first time. A significant voting bloc in states rich in presidential electoral votes, African Americans wielded critical influence in hotly contested campaigns for the White House.

Before becoming president following the sudden death of Franklin D. Roosevelt in April 1945, Truman had a reputation as a moderate on racial issues. A former senator from Missouri, he carefully balanced the interests of his black constituents from Kansas City with those of white residents in the state whose forebears had fought on the Confederate side in the Civil War. By the time he left the Oval Office in 1953, however, Truman had established himself as the chief executive most identified with civil rights.

Truman's appointment of the President's Committee on Civil Rights on December 5, 1946, launched the Second Reconstruction—the federal government's postwar effort to advance racial equality. The president summoned the committee to recommend "with respect to the adoption or establishment by legislation or otherwise of more adequate and effective means and procedures for the protection of the civil rights of the people of the United States."[2]

Both moral and political concerns motivated Truman. Earlier in the year the South had witnessed a white reign of terror against African Americans. New opportunities provided by the war for African Americans, along with the return of black veterans, made many whites in the South anxious about their ability to maintain political, social, and economic control. In February 1946, a white mob rampaged through the black section of Columbia, Tennessee, looting businesses, and attacking residents, killing two. That summer, whites in Georgia killed a newly enfranchised black voter, and near the town of Monroe two back men and their wives also were murdered. Perhaps most shocking of all, a recently discharged black soldier, Isaac Woodard, traveling by bus through South Carolina on his way home to New York City, was assaulted and had his eyes gouged out by a local police officer. Riding the momentum of World War II's democratic pronouncements, black leaders met with Truman in September 1946 to press their case for federal action to curb racial violence. Hearing their account of Woodard's suffering, a shocked Truman exclaimed: "My God! I had no idea that it was as terrible as that! We've got to do something!"[3]

The president carefully chose an outstanding group to investigate mob violence in particular and civil rights in general. Included in the fifteen-member, blue-ribbon panel were two African Americans: Sadie T. Alexander, a lawyer, and Channing H. Tobias, director of a major philanthropic foundation. Consisting of labor, religious, educational, and business leaders, the committee contained individuals from both the North and the South. Perhaps to show that his concern for racial justice was genuine, and to appeal to moderate white Southerners, Truman selected Frank Porter Graham, president of the University of North Carolina, and Dorothy Tilly of Georgia, a Methodist Church official, both of whom had liberal credentials. To head the group Truman chose Charles E. Wilson, the president of General Electric, a progressive businessman who would bring enormous legitimacy to the work of the committee.

On October 29, 1947, the panel submitted its report, *To Secure These Rights*, to the president. The 178-page document consisted of four sections. The first part examined the background of America's commitment to equal opportunity and basic rights of citizenship. The second surveyed the condition of civil rights in the nation and noted the gap between promises and reality. The third outlined the federal government's obligations to enforce the rights of citizens in light of state and local officials' unwillingness or inability to do so. Finally, the report contained recommendations aimed at strengthening the machinery of government to protect civil rights and extend the right to vote, furnishing the blueprint for civil rights in the following two decades. Setting the agenda for the future, *To Secure These Rights* called for "the elimination of segregation, based on race, color, creed, or national origin, from American life."[4]

Although Truman initially praised the work of his committee and crafted legislation based on its suggestions, he soon retreated. However reasonable the president may have considered the group's findings, the white South felt otherwise. Newspapers in the region joined politicians in denouncing the fruits of the committee's labor. In 1948, when Truman insisted on proposing civil rights legislation, the Senate, with Southern Democrats in the lead, easily defeated it. Concerned that white Southern Democrats would defect from the party in opposition to his civil rights offensive, thereby placing his chances for election in 1948 in jeopardy, Truman backed away from his progressive racial program.

At the same time, he still had to contend with powerful forces on his political left. The popular New Dealer Henry A. Wallace decided to run for president on the Progressive Party ticket and adopted a platform that embraced racial equality and an end to segregation, threatening to take away black support from the Democrats. Moreover, A. Philip Randolph, the African-American labor leader and civil rights activist, mounted a campaign to push the commander-in-chief to desegregate the military. Under pressure at the 1948 Democratic National Convention from liberal Democrats led by Hubert H. Humphrey of Minnesota, Truman embraced a stronger civil rights platform than he originally favored, based on the recommendations in *To Secure These Rights.* He also issued an executive order to integrate the armed forces after a number of Southern delegates to the Democratic nominating convention walked out and backed the independent presidential candidacy of segregationist Governor Strom Thurmond of South Carolina on the States' Rights (Dixiecrat) Party. Running on the recommendations inspired by his civil rights panel, Truman narrowly won the presidential election against the Republican Thomas E. Dewey, Wallace, and Thurmond. He clinched his victory by receiving critical votes from African Americans in key Northern States.[5]

In ways no one could have predicted at the time, *To Secure These Rights* became one of the most important milestones in the history of the modern civil rights movement. It established the civil rights legislative agenda for decades to come. The report created a benchmark with which both the federal government and civil rights groups could measure progress toward racial equality. Furthermore, the report set the precedent for strong federal action, which civil rights groups used to prod Washington to fulfill its historic and legal obligations to secure equality for all citizens.

PRESIDENT JOHNSON'S WHITE HOUSE CONFERENCE ON CIVIL RIGHTS

No politician at the national level did more than Lyndon B. Johnson (LBJ) to fulfill the civil rights agenda, including the recommendations of the Truman Committee. Yet he had not come swiftly to this position. As a Democratic congressman and senator from Texas, Johnson toed the segregationist line. At the same time, as leader of the Democratic Party in the Senate during the 1950s, he sought to unite its liberal and conservative factions around measures that would appeal to Northern blacks without offending Southern whites. In 1957 and again in 1960, Senator Johnson proved instrumental in steering passage of civil rights bills through Congress. These bills dealt mainly with voting rights, improving federal enforcement by the Department of Justice, and creating the U.S. Commission on Civil Rights.[6] He believed that the extension of first-class citizenship would free not only African Americans but also the entire South from racially imposed burdens of poverty and backwardness. Further, it would liberate Johnson as well to run for the White House less encumbered by the stigma of his Dixie origins. As vice president, Johnson's commitment to racial equality grew. He chaired President Kennedy's Committee on Equal Employment Opportunity and spoke out forcefully against racial discrimination. After LBJ assumed the presidency following Kennedy's assassination on November 22, 1963, he came into his own over the next five years as he signed into law three monumental civil rights acts combating racial segregation and discrimination in public accommodations, education, voting, and housing.

In these same years the civil rights movement in the South gained momentum as organizations and strategies multiplied. During the 1960s, the Southern Christian Leadership Conference (SCLC), an outgrowth of the 1955–56 Montgomery bus boycott and headed by Dr. Martin Luther King, Jr., and the Student Nonviolent Coordinating Committee (SNCC), which emerged from the sit-ins in 1960, had joined older organizations such as the National Association for the Advancement of Colored People (NAACP), the Urban League, and the Congress of Racial Equality (CORE) in waging the black freedom struggle. While the NAACP and Urban League focused on litigation and legislative lobbying to pursue their ends, the SCLC, SNCC, and CORE practiced more militant and disruptive, nonviolent, direct action protests that challenged white supremacy. Nonviolence may have been the official creed of the movement, but many Southern blacks kept firearms in their home for protection against white vigilantes, and others, such as Robert F. Williams of North Carolina, advocated armed self-defense as a means for both security and the assertion of black empowerment.[7]

Under these circumstances President Johnson could not control the direction of the black freedom movement. His vast accomplishments did not deter the growth of African-American militancy and the challenge it posed for mainstream civil rights leaders and the White House. Riots in black ghettos of Northern cities began in the summer of 1964 and spread westward to the Watts section of Los Angeles a week after Johnson signed the Voting Rights Act in August 1965. Urban violence shattered the political consensus on racial equality the president had forged.

Legislation alone did not furnish sufficient shelter from these swirling racial storms. Johnson still retained support from the NAACP, moderate black leaders, and the majority of African Americans, but this growing militancy and shifting direction of the civil rights movement ignited a white political backlash that threatened Johnson's Democratic Party. Seeking ways to cool off tensions, in mid-1965 the chief executive called for a White House Conference on Civil Rights rather than a Truman-style committee. Plans for the meeting quickly ran into trouble. A suggestion for scheduling discussion of the African-American family triggered angry dissent that nearly terminated the gathering before it began. Black leaders expressed considerable discomfort with a report written in 1964 by Assistant Secretary of Labor Daniel Patrick Moynihan that highlighted the "pathology of the Negro family" in retarding black economic progress. They feared that white opponents would interpret this as meaning that blacks caused their own impoverishment. The White House heeded their concern and dropped the contentious topic from the program.[8]

Apprehensive over the furor this issue produced, and upset over growing black militancy, Johnson pushed the conference back into a more moderate course. Seeking to delay the full gathering, the White House conducted a preliminary meeting of some two hundred participants on November 1–2, 1965, to hammer out an agenda for the subsequent convocation. From this meeting came the appointment of a blue-ribbon panel, which over the next six months prepared a program that included sessions on economic security and welfare, education, housing, and the administration of justice. LBJ took the extra precaution of selecting as conference chairman Ben Heineman, the head of the Chicago and North Western Railway, a white businessman whom he considered reliable on race issues.

The White House Conference finally took place on June 1–2, 1966. Planners tried to head off trouble by inviting more than 2,500 participants, a group representing broad segments of the black community, government officials, and business, civic, and religious leaders. A gathering of this size and scope made it impossible for more militant organizations to take charge and control the outcome. Also, Heineman's planning council had prepared recommendations in advance, which served as the basis for discussion. Although SNCC boycotted the meeting, representatives of other major civil rights groups, including the NAACP, the SCLC, and CORE, attended. Attempts by CORE to gain support for resolutions against the administration's escalation of the Vietnam War went down easily to defeat. The final report of the conference, "To Fulfill These Rights," recommended measures to remedy economic, social, and legal problems relating to racial discrimination through a combination of governmental and private action.[9]

The conference only temporarily defused the combustible racial situation. A Johnson adviser summed up the administration's thinking: "[The] White

House Conference, while sitting on a number of kegs of dynamite constantly was a strong plus and the press image that came out from this was most favorable."[10] Still, the administration did little to rally the nation behind a new offensive to deal with unresolved issues of racial inequality, especially if it involved massive government spending. Johnson supported legislation to protect civil rights workers in the South and curb housing discrimination everywhere it existed, but, increasingly preoccupied with the war in Vietnam, he did not move with any urgency.

The president soon faced new difficulties. A few days after the conference ended, James Meredith, whose admission in 1962 as the first African American to attend the University of Mississippi had spawned a riot and federal occupation of the campus, launched a "March Against Fear" from Memphis, Tennessee, to Jackson, Mississippi. Before he could get very far on his journey, on June 4, 1966, a would-be assassin shot him, leaving him wounded but alive. While Meredith recovered, Dr. King, together with leaders of SNCC and CORE, continued the march. By the time the pilgrimage came to an end several weeks later, SNCC staffers and their followers along the way were chanting "Black Power," in contrast to King and the SCLC's more mellow call for "Freedom Now." The Black Power battle cry, however, echoed more favorably than King's catchphrase among young and disaffected blacks throughout the nation, continuing to perplex the White House as to what to do.[11]

The rising popularity of Black Power, which rejected nonviolence and integration, drove a wedge within the civil rights coalition and distanced SNCC and CORE further from the president. Although Dr. King, the movement's most well-known leader, rejected the Black Power slogan, his escalating criticism of the war in Vietnam as a racist conflict also made him an outsider from the White House and he drew fire from Johnson's supporters in the NAACP.[12] Moreover, in October 1966 the Black Panther Party for Self Defense formed in Oakland, California, and stirred the racial cauldron further by taking up arms to safeguard blacks from police brutality and condemning the capitalist system for perpetuating racism and poverty.[13]

THE NATIONAL ADVISORY COMMISSION ON CIVIL DISORDERS

In 1966 and 1967, shouts of Black Power resonated in a new round of summer racial rebellions in cities across the country, ranging from Cleveland and Rochester (New York) to Cambridge (Maryland), Tampa, and San Francisco. In 1967 the two most destructive riots to date occurred in Detroit, Michigan, and Newark, New Jersey. In Detroit forty-three people died, two thousand suffered injuries, and five thousand lost their homes, while in Newark twenty-four perished and property damage totaled over $10 million.[14] With smoke still hanging over burned-out neighborhoods in black ghettos, on July 27, 1967, Johnson appointed the National Advisory Commission on Civil Disorders to investigate the causes of the uprisings and recommend measures to deter future riots. "The only genuine, long-range solution," the president declared, "for what has happened lies in an attack—mounted at every level— upon the conditions that breed despair and violence. All of us know what those conditions are: ignorance, discrimination, slums, poverty, disease, not enough jobs."[15]

This powerful rhetoric notwithstanding, the chief executive sought to deal with the issue by choosing another moderate, bipartisan, biracial committee. Chaired by Democratic governor Otto Kerner of Illinois, and with Republican mayor John V. Lindsay of New York City as vice-chair, the group consisted of eleven members. Johnson appointed two prominent African Americans, Republican senator Edward Brooke of Massachusetts and Roy Wilkins of the NAACP.[16] However, these two selections did not represent growing militancy among residents of the inner cities or the thinking of the most radical Black Power groups. After visiting Harlem, one of Johnson's aides recognized this dilemma and reported to the president that Brooke and Wilkins were considered "office leaders—they have no following on the streets; they neither understand nor are understood by people on the streets."[17] Still, the panel pushed ahead. The Kerner Commission held hearings at which over 130 witnesses testified. Despite the agency's moderate orientation, it did not exclude black radical leaders such as Stokely Carmichael of SNCC, but it balanced his appearance with that of such newly elected black officials as Mayor Carl Stokes of Cleveland, the kind of Black Power representation that Johnson preferred.

On February 29, 1968, the commission delivered its report. The document, at over five hundred pages, sketched the communities experiencing racial disorders, assessed the causes of the violence, and offered remedies. The report laid blame for the urban explosions primarily on white racism. "Our nation is moving toward two societies, one black, one white—separate and unequal," the committee concluded. Despite its moderate membership, the commission bluntly held whites responsible for impoverished ghettos, because "[w]hite institutions created it, white institutions maintain it, and white society condones it."[18] The commissioners supported traditional remedies contained in recently passed civil rights legislation, but they differed over whether to endorse proposals that moved beyond formal legal protection of civil rights to ensuring economic and social equality. Nevertheless, putting disagreements aside, the committee urged government spending of $30 billion to improve education, create jobs, standardize welfare payments across the nation, and build public housing. It also supported enactment of a controversial fair housing law, then pending in Congress, which many white Northerners opposed as the civil rights movement moved closer to their neighborhoods.

Johnson largely ignored the Kerner Commission recommendations. The escalating cost of the Vietnam War and Johnson's unwillingness to raise taxes sufficiently to support it meant that he had no interest in spending the kind of money proposed by the advisory body. The war and the protests that it generated had taken its toll on the chief executive personally and politically, and by the end of March 1968 he announced his intention not to seek reelection.[19] Johnson remained miffed because he considered his most enduring legacy to be achievements in civil rights and fighting the War on Poverty, and he resented the commission's report for insufficiently crediting him. The embattled president, increasingly isolated form former allies, privately believed that the riots resulted from a conspiracy of black agitators and communists. These considerations guaranteed that expensive proposals for national action remained unfulfilled, though Congress did pass the Civil Rights Act of 1968 with its controversial fair housing provision. In a further setback, rioting erupted with even greater vengeance in the aftermath of the assassination of Martin Luther King, Jr., in April 1968. The presidential election that same year of Republican Richard M. Nixon on a tough-minded platform of law and order further dimmed prospects for action on the commission's suggestions.

PRESIDENT CLINTON'S INITIATIVE ON RACE

African Americans did make significant advancements over the next two and a half decades. The civil rights coalition that had won landmark legislation, Supreme Court victories, and presidential backing fractured as the 1960s ended, but its triumphs had sunk roots deeply into the political soil. The civil rights movement inspired pride and encouraged standards of political participation in men and women that subsequently carried over to the electoral arena. From 1975 to 1993 the number of black elected officials in the United States leaped form around 3,500 to just over 8,000. In a remarkable turnabout, Mississippi, the state that had the lowest number of black adults registered to vote in 1965, recorded the highest number of black elected officials (897) of any state in the country by the year 2000. Nationwide, black male officeholders outnumbered females by more than double (5,683 to 2,332), but black women made greater percentage gains than did men (9.9 percent to 4.6 percent) during this eighteen-year period. In 1992, Carol Mosely Braun, a Democrat from Illinois, became the first black woman elected to the U.S. Senate. At the same time, the number of black women in Congress stood at ten, a gain of six, and they joined thirty black men in the national legislature. In addition, black mayors governed cities such as New York, Detroit, Birmingham, New Orleans, and Atlanta. And, from 1990 to 1994 L. Douglas Wilder of Virginia held the distinction of serving as the nation's only black governor.[20]

Economically, the situation for African Americans proved less promising. The Kerner Commission had spotlighted two separate and unequal societies in the United States divided by race, but many African Americans had made sufficient economic progress as a result of antidiscrimination laws and affirmative action to expand the size of the black middle class. In effect, two black societies also emerged: middle class and wealthy African Americans increasingly distanced themselves economically from the growing number of poor. Overall, however, racial distinctions prevailed. In 1992, the median annual income for blacks was $21,161, compared with $38,909 for whites. To make matters worse, the percentage of black to white median income had dropped steadily, from 61.5 in 1975 to 54.4 in 1992. By the end of the 1990s, approximately 24 percent of African Americans lived in poverty, nearly double the national rate of 12.7 percent and compared with only 8 percent of non-Hispanic whites.[21]

African Americans also lagged behind educationally. In 1999 almost twice as many whites received a bachelor's degree as did blacks, 28 to 15 percent of the total number receiving degrees. Among blacks, more women than men earned at least a bachelor's degree—16 percent as opposed to 14 percent. For whites, this was reversed—more men received at least a bachelor's degree (31 percent) than women (25 percent). The figures for African-American men reflected a tragic reality particularly for youth and young adults. African Americans were six times more likely to go to prison during their lifetime than whites and could expect to serve longer sentences for the same offenses. More than 28 percent of African-American men were expected to be incarcerated over their lifetime, while white males had only a 4 percent chance of imprisonment. In 1996, African Americans represented 30 percent of all convicted federal offenders despite the fact that they made up only 13 percent of the population. In the decade between 1985 and 1995 the percentage of African Americans under correctional supervision increased 81 percent.[22]

Within this context William Jefferson Clinton came to the White House in 1993 for his first of two terms as president. The former governor of Arkansas, Clinton had entered politics in the post–civil rights era. For him the battle cry of white supremacy, which had vaulted his state into the national limelight during the 1950s for its defense of school segregation in Little Rock, had become a discarded legacy of an unwelcome past. Eleven years old at the time of

Little Rock, Clinton had developed an awareness of racial inequality that was rare among Southern whites. He was "bothered" that his high school in Hot Springs remained segregated following the Little Rock crisis. During this period, he often lived with his grandparents and worked at his grandfather's grocery store, where Clinton saw him dealing fairly with black and white customers alike. At the age of sixteen, Clinton attended an American Legion Boys Nation retreat and worked to include civil rights in his party's platform. During a summer break from attending Yale Law School in 1969, the saxophone-playing Clinton visited Hot Springs and formed an interracial band to help ease racial tensions. When Clinton began his political career as attorney general of Arkansas in 1975, he hired more African Americans and female attorneys than ever before. Elected governor three years later, he continued to appoint women and minorities to his Cabinet and to state boards. In a significant moment of symbolism, in 1987 Clinton invited the Little Rock Nine to a reception at the governor's mansion to commemorate the thirtieth anniversary of their heroic challenge to segregation.[23]

Black voters responded positively to this record and helped elect Clinton president in 1992 by casting 80 percent of their ballots for him, thereby providing the margin of victory he needed in key electoral states. As president, Clinton expressed his gratitude by appointing four African Americans to sit in his Cabinet at the same time, an historic first. He worked closely with the forty-member Congressional Black Caucus (CBC) and won its approval by invading Haiti in 1994 to force the replacement of the oppressive government with a democratic regime. He also scored points by enacting legislation expanding opportunities for voter registration at motor vehicle offices, which made it more convenient for minorities and the poor to sign up to vote.

However, Clinton made a major misstep, affecting his relations with African Americans. His nomination in 1993 and subsequent withdrawal of Lani Guinier as assistant attorney general for civil rights topped the list in his first term. A law school professor and expert on voting rights, Guinier had litigated and won cases challenging suffrage measures that diluted the power of black ballots, such as at-large elections. Based on her experience, she had increasingly come to the conclusion that black elected officials alone, destined by demographic considerations to remain limited in numbers, could not advance black fortunes much further. Guinier suggested alternative election methods and legislative procedures that remove the "winner-take-all" effect of American politics. Conservative opponents branded her a "quota queen," referring to affirmative action, which they opposed, and denouncing what they interpreted as her "race-conscious" ideas. They distorted Guinier's proposals, which were designed to create interracial coalitions of like-minded interests and not separate blacks from whites. Whatever the reality, legislative opposition mounted, and, instead of giving Guinier a full hearing, Clinton decided to scuttle her nomination, which incurred criticism from the CBC and civil rights groups.[24]

A centrist Democrat, the president also departed from traditional liberal principles. Clinton supported an omnibus crime measure (the Violent Crime Control and Law Enforcement Act of 1994), usually the trademark of Republican politicians, which provided both progressive and draconian provisions: funds for community policing, a ban on the sale of assault weapons, expansion of the death penalty for federal criminal offenses, and grants to states for prisons. The president also succeeded in reducing the federal deficit and signed into law a "welfare reform measure" (Personal Responsibility and Work Opportunity Act of 1996) calculated to move recipients off public rolls and into jobs within a prescribed five-year period, while cutting funds for food stamps and emergency medical programs. Many liberals predicted that these policies would produce dire consequences for the black poor, but Clinton's management of the economy fueled prosperity and forestalled some of his critics' worst expectations.[25]

Still, the president retained the overwhelming support of African-American politicians and their constituents. His reelection in 1996 garnered 84 percent of the black electorate, a 4 percent increase from 1992 and a figure vastly higher than any other group in his winning coalition.[26] Later, when Clinton ran into difficulty over his extramarital affair with a young White House intern, Monica Lewinsky, and when his sworn testimony to a special prosecutor investigating this and other accusations against him resulted in his impeachment by the House of Representatives, African Americans stood by him steadfastly.[27] No matter the charges against him and whatever personal and legal transgressions he committed, blacks identified with Clinton as a victim of injustice, accepted him as a reconstructed, white Southerner, and embraced him in the spirit of Christian redemption. The African-American writer Toni Morrison proclaimed Clinton the "first black president," acknowledging the rapport he had established with African Americans.[28]

Much of Clinton's troubles resulted from the Republican takeover of Congress beginning in 1994. Gaining control of the House and Senate for the first time since 1953, the GOP called for a balanced budget and pledged to roll back government welfare and affirmative action programs, measures closely identified with African Americans. GOP leaders also succeeded in tying down Clinton in legal troubles for much of the last three years of his presidency.

As the nation moved through the final decade of the twentieth century, racial friction, never wiped out entirely by the civil rights movement, magnified in intensity. The 1992 riot in south central Los Angeles—following the acquittal of policemen whose beating of Rodney King had been videotaped by a by-stander—harked back three decades to the racial explosions shattering the urban landscape in the 1960s. The acquittal of ex-football star O. J. Simpson in 1995 by a predominantly black jury for murdering his white wife and her friend exposed a wide gap between whites and blacks in their perception of whether justice was carried out. At the same time, the holding of the Million Man March in Washington, D.C., organized by the controversial Black Nationalist organization the Nation of Islam, expressed growing discontent among African Americans with the unwillingness of whites to grapple with racial bias in employment, education, housing, and criminal justice. Furthermore, illegal immigration from Mexico and Central America heightened antagonism not only from whites but also from blacks who believed their chances of employment were threatened and their access to educational and social services systems handicapped by the influx of tens of thousands of impoverished foreigners.

Disputes over affirmative action programs sharpened these tensions. Designed at the tail end of the civil rights movement in the late 1960s to remedy the effects of past racial and sexual discrimination, affirmative action drove a political wedge between whites and blacks. African Americans largely endorsed these programs for creating a level playing field to provide equal access to economic and political opportunities. In contrast, a growing number of whites, some of whom had supported the civil rights movement in its goal of a color-blind society, rejected the notion that blacks as a group should be granted preferential treatment in employment, university admissions, or electoral competition. A 1995 national survey undertaken by the *Washington Post* and ABC News underscored the deep racial divide concerning opinions on affirmative action. The poll found Americans sharply split over whether affirmative action hurt white males. Half of those interviewed—51 percent—said white men had been adversely affected by preference programs, while 46 percent disagreed. These views differed greatly by race. Fifty-seven percent of all whites interviewed and 63 percent of all white males thought affirmative action had hurt white men, a view shared by just 19 percent of all blacks.[29]

The Supreme Court fanned the flames of racial passions as it increasingly upheld the complaints of disgruntled whites and reversed the gains minorities and women had made. Throughout the 1970s and up to the mid-1980s, the justices had generally espoused an expansive interpretation of affirmative action. However, the conservative administrations of Ronald Reagan and George H. W. Bush changed the shape of the lower federal courts and the Supreme Court through the appointment of judges who gradually narrowed the scope of affirmative action.[30]

Against this backdrop of increased racial stress, President Clinton resurrected an approach from the earlier civil rights era. Furthermore, with Congress controlled by Republicans and so any legislative initiative to promote black advancement found itself on the back burner, Clinton relied on his executive power to create a committee to promote racial reform. On June 13, 1997, he appointed a distinguished, seven-member national commission to advise him "on matters involving race and racial reconciliation [and to] promote a constructive national dialogue to confront and work through challenging issues that surround race." Clinton also authorized the council to "[i]dentify, develop, and implement solutions to problems in areas in which race has a substantial impact, such as education, economic opportunity, housing, health care, and the administration of justice."[31] The next day, June 14, in a commencement address at the University of California–San Diego, the president declared: "More than 30 years ago, at the high tide of the civil rights movement, the Kerner Commission said we were becoming two Americas: one white, one black, separate and unequal. Today, we face a different choice: Will we become not two but many Americas, separate, unequal, and isolated? Or will we draw strength from all our people and our ancient faith in the quality of human dignity to become the world's first truly multiracial democracy?"[32] The statement reflected the ideology Clinton brought with him to the White House, the one he construed as restoring Democrats as the majority party. Toward this end, he sought to appeal to what journalist E. J. Dionne called the "language of common citizenship" and an emphasis on "values of generosity and tolerance."[33]

To establish complete credibility among civil rights leaders, the president selected the eminent African-American historian John Hope Franklin to chair the group. Originally from Oklahoma, where his father had survived the Tulsa race riot in 1921, Franklin earned his doctorate from Harvard University and gained his reputation as a noted scholar of the South and a pioneer in the field of African-American history. His textbook *From Slavery to Freedom,* first published in the 1940s, has gone through seven editions and is still the best-selling book of its kind in the field. Franklin taught at a number of historically black colleges before teaching at Brooklyn College, the University of Chicago, and Duke University. Committed to placing his scholarship in the cause of social justice, he had engaged in research for the historic *Brown v. Board of Education* decision (1954) and marched during the voting rights campaign in Selma, Alabama, in 1965. In his early eighties, Franklin accepted Clinton's offer to come up with a racial blueprint designed to lead the nation into the twenty-first century.[34] In doing so, Franklin became the first African American to chair a presidential commission on race relations. More than any other past chairman of a presidential racial advisory board, both personally and professionally Franklin possessed the qualifications to undertake the task.

Representation on this presidential advisory board reflected the changing face of race in the United States, no longer confined to black and white. The committee included persons of Asian-American and Hispanic-American descent, with the latter group just about poised to surpass African Americans as the nation's largest minority. Despite its multicultural make up, the group did not contain an American Indian, an omission that evoked criticism from leaders of that community. Nevertheless, the board strived to include ample testimony from Indians in its discussions (and Professor Franklin pointed out and took pride in his Cherokee ancestry).[35] As was common with such panels in the past, the committee balanced its membership between men and women, labor and business, North and South, secular and religious. Taken together, the members of the board were moderates, influential professionals, and respected politicians; yet within an era when the political mainstream had moved to the right, this group certainly consisted of liberals sensitive to the need for fostering racial diversity and reducing racial inequality through both government and corporate action.

The advisory board encountered considerable criticism from political conservatives for not including them on the panel. There was no shortage of scholars and activists who would have qualified to serve; however, appointing right-wing adherents would have been unprecedented if not counterproductive. Though previous presidents had selected such committees with moderation in mind, they had chosen appointees generally supportive of civil rights. The right-wing agenda conflicted with the main tenets around which racial equality pivoted at the turn of the century: affirmative action, race-conscious voting rights remedies, and government spending to expand economic opportunity. It is true that in creating the advisory board Clinton had called for a dialogue on race in which all Americans should be engaged. Still, neither he nor the panel wanted to have a fractious debate on the subject, which they thought would do more harm than good. When John Hope Franklin was asked why Ward Connerly, the leader of anti–affirmative action campaigns at the University of California and elsewhere, had not been invited to speak to the committee, Franklin replied that Connerly was "not addressing the subject as to how to make the university more diverse." Abigail Thernstrom, a scholar, conservative member of the United States Civil Rights Commission, and foe of affirmative action, did attend one of President Clinton's town hall meetings in Akron, Ohio. During the conversation, the president treated her dismissively and cut her off several times, prompting the *Philadelphia Inquirer* to call Clinton an "inquisitor" who tried to "corner the group's lone outspoken conservative."[36]

Over fifteen months, members of the board traversed the nation holding meetings in local communities, talking with experts and ordinary citizens alike, and engaging in "a great and unprecedented conversation about race." The committee initiated dialogues on race, "One America Conversations," in thirty-nine states and eighty-nine cities, attracting some seventeen thousand participants. In April 1998, faculty, students, staff, and administrators conducted a week of lively discussions on over six hundred college campuses. Clinton backed his "Initiative on Race" with three televised presidential assemblies and dispatched administration officials to speak at hundreds of gatherings nationwide.[37] On September 18, 1998, the Franklin Commission issued its report, *One America in the 21st Century: Forging a New Future.* Consisting of one hundred and four pages of text, sixteen pages of footnotes, eight pages of exhibits, and ninety-six pages of appendices, the document underscored the growing complexity of racial issues in a multicultural society and the continuing legacy of racial discrimination. No longer a simple matter of black and white, the conversation about race included Hispanics, American Indians, Alaska Natives, Asian-Pacific Americans, and the rising number of offspring of interracial marriages. In a nation whose motto is *e pluribus unum* (out of many, one), the panel emphasized the strength of racial diversity at the same time as it promoted national unity. "Our greatest challenge," the report declared, "is to work as one community to define ourselves with pride as a multiracial democracy."[38] The board reported finding consensus among Americans in support of "justice, equality of opportunity, respect, responsibility, honor, integrity, civility, and inclusion,"[39] but it also observed that race still mattered in keeping these principles from becoming reality. The Franklin Committee's assumptions mirrored those of Truman's board, the pioneer of presidential studies on race. Both agreed that a fundamental American creed of fairness and morality existed, and the gap between theory and practice could be closed through education, collection and dissemination of information to dispel racial stereotyping, and appeals to the goodwill of all citizens.

Yet, like its predecessor, the committee did not rely solely on education and conversation to foster change. It also offered specific recommendations for strengthening civil rights enforcement by the government, maintaining affirmative action programs, improving housing, health care, and education for the poor, raising the minimum wage, extending collective bargaining for workers, ending racial profiling in law enforcement, strengthening laws against hate crimes, and monitoring the consequences of welfare reform. In the more than fifty years since *To Secure These Rights,* the committee recognized that much had been accomplished, but it continued to look to government—national, state, and local—to devise methods to overcome persistent racial inequities that separated whites and racial minorities in their quest for jobs, housing, education, health insurance, and criminal justice.

However, in an era when many Americans had lost respect for government officials and the ability of Washington politicians to solve their problems, the advisory board put its ultimate faith in ordinary people and the power of reason and persuasion more than in government. Echoing Clinton's 1996 State of the Union message that "the era of big government is over,"[40] the Franklin Commission concluded that "[o]ne of the best tools for forging common ground and developing new understanding among people of different races is dialogue."[41] To that end, the board produced the *One America Dialogue Guide* to facilitate the exchange of ideas, and it compiled a list of civic, religious, and community organizations that interested citizens could join in pursuit of racial and economic justice. It also called for vigorous educational and media advertising campaigns to promote racial reconciliation and proposed establishment of a permanent President's Council for One America to continue its work.

The report drew mixed reviews. "This board has raised the consciousness and quickened the conscience of America," Clinton remarked in receiving the report. Civil rights advocates greeted the committee document with milder enthusiasm. A leading official of the National Council of La Raza, a Hispanic group, noted: "There are not a lot of bold, new or exciting recommendations in the report. But it is important to understand that this is not the final step in the process." Similarly, the director of the Black Leadership Forum praised the board for achieving "a measure of success" and creating "some kind of momentum."[42] The *New York Times* echoed these comments, calling the board's recommendation "modest" and "break[ing] little new ground." The *Los Angeles Times* agreed that the commission report suggested "too obvious solutions."[43] These assessments were glowing compared to those by conservatives who had criticized the president's race initiative from the beginning and did not change their minds. They found fault with what they considered a limited dialogue. "For this commission, nothing has changed since the 1960s," conservative commentator Clint Bollick groused. "So long as we fail to address such problems as out-of-wedlock births, abysmal inner-city public education and . . . violent crime, we will not achieve real equal opportunity."[44]

In a significant sign of the times, *One America in the 21st Century: Forging A New Future,* did not get published commercially or receive wide distribution, as had both the Truman Committee and Kerner Commission reports. Part of the reason was that the Franklin Commission's report emerged with the president embroiled in the Monica Lewinsky scandal, a battle that consumed his time, diminished his credibility and political capital, and, within a few months of the issuance of the report, led to his impeachment by the House of Representatives. Clinton discusses the Franklin Commission in his memoir *My Life*[45] only cursorily, briefly mentioning it twice, its work once again crowded out by the Lewinsky affair.

Still, in many ways the failure of the president and the nation to follow up on this report is curious. Written to appeal to unity and reconciliation, the text was carefully constructed to avoid confrontational language or cast blame. The commission did not propose extravagant, costly programs along the lines of Lyndon Johnson's Great Society; nor did it call for much in the way of new legislation. The core of its recommendations concerns education and healing, ongoing dialogue among racial and ethnic groups rather than divisive debate. That politicians and the public did not more eagerly embrace such a moderate and largely inoffensive approach suggests a great deal about the racial attitudes and complacency that existed and that continue to do so.

Commentators have provided several reasons beyond the diversion of the Lewinsky scandal to explain the committee's limited effect. Franklin and his colleagues blamed the media for inadequate coverage and lack of support.[46] Others attributed some of the shortcomings to poor planning in establishing the presidential initiative and the slow pace in setting the inquiry in motion. The president deserves responsibility not only for getting into the Lewinsky mess in the first place but also for generally failing to follow through on implementing the commission's recommendations.[47] Furthermore, the emphasis by Clinton and the committee on conversation and dialogue proved insufficient. This approach "invited Americans to think of the race problem as a matter of intergroup miscommunication rather than a stain on the national character."[48] By focusing on race relations rather than on institutional racism, the Clinton initiative left the fundamental problem of embedded racial injustice unresolved.

Most important, despite considerable effort and good intentions, the committee's report did not have a greater impact because it emerged outside of a supportive historical context. Previous race commissions in the late 1940s and 1960s came about during the growth and development of an organized civil rights movement both at the local and national levels. In many respects, appointment of presidential committees resulted form demands by civil rights groups for Washington to take action against escalating racial violence. Presidents responded favorably because they believed that creation of such agencies could defuse both white hostility and black militancy. These committees also arose during the Cold War era, when racial disturbances at home figured greatly into diplomatic calculations of the United States and the Soviet Union. With the Cold War over, conservatives in control of Congress, and the Supreme Court retreating from extending racial equality, and without a broad-based, civil rights movement, the Clinton initiative stalled. In effect, *One America* failed to spark great change because it lacked a dynamic social movement to propel it and a supportive national constituency to demand its implementation.

Yet *One America* stands as a valuable document on the state of race relations in the United States at the turn of the twenty-first century. The report provides the first comprehensive assessment of racial progress (or lack thereof) since the heyday of the civil rights movement. As such, it constitutes an important benchmark for gauging the effects of civil rights measures instituted in the 1950s and 1960s. Considerable progress has certainly occurred since the dark days of rigid segregation and disfranchisement fifty years ago, but the story remains unfinished. Since its completion in 1998, the Franklin Commission's report remains current, as very little has changed.

In April 2007 the popular radio talk show host Don Imus insulted the Rutgers University women's basketball team that had just competed for and lost a national championship. Using racist and sexist language, he referred to the largely African-American team (eight blacks and two whites) as "nappy-headed 'hos." This slur instigated an outcry of condemnation and protests, which resulted in Imus's firing. The publicity generated a public uproar over hate speech. However, the ensuing debate did not recall the existence just a decade earlier of the work of the Franklin commission and its effort to conduct the same kind of discussion that many were again calling for. (Imus returned to radio later that year, though he did add two African-American on-air personalities to his program.)

Nevertheless, as this episode demonstrates, the Franklin committee's findings are as relevant today as they were when first presented. Even if, in 2008, Barack Obama wins the Democratic nomination and general election and becomes the first African-American president, he will face the same protracted economic and social problems enumerated in the Franklin Committee report. Indeed, Obama is inspiring and making a connection with millions of white voters, but it remains to be seen whether, if successful in winning the election, he can turn this unprecedented support into concrete action to overcome the continuing legacy of racial inequality. Yet his candidacy sparked the kind of racial conversation that has rarely surfaced since the appointment of the Franklin Commission. Ironically, supporters of Hillary Clinton, his chief rival for the Democratic nomination, whose husband had promoted a national racial dialogue a decade earlier, stirred up racial antagonism. They charged Obama's pastor, Jeremiah Wright, with making controversial remarks from the pulpit of his predominantly black Trinity United Church of Christ in Chicago. Fueled by a media frenzy, Obama sought to quell this controversy and do much more. On March 18, 2008, speaking in Philadelphia, the cradle of the Constitution, Obama used the occasion not only to place his pastor's remarks in context, but to ask Americans, black and white, to confront their own and their nation's racial history and prejudices. Rather than dwelling on past grievances, he urged all Americans to join together and create "the more perfect union" that the founding fathers had envisioned. This would mean using race not as a divisive issue but as an opportunity "to come together and solve challenges like health care, or education, or the need to find good jobs for every American."[49] No matter the outcome of the presidential contest, it still makes sense to ponder the words of W. E. B. Dubois about the color line, which reverberate in Bill Clinton's eloquent San Diego speech: "That is the unfinished work of our time, to lift the burden of race and redeem the promise of America."[50]

NOTES

[1] W. E. B. DuBois, *The Souls of Black Folk* (New York, New American Library, 1969, xi.

[2] Steven F. Lawson, ed., *To Secure These Rights: The Report of President Harry S Truman's Committee on Civil Rights* (Boston: Bedford/St. Martin's, 2004), 44.

[3] Ibid., 12.

[4] Ibid., 179.

[5] Kari Frederickson, *The Dixiecrat Revolt and the End of the Solid South, 1932–1968* (Chapel Hill, University of North Carolina Press, 2001), 150–96; Harold Gullen, *The Upset That Wasn't: Harry S. Truman and the Crucial Election of 1948* (Chicago, Ivan R. Dee, 1998).

[6] The United States Commission on Civil Rights (CCR) was created under the Civil Rights Act of 1957 and signed into law by President Dwight D. Eisenhower. Congress originally conceived of it as a temporary organization, requiring the commission to turn in a final report within two years. However, beginning in 1959, federal lawmakers extended the life of the body through periodic renewals, and in 1983 the CCR became a permanent federal agency. Originally, it focused its attention primarily on voting discrimination and issued several reports that laid the basis for passage of the 1965 Voting Rights Act. See Foster Rhea Dulles, *The Civil Rights Commission, 1957–1965* (Ann Arbor, University of Michigan Press, 1968).

[7] On the SCLC, see Adam Fairclough, *"To Redeem the Soul of America": The Southern Christian Leadership Conference and Martin Luther King, Jr.* (Athens, University of Georgia Press, 1987); on SNCC, see Clayborne Carson, *SNCC and the Black Awakening of the 1960s* (Cambridge, Harvard University Press, 1981); on CORE, see August Meier and Elliott Rudwick, *CORE: A Study in the Civil Rights Movement, 1942–1968* (New York, Oxford University Press, 1973); and on Robert F. Williams, see Timothy B. Tyson, *Radio Free Dixie: Robert F. Williams and the Roots of Black Power* (Chapel Hill, University of North Carolina Press, 2000).

[8] Lee Rainwater and William L. Yancey, *The Moynihan Report and the Politics of*

Controversy (Cambridge, M.I.T. Press, 1967). On June 4, 1965, Johnson had delivered the commencement address at Howard University, based in part upon the assumptions in Moynihan's report. The president declared: "We seek not just freedom but opportunity. We seek not just legal equality but human ability, not just equality as a right and a theory but equality as a fact and equality as a result." These ideas became the underpinnings for subsequent affirmative action policies. Terry H. Anderson, *The Pursuit of Fairness: A History of Affirmative Action* (New York, Oxford University Press, 2004), 87–88.

[9] Steven F. Lawson, *In Pursuit of Power: Southern Blacks and Electoral Politics, 1965–1982* (New York, Columbia University Press, 1985), 43–48. Kevin L. Yuill, "The 1966 White House Conference on Civil Rights," *The Historical Journal*, 41 (March 1998): 259–82.

[10] Lawson, *In Pursuit of Power*, 47.

[11] Ibid., 49–62. Meredith had attended the White House Conference.

[12] On the relationship between LBJ and King, see Nick Kotz, *Judgment Days: Lyndon Baines Johnson, Martin Luther King, Jr., and the Laws That Changed America* (Boston, Houghton Mifflin, 2005).

[13] Steven F. Lawson, *Civil Rights Crossroads: Nation, Community, and the Black Freedom Struggle* (Lexington, University of Kentucky Press, 2003), 71–94.

[14] Steven F. Lawson, *Running for Freedom: Civil Rights and Black Politics in America Since 1941*, 2d ed. (New York, McGraw Hill, 1997), 127.

[15] *Report of the National Advisory Commission on Civil Disorders* (New York, Bantam Books, 1968), xv.

[16] The other members of the committee were Senator Fred R. Harris of Oklahoma; Representative John C. Corman of California; Representative William M. McCulloch of Oho; I. W. Abel, president of the United Steelworkers of America; Charles B. Thornton, Chief executive officer of Litton Industries; Katherine Graham Peden, Kentucky Commissioner of Commerce; and Herbert Jenkins, Atlanta chief of police.

[17] Lawson, *Civil Rights Crossroads*, 88.

[18] *Report of National Advisory Commission on Civil Disorders*, 2.

[19] Richard Godwin, *Remembering America: A Voice from the Sixties* (New York, Harper and Row, 1988), 402–3.

[20] Lawson, *Civil Rights Crossroads*, 171–72.

[21] *http://www.census.gov/hhes/www/poverty/histpov/hstpov2.html*. The 1999 figure for Hispanics was 22.7, and 10.7 for Asian/Pacific Islanders.

[22] Lawson, *Civil Rights Crossroads*, 172.

[23] Bill Clinton, *My Life* (New York, Alfred A. Knopf, 2004), 37, 55, 156; Cheryl Citera, "Bill Clinton's Race Initiative and Its Limited Legacy," thesis, Henry Rutgers Scholars Program, April 2007, Rutgers University, 16–19.

[24] Lani Guinier, *Lift Every Voice: Turning a Civil Rights Setback into a New Vision of Social Justice* (New York, Simon and Schuster, 1998), 23–56. For Clinton's viewpoint, see Clinton, *My Life*, 523–24.

[25] Darlene Clark Hine, "African Americans and the Clinton Presidency: Reckoning with Race, 1992–2000," in *The Clinton Riddle: Perspectives on the Forty-second President*, ed. Todd G. Shields, Jeannie M. Wayne, and Donald R. Kelley (Fayetteville, University of Arkansas Press, 2004), 79–91; and Dan Carter, "Rightward Currents: Bill

Clinton and the Politics of the 1990s," in ibid., 111–34. Temporary Assistance for Needy Families (TANF) replaced the former cash assistance program known as Aid to Families with Dependent Children (AFDC). Ironically, both liberals and conservatives criticize the implementation of welfare reform. The former emphasize that poverty will persist because families that have gone off welfare recently are less likely to have jobs than those who left welfare earlier; poverty rates among former welfare recipients remain high; families forced off welfare for failing to find a job within the time limit are in worse shape economically than those who leave because of other reasons; and more than half of impoverished families with children who are eligible for assistance do not receive it, and the figure is rising. The latter, which focus on those who have found work, believe that not enough is being done to force recipients to obtain employment. They applaud reductions in welfare caseloads and increased employment among former recipients of assistance, especially single mothers. However, they complain that some states allow recipients to refuse work and still receive benefits, and that not enough is being spent on encouraging marriage and sexual abstinence among teenagers. Shawn Fremstad, "Recent Welfare Reform Research Finding: Implications for TANF Reauthorization and State TANF Policies," Center on Budget and Policy Priorities, http:www.cbpp.org/pubs/welfare/htm; Robert E. Rector, "Welfare Reform: Progress, Pitfalls, and Potential," The Heritage Foundation, http://www .heritage.org.Research/Welfare/wm421.cfm. It should be noted that much of the research on welfare reform involves data from the late 1990s, during which time a strong economy prevailed. The results might prove different if based on information from a period of economic decline.

[26] David A. Bositis, *The Black Vote in 2000* (Washington D.C.: Joint Center for Political and Economic Studies, 2001), 3.

[27] Monica Lewinsky came to the White House as an intern in 1995. Three years later, it was publicly revealed that she and the president had sexual trysts inside the White House on a number of occasions. At first Clinton denied having had "sexual relations with that woman. Miss Lewinsky." After receiving immunity for grand jury testimony, Lewinsky, who at first had stood by the president's denial, admitted to the federal panel that she indeed had performed oral sex on the president. On August 17, 1998, Clinton admitted in taped testimony from a sexual harassment case involving Paula Jones, dating back to his governorship, that he had had an "improper physical relationship" with Lewinsky. The problem for Clinton was that, in a deposition in the Jones case, he denied having sexual relations with Lewinsky. The special prosecutor, Kenneth Starr, appointed to look into these and other allegations against Clinton, concluded that the president had committed perjury and obstruction of justice, which became the basis for his impeachment by the House. In 1994, Starr had been appointed to investigate the involvement of the president and his wife, Hillary, in a real estate venture in the Arkansas Whitewater Development Corporation during the 1970s. The president and first lady were accused of fraud, receiving improper tax benefits, securities manipulation, and receiving illegal campaign contributions. While this investigation was taking place, the Lewinsky affair broke and Starr was granted authority to add it to his inquiry. Unlike "Monica-gate," the special prosecutor did not charge Clinton with criminal wrongdoing with respect to Whitewater. James B. Stewart, *Blood Sport: The President and His Adversaries* (New York, Simon and Schuster, 1996), and Michael Isikoff, *Uncovering Clinton: A Reporter's Story* (New York, Crown, 1999).

[28] Toni Morrison, "Talk of the Town," *New Yorker*, October 5, 1998, 31–32. See also, DeWayne Wickham, *Bill Clinton and Black America* (New York, Ballantine, 2002). In 2001 the Congressional Black Caucus honored Clinton at its annual dinner "as the nation's first black president." Marc Morano, "Clinton Honored as 'First Black President' at Black Caucus Dinner," CNSNews.com, October 1, 2001, http://www .cnsnews.com/ViewNation.asp?Page+Nation/archive/200.

29 Richard Morin and Sharon Warden, "Americans vent Anger at Affirmative Action," March 24, 1995, *Washington Post,* A1.

30 Anderson, *The Pursuit of Fairness,* 161–273; J. Morgan Kousser, *Colorblind Injustice: Minority Voting Rights and the Undoing of the Second Reconstruction* (Chapel Hill, University of North Carolina Press, 1999).

31 The President's Initiative on Race, The Advisory Board's Report to the President, *One America in the 21st Century: Forging a New Future,* unpublished copy, 1998, Appendix, A-1, hereafter referred to as "unpublished version."

32 *Public Papers of the Presidents: Administration of William J. Clinton, 1997* (Washington, Government Printing Office, 1998), 741.

33 E. J. Dionne, *Why Americans Hate Politics* (New York, Simon and Schuster, 1991), 330–31; Carter, "Rightward Currents," 112–14.

34 John Hope Franklin and Alfred Moss, Jr. *From Slavery to Freedom: A History of African Americans,* 7th ed. (New York, McGraw-Hill, 1994); John Hope Franklin, *Mirror to America* (New York, Farrar, Straus, and Giroux, 2005), 15–16. The Tulsa riot began on June 1 after the local newspaper printed an inflammatory story of a black man allegedly raping a white woman. The violence may have produced over three hundred deaths. The riot resulted in the burning of thirty-five city blocks in the black area of the city, resulting in the destruction of over twelve hundred homes.

35 The other members of the panel were Linda Chavez-Thompson, executive vice president of the AFL-CIO; Suzan D. Johnson Cook, senior pastor of the Bronx Christian Fellowship; Thomas H. Kean, former governor of New Jersey and currently president of Drew University; Angela E. Oh, a Los Angeles attorney; Bob Thomas, executive vice president for marketing for Republic Industries; and William F. Winter, former governor of Mississippi. The executive director was Judith A. Winston, a civil rights lawyer.

36 Quoted in Citera, "Bill Clinton's Race Initiative," 41 (first quote), 47 (second quote).

37 Unpublished version of report, 10–11.

38 Ibid., 9.

39 Ibid., 16.

40 The president also remarked: "But we cannot go back to the time when our citizens were left to fend for themselves. . . . We know that big government does not have all the answers. We know that there is not a program for every problem." http://clinton2 .nara.gov/WH/New/other/sotu.html.

41 Unpublished version of report, 16.

42 Michael A. Fletcher, "President Accepts Report on Race," *Washington Post,* September 19, 1998, http://www.washingtonpost.com/wp-srv/national/longterm/race .htm.

43 Quoted in Citera, "Bill Clinton's Race Initiative," 84–85.

44 Fletcher, "President Accepts Report on Race."

45 Clinton, *My Life,* 758, 813.

46 Franklin, *Mirror to America,* 351–52.

47 Citera, "Bill Clinton's Race Initiative," 105–9. The president was supposed to write up and publicize the committee's work, but he did not do so until his final week in office. Steven A. Holmes, *New York Times,* January 15, 2001, A11. Clinton did create a White House Office on One America, but it had little support or success.

48 Patricia A. Sullivan and Steven R. Goldzwig, "Seven Lessons from President Clinton's Race Initiative: A Post-Mortem on the Politics of Desire," in *Images, Scandal, and Communication Strategies of the Clinton Presidency,* ed. Robert E. Denton, Jr. and Rachel L. Holloway (Westport, CT: Praeger, 2003), 161.

49 Barack Obama, "A More Perfect Union, March 18, 2008," http://my.barackobama.com/page/content/hisownwords.

50 *Public Papers of the Presidents,* 741.

Timeline

1947

- Truman's Committee on Civil Rights delivers its report, *To Secure These Rights.*

1965

- Passage of Voting Rights Act on August 6.
- Race riot in Watts, Los Angeles, on August 11.

1966

- Meredith March and SNCC's call for Black Power.
- President Lyndon B. Johnson convenes the White House Conference on Civil Rights.

1967

- Racial uprisings in major cities throughout the nation, most notably Detroit, Michigan; Newark, New Jersey; and Tampa, Florida.
- President Johnson appoints the National Advisory Commission on Civil Disorders, known as the Kerner Commission, to investigate the riots.

1968

- The Kerner Commission issues its report and places responsibility on white racism for causing the urban rebellions. The report calls for major reforms, but Johnson, preoccupied with the Vietnam War and upset with the commission for neglecting to emphasize his civil rights accomplishments, ignores its recommendations.
- Following the assassination of Martin Luther King, Jr., rioting breaks out in Washington D.C., Chicago, Baltimore, and in other cities across the nation.
- Congress passes the Civil Rights Act of 1968, banning racial discrimination in housing.

1978

- *Regents of the University of California v. Bakke* upholds affirmative action on the grounds of promoting diversity but prohibits racial quotas.

1992

- Riots in South Central Los Angeles following the acquittal of police officers in the beating of Rodney King.
- Election of Arkansas governor Bill Clinton as president.

1993

- Nomination and withdrawal of Lani Guinier to head the Civil Rights Division of the Justice Department.
- In *Shaw v. Reno,* Supreme Court outlaws the drawing of congressional districts based primarily on race. This ruling limits the possibilities for the creation of additional majority African-American legislative districts.

1994

- Passage of Omnibus Crime measure.

• Republican Party wins midterm elections and controls House and Senate.

1995

• O. J. Simpson acquitted by a jury on charges of murdering his wife and her friend.

• Million Man March on Washington organized by the Nation of Islam.

1996

• Passage of Welfare Reform law.

• Bill Clinton reelected with 84 percent of the black electorate, up 4 percent from 1992.

1997

• June 13: President Clinton issues Executive Order 13050, creating an Initiative on Race and an advisory board to report to the president on how to achieve "One America in the Twenty-first Century." Clinton appoints John Hope Franklin to chair the advisory panel.

• June 14: President Clinton delivers the commencement speech at the University of California–San Diego, extolling the virtues of a multiracial society.

1998

• September 18: Franklin Commission issues its report, *One America in the 21st Century: Forging a New Future.*

• December 19: Clinton impeached by the House of Representatives on charges of perjury and obstruction of justice, arising from the Monica Lewinsky sex scandal.

1999

• February 12: Clinton acquitted by the Senate.

2003

• In *Gratz v. Bollinger*, the Supreme Court ruled unconstitutional the University of Michigan's affirmative action program for undergraduate admission, which awarded bonus points to minorities. At the same time, in *Grutter v. Bollinger*, the Supreme Court upheld the affirmative action admissions' policy of the University of Michigan Law School, which permitted "race conscious" considerations if they were applied as one of many factors in a student's admission.

One America in the 21st Century

Century

Forging a New Future

The President's Initiative on Race

The Advisory Board's
Report to the President

ADVISORY BOARD MEMBERS

President Clinton has called together seven distinguished Americans to help him with this Initiative. The members of the Advisory Board are reaching out to all Americans to talk about race, learn about our existing perceptions and misperceptions, and recommend solutions to create One America.

JOHN HOPE FRANKLIN
Durham, NC • Chairman

LINDA CHAVEZ-THOMPSON
Washington, DC

SUZAN D. JOHNSON COOK
Bronx, NY

THOMAS H. KEAN
Madison, NJ

ANGELA E. OH
Los Angeles, CA

ROBERT THOMAS
Fort Lauderdale, FL

WILLIAM F. WINTER
Jackson, MS

September 1998

ONE AMERICA IN THE 21ST CENTURY
The President's Initiative on Race

The New Executive Office Building
Washington, D.C. 20503
202/395-1010

Dear Mr. President:

On behalf of the Advisory Board, I am pleased to present you with these observations, insights, and recommendations that reflect our work during this past year. We hope this final submission will convey to you the breadth and richness of our experience. We have traveled to many places, talked with countless Americans, heard many opinions and concerns, studied many issues related to race and race relations, and seen much that is quite promising. None of our work would have been possible without your strong and sustained leadership. The bold step that you, the Vice President, and the First Lady have taken is making an enormous difference in bringing us closer to becoming One America in the next century.

We hope that what we have learned, along with our recommendations, will help you as you write your report to the American people and develop a work plan to build one America in the 21st century for people of all races. While we prepared these observations and recommendations for you, we know that members of the public will also be interested in them. We, therefore, included a contextual and factual background that covers much that you already know about the legacy of race and color and the demographic trends that signal who we will be in future years.

Mr. President, when we embarked on this endeavor almost 15 months ago, we expected that many people would share our commitment to your Initiative. I speak for the entire Advisory Board when I say we were not prepared for the overwhelming support and interest we encountered at a time when, to most people, there was no crisis and, therefore, no reason to raise issues related to race. We were met at every event with thoughtful people who are greatly concerned that race still divides our country and who want to know how they can help move our Nation toward one America in the 21st century.

We were met with challenges during the year as well. However, we did not expect our task to be easy. Race is a complex and emotional subject. Our experience this year reinforced our view that while there has been much progress in eliminating racial discrimination, disparities, and stereotypes, many challenges remain and these challenges cannot be resolved overnight. We believe, as you do, that the measure of the Initiative's success will be whether it made a difference for our Nation, but this will be known only in the long-term, not in the coming weeks or months. The country still has much work to do if we are to become, "one America respecting, even celebrating, our differences, but embracing even more what we have in common." The Nation must focus on creating equal opportunities to quality education for all and on giving our young people tools to become leaders and role models able to pilot our increasingly diverse society into the next century and beyond as one America.

It has been a great honor and a pleasure to serve as your "eyes and ears" on issues of race this year. We wish you much success in your continuing efforts to create equality of opportunity and justice for all Americans regardless of race and look forward to reading your report. We pledge that each of us will continue to work to build one America in the 21st century and stand ready to assist you.

Yours truly,

John Hope Franklin

John Hope Franklin
Chairman

ACKNOWLEDGMENTS

The Advisory Board to the President's Initiative on Race wishes to thank the countless individuals and organizations across the country who work to improve race relations in America. We were heartened to find so many people striving every day to reduce disparities, combat stereotypes, and fight discrimination. We were particularly inspired by our Nation's young people who answered the President's call to action in so many ways and by their commitment to carry forward this critical effort to improve race relations as we enter the next century.

We are deeply appreciative of the organizations and individuals who gave their time and energy to assist us with Advisory Board meetings, community forums, conversations about race, the Campus Week of Dialogue, the Statewide Days of Dialogue, and many other events and activities. We are grateful to all of them, including members of the Cabinet and Congress; state and local elected officials; people in Federal, State, and local agencies; higher education institutions; national non-profit organizations; foundations; the corporate and faith communities; local and regional community organizations; and the legions of other individuals who contributed to our efforts. In addition, thousands of people shared articles, books, letters, and videos with us. Their contributions taught us about what people are thinking, feeling, and doing about race. We welcomed and learned from all of them.

We would like especially to thank the Leadership Conference Educational Fund for producing an award-winning public service announcement on race relations and the following organizations for their support in producing the *One America Dialogue Guide*: Hope In The Cities, National Conference on Community and Justice, National Days of Dialogue, National Multicultural Institute, Study Circles Resource Center, and the YWCA.

The Executive Director of the Initiative, Judith Winston, deserves a special tribute. Her stewardship and expertise were our compass. We could not have accomplished our work without her tireless dedication, commitment, wisdom, insight, and assistance.

We also want to thank Erskine Bowles; Sylvia Mathews; Maria Echaveste; Minyon Moore; Ann Lewis; Mickey Ibarra; Thurgood Marshall, Jr.; Bob Nash; other members of the President's staff; and consultants Christopher Edley, Jr., Laura Harris, and Sonia Jarvis, who filled in many of the details from the President's original vision. We would be remiss if we did not recognize their contributions to building one America.

Finally, we would like to thank everyone who—because of this Initiative—has a better appreciation of our continuing individual and community challenges on race and who is willing to accept those challenges as their own. Each person who takes some action to improve race relations and reduce racial disparities makes a difference. It is that citizen service at home, at work, and in neighborhoods and communities that is the hope and promise of this Initiative, Nation, and our future. To all of you, we urge you to continue your work, to reach out to others, and to help build one America in the 21st century.

The members of the Advisory Board would like to thank the staff
of the President's Initiative on Race for their contributions.

Bruce Andersen
Randy Ayers
Patrick Aylward
Elizabeth Belenis
Lee Boyle
Karen Burchard
David Campt
Rhonda Carney
Elizabeth Castle
Michele Cavataio
David Chai
Jennifer Dolan
Grace Garcia
Danielle Glosser
John Goering
Claire Gonzales
Roderick Harrison
Suzanne Hodges

Audrey Hutchinson
Allison King
D. Bambi Kraus
Stacey Ladman
Lin Liu
Ana Lopez
Jacinta Ma
Elizabeth Martinez
Tamara Monosoff
Scott Palmer
Barbara Semedo
Lydia Sermons
Michael Sorrell
Maria Soto
Chandler Spaulding
Brenda Toineeta
Michael Wenger
Rob Wexler

Judith Winston
Executive Director

The Board would like to express its gratitude to the following
individuals for their administrative assistance over the last year.

Elizabeth Asher
Marjorie Black
Cedra Eaton
Linda Gray
Andrew Holzapfel
Wanda Johnson
Diana Kappner

Evelina Mosby
Brent Oliver
Jane Price-Smith
Daphne Pringle
Matthew Roper
Katherine Sheckells
Michelle Waldron

EXECUTIVE SUMMARY

ONE AMERICA IN THE 21ST CENTURY: FORGING A NEW FUTURE

Today, I ask the American people to join me in a great national effort to perfect the promise of America for this new time as we seek to build our more perfect union....That is the unfinished work of our time, to lift the burden of race and redeem the promise of America.

—President Clinton, June 14, 1997

America's greatest promise in the 21st century lies in our ability to harness the strength of our racial diversity. The greatest challenge facing Americans is to accept and take pride in defining ourselves as a multiracial democracy. At the end of the 20th century, America has emerged as the worldwide symbol of opportunity and freedom through leadership that constantly strives to give meaning to democracy's fundamental principles. These principles—justice, opportunity, equality, and racial inclusion—must continue to guide the planning for our future.

On June 13, 1997, President William Jefferson Clinton issued Executive Order No. 13050 (the "Executive Order"), which created the Initiative on Race (the "Initiative") and authorized the creation of an Advisory Board to advise the President on how to build one America for the 21st century. The Board, consisting of Dr. John Hope Franklin (chairman), Linda Chavez-Thompson, Reverend Dr. Suzan D. Johnson Cook, Thomas H. Kean, Angela E. Oh, Bob Thomas, and William F. Winter, was tasked with examining race, racism, and the potential for racial reconciliation in America using a process of study, constructive dialogue, and action.

Board members have spent the last 15 months seeking ways to build a more united and just America. They have canvassed the country meeting with and listening to Americans who revealed how race and racism have impacted their lives. Board meetings focused on the role race plays in civil rights enforcement, education, poverty, employment, housing, stereotyping, the administration of justice, health care, and immigration. Members have convened forums with leaders from the religious and corporate sectors.

This Report, a culmination of the Board's efforts, is not a definitive analysis of the state of race relations in America today. Board members had no independent authority to commit Federal resources to a particular problem, community, or organization. Rather, this Report is an account of the

Board's experiences and impressions and includes all of the recommendations for action submitted by the Board to the President following its formal meetings. Many have already been implemented or are awaiting congressional action.

CHAPTER ONE—SEARCHING FOR COMMON GROUND

Throughout the year, the Board heard stories and shared experiences that reinforced its belief that we are a country whose citizens are more united than divided. All too often, however, racial differences and discrimination obstruct our ability to move beyond race and color to recognize our common values and goals. Common values include the thirst for freedom, desire for equal opportunity, and a belief in fairness and justice; collective goals are securing a decent affordable home, a quality education, and a job that pays decent wages. All people, regardless of race, want financial and personal security, adequate and available health care, and children who are healthy and well-educated. Chapter One discusses these shared goals and values and also describes how the Initiative used dialogue as a tool for finding common ground. Through One America Conversations, the Campus Week of Dialogue, Statewide Days of Dialogue, tribal leaders meetings, and the *One America Dialogue Guide*, the Initiative was able to spark dialogue across the country. The chapter also points to the importance of recruiting a cadre of leaders to provide strong leadership in the corporate, religious, and youth sectors of our society and provides examples of Promising Practices.

CHAPTER TWO—STRUGGLING WITH THE LEGACY OF RACE AND COLOR

Chapter Two confronts the legacy of race in this country and in so doing, answers the question of whether race matters in America. Our Nation still struggles with the impact of its past policies, practices, and attitudes based on racial differences. Race and ethnicity still have profound impacts on the extent to which a person is fully included in American society and provided the equal opportunity and equal protection promised to all Americans. All of these characteristics continue to affect an individual's opportunity to receive an education, acquire the skills necessary to maintain a good job, have access to adequate health care, and receive equal justice under the law.

Americans must improve their understanding of the history of race in this country and the effect this history has on the way many minorities and people of color are treated today. Each minority group shares a common history of legally mandated and/or socially and economically imposed subordination to white European-Americans and their descendants. In this chapter, the experiences of American Indians and Alaska Natives, African Americans, Latinos, Asian Pacific Americans, and white immigrants are highlighted.

The lesson of this chapter is that the absence of both knowledge and understanding about the role race has played in our collective history continues to make it difficult to find solutions that will improve race relations, eliminate disparities, and create equal opportunities in all areas of American life. This absence also contributes to conflicting views on race and racial progress held by Americans of color and white Americans.

This is especially relevant in the context of race-conscious affirmative action programs. Lack of knowledge and understanding about the genesis and consequences of racial discrimination in America often make it difficult to discuss affirmative action remedies productively. It also obscures the significant progress made in the last two decades in eliminating racial disparities in the workplace and in educational institutions through the use of properly constructed affirmative action strategies.

CHAPTER THREE—THE CHANGING FACE OF AMERICA

In Chapter Three, the Board examines the changing face of America. The discussion of race in this country is no longer a discussion between and about blacks and whites. Increasingly, conversations about race must include all Americans, including, but not limited to, Hispanics, American Indians and Alaska Natives, and Asian Pacific Americans. Statistics show that by the year 2050, the population in the United States will be approximately 53 percent white, 25 percent Hispanic, 14 percent black, 8 percent Asian Pacific American, and 1 percent American Indian and Alaska Native. This represents a significant shift from our current demographics of 73 percent white, 12 percent black, 11 percent Hispanic, 4 percent Asian Pacific American, and 1 percent American Indian and Alaska Native.

Further complicating the discussions of race is the increasing amount of interracial marriages. Americans are marrying persons of a different race at consistently high rates. U.S. Census data show that 31 percent of native-born Hispanic husbands and wives, between ages 25 and 34, have white spouses. In the native-born Asian Pacific American category, 36 percent of the men and 45 percent of the women marry white spouses.

The complexities, challenges, and opportunities that arise from our growing diversity point to the need for a new language, one that accurately reflects this diversity. Our dialogue must reflect the steps being taken to close the gap in data reporting on America's less visible racial groups—American

Indians, Alaska Natives, Native Hawaiians, and all of the subgroups of
Asian Pacific Americans and Hispanics.

CHAPTER FOUR—BRIDGING THE GAP

Chapter Four summarizes key facts and background information that
emerged from each of the Board's formal meetings and the recommendations made to the President on civil rights enforcement, education, economic opportunity, stereotypes, criminal justice, health care, and the immigrant experience. The data show that although minorities and people of
color have made progress in terms of the indicators used to measure quality
of life, persistent barriers to their full inclusion in American society remain.

In the area of civil rights enforcement, the Board made the following recommendations:

- Strengthen civil rights enforcement.

- Improve data collection on racial and ethnic discrimination.

- Strengthen laws and enforcement against hate crimes.

Two of the early Board meetings focused on the role of education in helping to overcome racial disparities. These meetings stressed the importance
of educating children in high-quality, integrated schools, where they have
the opportunity to learn about and from each other. These meetings served
as the basis for the following recommendations:

- Enhance early childhood learning.

- Strengthen teacher preparation and equity.

- Promote school construction.

- Promote movement from K–12 to higher education.

- Promote the benefits of diversity in K–12 and higher education.

- Provide education and skills training to overcome increasing income
  inequality that negatively affects the immigrant population.

- Implement the Comprehensive Indian Education Policy.

The Board analyzed the issue of economic opportunity through formal
meetings on employment and poverty. Information gathered showed that a
substantial amount of disparity remains between the economic prosperity
of whites and most minority groups. Also, the Board found clear evidence
of active forms of discrimination in employment, pay, housing, and consumer and credit markets. The Board made the following recommendations
for correcting these disparities:

- Examine income inequality.

- Support supplements for Small Business Administration programs.

- Use the current economic boom to provide necessary job training and to increase the minimum wage.

- Evaluate anti-poverty program effectiveness.

- Provide a higher minimum wage for low-wage workers and their families.

- Improve racial data collection.

- Evaluate the effectiveness of job-training programs designed to reach minority and immigrant communities.

- Commission a study to examine American Indian economic development.

- Support the right of working people to engage in collective bargaining.

The U.S. Department of Housing and Urban Development convened a meeting for the Board on race and housing. Active forms of racial discrimination continue to plague our housing markets. According to current statistics, blacks and Hispanics are likely to be discriminated against roughly half of the time that they go to look for a home or apartment. The recommendations for addressing the disparities in the area of housing follow:

- Continue to use testing to develop evidence of continuing discrimination.

- Highlight housing integration efforts.

- Support the increase and targeting of Federal funds for urban revitalization.

- Support community development corporations.

- Promote American Indian access to affordable housing.

In one meeting, the Board addressed the issues surrounding negative racial stereotypes, which are the core elements of discrimination and racial division. Stereotypes influence how people of different races and ethnicities view and treat each other. The Board's recommendations on stereotypes, which follow, focus on using both public and private institutions and individuals to challenge policymakers and institutional leaders to examine the role stereotypes play in policy development, institutional practices, and our view of our own racial identity:

- Hold a Presidential event to discuss stereotypes.

- Institutionalize the Administration's promotion of racial dialogue.

- Convene a high-level meeting on the problem of racial stereotypes with leaders from the media.

At the Board meeting on race, crime, and the administration of justice, experts explained how racial disparities and prejudices affect the way in which minorities are treated by the criminal system. Examples of this phenomenon can be found in the use of racial profiling in law enforcement and in the differences in the rates of arrest, conviction, and sentencing between whites and minorities and people of color. These discoveries led to the following recommendations:

- Expand data collection and analysis.

- Consider restricting the use of racial profiling.

- Eliminate racial stereotypes and diversify law enforcement.

- Reduce or eliminate drug sentencing disparities.

- Promote comprehensive efforts to keep young people out of the criminal justice system.

- Continue to enhance community policing and related strategies.

- Support initiatives that improve access to courts.

- Support American Indian law enforcement.

The U.S. Department of Health and Human Services sponsored a meeting on race and health for the Board. Disparities in the treatment of whites and minorities and people of color by the health care system can be attributed to disparities in employment, income, and wealth. The Board made the following recommendations as a result of information received at this meeting:

- Continue advocating for broad-based expansions in health insurance coverage.

- Continue advocacy of increased health care access for underserved groups.

- Continue pushing Congress for full funding of the Race and Ethnic Health Disparities Initiatives.

- Increase funding for existing programs targeted to under served and minority populations.

- Enhance financial and regulatory mechanisms to promote culturally competent care.

- Emphasize the importance of cultural competence to institutions training health care providers.

The Carnegie Endowment for International Peace and the Georgetown University Law Center jointly sponsored a meeting for the Board that explored immigration and race. Evidence showed that race is the source of a fundamental rift in American society that affects immigrants and their experiences with discrimination. The Board issued the following recommendations as a result of the information it received in this meeting:

- Strongly enforce anti-discrimination measures on behalf of every racial and ethnic minority group.

- Back programs that would promote a clear understanding of the rights and duties of citizenship.

- Support immigrant-inclusion initiatives.

CHAPTER FIVE—FORGING A NEW FUTURE

Chapter Five calls for the continuation of the Initiative to complete the work already begun. The following elements are the most critical in developing a meaningful long-term strategy to advance race relations in the 21st century:

- **A President's Council for One America.** This year's effort has been vital in laying the foundation for the larger task that lies ahead. The creation of a President's Council for One America speaks to the need for a long-term strategy dedicated to building on the vision of one America. Its main function would be to coordinate and monitor the implementation of policies designed to increase opportunity and eliminate racial disparities.

- **A public education program using a multimedia approach.** A public education program could assist in keeping the American public informed on the facts about race in America, pay tribute to the different racial and ethnic backgrounds of Americans, and emphasize and highlight the common values we share as a racially diverse Nation.

- **A Presidential "call to action" of leaders from all sectors of our society.** A call to action should come from the President to leaders in State and local government and private sector organizations to address the racial and ethnic divides in their communities. Public/private partnerships can demonstrate leadership by working collaboratively to make racial reconciliation a reality in all communities across America.

- **A focus on youth.** Young Americans are this Nation's greatest hope for realizing the goal of one America. Young people must be engaged in efforts to bridge racial divides and promote racial reconciliation. Organizations and groups that encourage the development of youth leaders must be supported.

This chapter also includes a brief discussion of other critical issues, such as environmental justice, media and stereotyping, and police misconduct, that the Advisory Board believes deserve further dialogue. Among these issues is affirmative action, which the Board believes remains an important tool among many for overcoming racial discrimination and promoting the benefits of diversity in education, employment, and other contexts.

Chapter Five concludes with the 10 suggestions on how Americans can help to build on the momentum that will lead our Nation into the 21st century as one America.

INTRODUCTION—ONE AMERICA IN THE 21ST CENTURY: FORGING A NEW FUTURE

Today, I ask the American people to join me in a great national effort to perfect the promise of America for this new time as we seek to build our more perfect union.... That is the unfinished work of our time, to lift the burden of race and redeem the promise of America.

—President Clinton, June 14, 1997

America's greatest promise in the 21st century lies in our ability to harness the strength of our racial diversity. Our greatest challenge is to work as one community to define ourselves with pride as a multiracial democracy. At the end of the 20th century, America has emerged as the worldwide symbol of opportunity and freedom through leadership that constantly strives to give meaning to the fundamental principles of our Constitution. Those principles of justice, opportunity, equality, and inclusion must continue to guide the planning for our future.

Members of the Advisory Board to the President's Initiative on Race have spent the past 15 months engaged in a process designed to examine race relations in America. Through study, dialogue, and action we have begun to engage the American people in a focused examination of how racial differences have affected our society and how to meet the racial challenges that face us. Our task was to take this necessary first step in the President's effort to articulate and realize a vision of a more just society.

THE ADVISORY BOARD AND ITS MANDATE

In June 1997, through Executive Order No. 13050, President Clinton appointed John Hope Franklin (chairman), Linda Chavez-Thompson, Reverend Dr. Suzan D. Johnson Cook, Thomas H. Kean, Angela E. Oh, Bob Thomas, and William F. Winter to serve as members of the Advisory Board. Each member brought to this effort the experience of having engaged in the work of building relationships and creating opportunities to bridge racial divides in their communities, professions, and workplaces.

This Initiative represents an example of leadership that seeks to move America toward its highest aspirations. No other President in the history of this Nation has had the courage to raise the issue of race and racism in American society in such a dramatic way.

The Board struggled with the fact that there currently does not exist a language or vocabulary that respects differences of opinion and experience that often materialize during conversations about race and racism in this country. The absence of such a language created tensions and opportunities to expand the dialogue. Despite the inadequacy of our existing language, the Board forged ahead to meet the objectives set out by the President through his Executive Order. Those objectives included the following:

- Promote a constructive national dialogue to confront and work through the challenging issues that surround race.

- Increase the Nation's understanding of our recent history of race relations and the course our Nation is charting on issues of race relations and racial diversity.

- Bridge racial divides by encouraging community leaders to develop and implement innovative approaches to calming racial tensions.

- Identify, develop, and implement solutions to problems in areas in which race has a substantial impact, such as education, economic opportunity, housing, health care, and the administration of justice.

In addition, the Advisory Board examined issues related to race and immigration, the impact of the media on racial stereotyping, and enforcement of civil rights laws.

We wish to make it clear that this Report is not a definitive analysis of the state of race relations in America today. That task should be undertaken by the many scholars and experts on race relations, only a few of whom we had the opportunity to meet during the course of this past year. We had no independent authority to commit Federal resources to a particular problem, community, or organization. Rather, we were engaged in the task of assisting with the initial stages of this new America's journey toward building a more just society in the 21st century. It is our hope that the information contained in this Report will present a more realistic view of how race has affected our national unity. Ideally, we hope that it will be used to create a more detailed blueprint for the future.

ACCOMPLISHMENTS, CHALLENGES, AND OPPORTUNITIES

The year of study and dialogue produced a number of outcomes that are directly attributable to the President's Initiative on Race. Some of these include:

- One America Conversations in which approximately 17,000 people in 39 States and 89 cities participated.

- Campus Week of Dialogue in April 1998, which involved students, faculty, and administrators on nearly 600 campuses.

- Statewide Days of Dialogue in April 1998, which involved 110 communities, governors of 39 States and 2 territories, and 25 mayors.

- Meetings between Advisory Board members and/or Initiative staff with approximately 600 tribal leaders and members around the country to discuss race and sovereignty. This included special meetings and conferences with 60 tribal leaders and visits to the Standing Rock Sioux Reservation in North Dakota and the Lummi Reservation in Washington State.

- The *One America Dialogue Guide,* which was produced to facilitate discussions about race.

- Four forums for corporate leaders and 2 forums for religious leaders that engaged more than 1,000 leaders in the corporate and faith communities in discussions of race, racial and cultural barriers, opportunities, and leadership.

- Outreach to more than 30,000 young Americans in 48 States and Puerto Rico through the President's "Call to Action" letter, the Vice Presidential Briefing for Youth-Oriented Media, and numerous other youth activities.

- Identification of more than 300 Promising Practices—community efforts designed to bridge racial divides.

- Two nationally televised public service announcements, including one that received the advertising industry's honor for best public service announcement.

- On average, approximately 1,000 "visits" per week on the One America Web site and the receipt of more than 1,000 e-mail messages from people around the country.

- The White House Conference on Hate Crimes in November 1997.

- More than 2,200 news and magazine articles written during the period from June 1997 through April 1998 that made reference to the Race Initiative.

Many challenges lie ahead. As America's racial diversity grows, the complexity of giving meaning to the promise of America grows as well. It is these challenges that signal where opportunities may exist. This Report attempts to frame the challenges, identify the opportunities, and recommend action. It provides an overview of information gathered from communities across the Nation, including diverse points of view about racial differences and controversial issues that are currently being debated and ideas for how strong leadership can continue to move our Nation closer to its highest aspirations.

REPORT OVERVIEW

In Chapter One, the common values and concerns that people share, regardless of racial background, are discussed. The chapter highlights the leadership being demonstrated in almost every sector of our Nation, including schools, businesses, labor organizations, community-based organizations, local government, and faith-based organizations.

Chapter Two presents a discussion on why it is important for America to grapple with the difficult subject of race and racism at the end of the 20th century. We present our observations on how the goal of achieving racial justice and reconciliation requires us to deepen our understanding of different points of view about how race affects individual and institutional biases.

Chapter Three provides information about racial demographics in America. It focuses on how the predicted shift in the Nation's demographic profile will require us to expand the race relations framework to reflect America's growing diversity.

In Chapter Four, the focus shifts to select issues addressed by the Advisory Board in its meetings throughout the year and relevant data concerning civil rights enforcement; racial disparities in education, economic opportunity, housing, the criminal justice system, and health care; the immigrant experience; and the impact of stereotypes on racial attitudes. These data demonstrate the reality of the racial divides among us and the need to set priorities in taking action for the future. The chapter also includes all of the recommendations for action submitted to the President following the formal Board meetings. Many have already been implemented or are awaiting congressional action.

Chapter Five captures our sense of the transition to the next phase rather than closure of this 15-month effort. It includes final observations and recommendations as we build on the President's vision of one America in the 21st century.[1] It also identifies other critical issues that the Advisory Board believes deserve further dialogue. Among these issues is affirmative action, which the Board believes remains an important tool for overcoming racial discrimination and promoting the benefits of diversity in education, employment, and other contexts.

Although this Report concludes our year-long exploration of race and racism, our work is only the foundation for building one America. The work that lies ahead cannot be accomplished by a single group. Our experience has provided the Nation with the chance to identify leaders in many parts of this country, working in numerous fields, who will promote a vision of a unified, strong, and just society. The Race Initiative affirmed the efforts of Americans who have been, are, and will continue to give meaning to the words "justice," "equality," "dignity," "respect," and "inclusion." We urge bold and decisive action to further the movement toward "redeeming the promise of America."

In addition to this Report, a major report on racial disparities prepared by the Council of Economic Advisers (CEA) has been released to the public.[2] Copies of that report may be obtained through the CEA Web site at www.whitehouse.gov/WH/EOP/CEA. In addition, attached to this Report are 11 appendixes that provide supporting and clarifying material related to the substance of our report.

CHAPTER ONE—SEARCHING FOR COMMON GROUND

I just hope that the Board and its report... talks not only about the need to respect the differences among our communities, but also to dwell on those principles that unify us and how we got to those principles... The best way of bridging these issues is to focus on solving problems that are, in fact, common to all of us. We are all concerned about personal safety and crime. We are all concerned about education. We are all concerned about economic development and income differences.

Karen K. Narasaki, Executive Director of the National Asian Pacific American Legal Consortium, statement at the Carnegie Endowment for International Peace and Georgetown University Law Center meeting on immigrants and race, Washington, D.C., July 13, 1998

Although America confronts a variety of racial and cultural barriers, common themes and concerns emerged throughout the year that reinforced our view that we are indeed more united as a country than divided. Too often, however, race prevents us from moving beyond our differences to see our common interests. In this chapter, we highlight some of the common ground we discovered, the importance of dialogue in breaking down barriers and finding common ground, the role of leaders in bringing people together, and the efforts in which people across the Nation came together despite racial differences. These efforts, which we call Promising Practices, give us hope that the Nation can make a serious commitment to overcome our history of racism and has the will to eliminate persisting racial disparities, allowing us to move beyond destructive myths, stereotypes, and discrimination and its vestiges.

AMERICANS SHARE COMMON VALUES AND ASPIRATIONS

Some common values and aspirations that Americans share became evident as we traveled throughout the Nation. We all share common values—a thirst for freedom, the desire for equal opportunity, a belief in fairness, and the need for essential justice. We all possess common aspirations—a decent and affordable home, a good education, a fulfilling job, financial and personal security, adequate and available health care, and healthy and educated children whose dreams for a bright future are a vision of reality, not a mirage. We all feel the same emotions—joy at the birth of a child, sadness at the death of a loved one, love for our family, fear of conditions beyond our control, anger at people who disrespect us, hope for the future, and frustration at the daily barriers we encounter. We all should aspire to the vision of an America in which we honor and respect the differences that make each of us unique and celebrate the common threads that bind us together.

Based on the common themes we heard throughout the year, a set of fundamental principles that we believe all Americans either do or can embrace as ideals for American society—justice, equality of opportunity, respect, responsibility, honor, integrity, civility, and inclusion—has been articulated. Through our work this year, we have established partnerships with individuals, communities, businesses, schools, religious institutions, Administration officials, and tribal governments from across the country to promote these principles and to ensure they become a reality for all Americans.

DIALOGUE IS A TOOL FOR FINDING COMMON GROUND

One of the best tools for finding common ground and developing new understanding among people of different races is dialogue. One goal for this year was to spark an extensive dialogue in which people throughout America could freely discuss how problems of race have impinged on their lives and affected the Nation in ways that could impede progress in other areas. We hoped that these dialogues would help refute stereotypes and provide opportunities for people to share their individual experiences and views, which may be different from others because of their race. Although statistics on discrimination and racial disparity show continuing inequality, it was hearing the personal experiences that had the most effect on us. They are the most useful in bringing people closer together to work for a Nation where people are given equal opportunities and treated fairly regardless of race.

When the President called for a great national conversation about racial issues, he was not calling for more debates about race, which have a long and valued tradition in this country.[3] Today, debates on race often take the form of politicians, experts, pundits, and the public arguing for their positions on issues such as affirmative action, immigration, and bilingual education. Alternatively, dialogue offers an opportunity to talk about race and issues related to race in a way that leads to a better understanding of differing views, experiences, and cultures. We hope the dialogue that began this year will continue with civility and respect for each other's views and that it will extend to all parts of the country and to all segments of our society.

In our discussions with experts on and facilitators of racial dialogue, we learned two important differences between debate and dialogue:

- The object of debate is to persuade others to one's point of view. The object of dialogue is to exchange ideas and find common ground.

> *I believe we're engaged in a task that's about reaching the hearts, not just the minds, of America*
>
> **Angela Oh, Advisory Board meeting, Washington, D.C., June 18, 1998**

- In debate, the role of the average person is to observe and eventually take sides. In dialogue, each person actually participates, offering his or her experience and perspective regarding an issue.

Dialogue helps to illuminate the areas of disagreement and common ground. The success of a dialogue should be measured by how well the participants develop a tolerance for differing perspectives and a shared insight of the issue.

One example of effective dialogue that we witnessed occurred during a forum on race sponsored by the University of Mississippi. Ten dialogue groups, composed of people from diverse racial backgrounds, were convened in preparation for the public forum, which was held on the campus on March 16, 1998. Most of these groups focused on a specific issue related to race (such as labor, business, and education). Many conducted several meetings in the weeks preceding the forum. During the inspiring public forum, leaders from each group presented specific recommendations for action and committed themselves to ongoing efforts to implement these recommendations.

Another example of how dialogue can deepen understanding occurred during the Annual Session of the National Congress of American Indians in Sante Fe, New Mexico. Advisory Board members Angela Oh and William Winter participated in a conversation with more than 20 representatives of tribal governments and Indian organizations from across the country. Not only was the substance of the conversation remarkably honest, the physical format used was a reflection of the values held by many American Indians. Sitting in a circle, without a dais or microphones, the Board members learned that there was a divide among tribes about the Race Initiative. Specifically, some were angry that an American Indian or Alaska Native was not asked to serve on the Board. Others expressed the view that it was better that way because American Indians and Alaska Natives are not "minorities," rather they are people of sovereign nations. Thus, any input from American Indians and Alaska Natives should be in the form of an appropriate government-to-government exchange.

Two Ole Miss women students, one black and one white, faced an angry man at a forum on race on the campus and calmly explained to him why waving the Rebel flag at football games was offensive to many students, whereupon he agreed not to wave his flag anymore.

William Winter on his experience at a forum on race at the University of Mississippi, Spring 1998

HONEST, OPEN RACIAL DIALOGUE IS DIFFICULT

As we began to organize and participate in dialogues, it was apparent that few citizens have been involved in or have organized conversations in which genuine dialogue on racial issues has taken place. Many people are uncomfortable examining the complexities of racial issues with those who may see them differently. Many people fear saying the wrong thing or being misunderstood and, therefore, being labeled a racist. Many minorities and people of color[4] may be tired of constantly talking about race without seeing concrete action to reduce disparities. Some may also be concerned about being labeled as traitors to their race or too sympathetic to the perspectives or views of those of other races. Dialogue is not always easy; often, it is quite difficult. Yet, most of those who did participate in these dialogues found them beneficial, insightful, and a welcome opportunity to discuss difficult issues in an environment in which it was safe to express their views.

For example, some Board members were able to participate in the Central High School 40th Anniversary Observance in Little Rock, Arkansas, sponsored by the National Conference for Community and Justice. We were struck by the ability of the people of Little Rock—particularly the Little Rock Nine, who were the first to desegregate Central High School—to share their experiences and examine a painful chapter in their lives and in the Nation's history. It was powerful and touching to see an apology from one who vehemently opposed and protested the desegregation to one of the Little Rock Nine result from the dialogue surrounding the commemoration.[5]

In fact, coinciding with our September 1997 Board meeting, the Center for Living Democracy released its year-long study which identified more than 80 interracial dialogue groups in more than 30 States and the District of Columbia. The Center estimated that hundreds of thousands of Americans were engaging in sustained dialogues.[6]

DIALOGUE HELPS TO DISPEL STEREOTYPES

The dialogues in which the Board participated involved interaction and communication among people of different racial backgrounds. This type of interaction was particularly important because it served as a means for confronting and dispelling stereotypes. One of the more formidable barriers to bridging our continuing racial divide is negative racial stereotypes. These stereotypes are endemic in our culture; we learn them from our friends and family, in school, and through the media. One of the most effective ways to confront and dispel racial stereotypes is through continuous, meaningful interaction among people of different racial backgrounds. Unfortunately,

As a civil rights baby, I was particularly moved by the experience at the commemoration of the 40th anniversary of the desegregation of Central High School. It was a powerful example of the difficulty of overcoming racial divides and of our ability to achieve our goal. It was a significant way for the Initiative to begin.

Reverend Dr. Suzan D. Johnson Cook, about the 40th anniversary of the desegregation of Central High School, Little Rock, Arkansas, September 26B27, 1997

opportunities for such interaction are often limited. More opportunities for these types of sustained dialogues are necessary to build a foundation for racial reconciliation.[7]

In addition to enabling people to find common ground, we believe that increased dialogue on race will make today's debates on race less divisive. Debates on the effect of affirmative action on minority college admissions will have more meaning if people also engage in dialogue on the amount of discrimination faced by elementary and high school students and the larger societal goals of affirmative action programs. Debates on bilingual education will be more productive if people engage in dialogue with those who have limited English ability about their desire to become fluent and the best means for accomplishing that goal. Because most people are not engaged in dialogue about the underlying perceptions of race, debates about future strategies often become divisive or remain stagnant. Dialogue also may be impeded by the failure to include empirical data about race and racial disparities. Although all may not agree on the meaning of the facts, they provide a basis for illuminating participants' opinions.

SPARKING THE DIALOGUE

Recognizing the importance of dialogue and the need to bring people together to begin these conversations, the Board, in partnership with Administration officials, engaged in several outreach efforts to initiate dialogues on racial issues throughout the Nation. These outreach efforts took the form of One America Conversations, Campus Week of Dialogue, Statewide Days of Dialogue, and meetings with tribal leaders.

One America Conversations consisted of a grassroots outreach effort to engage Americans across the country in the President's national dialogue on race. Initially, Administration officials, as they traveled on routine business, were encouraged to organize groups of 10–20 people at each location to participate in conversations on race. Some Board members also hosted One America Conversations during their travels. Since late November 1997, Federal agency officials, the Office of the President, and other Administration offices have hosted 175 conversations across the country. Subsequently, the Initiative has branched out beyond Administration officials to expand the One America Conversations effort into other parts of the public and private sectors. In total, more than 17,000 people have taken part in more than 1,300 dialogues on race.

During a meeting of college and university presidents attending an American Council of Education and Association of American Colleges and Universities Conference in October 1997 in Miami, Florida, Board members

John Hope Franklin, Reverend Dr. Suzan D. Johnson Cook, and William Winter laid the groundwork for a larger effort at sparking dialogue among college and university presidents, students, faculty, and administrators. This resulted in the Campus Week of Dialogue, which took place in April 1998.

America becomes more racially and ethnically diverse every year; it is clear that young people, America's future leaders, are the most important constituency in our effort to create one America. John Hope Franklin and U.S. Secretary of Education Richard Riley asked college and university presidents across the Nation to organize race dialogue events, including town hall meetings, meetings between campus leaders and community leaders, meetings of students from diverse races and ethnicities, and other activities such as service events, film screenings, and faculty lectures. Nearly 600 colleges and universities, including community colleges, tribal colleges, and minority-serving institutions, responded to the call to action by organizing activities in every State, the District of Columbia, and Puerto Rico. (See Appendix E for a list of participating institutions.) An example of such an activity was when Advisory Board member Thomas Kean hosted a town hall meeting at Drew University where he is president.

In an effort to engage more State and local government officials and community organizations in dialogue, we partnered with the Young Women's Christian Association (YWCA) to sponsor the Statewide Days of Dialogue in conjunction with the National Day of Commitment to End Racism and Erase the Hate. To broaden the impact, make the most effective use of limited resources, and institutionalize the process, we again worked with 110 YWCA affiliates that collaborated with local partners to organize dialogues on race in their communities. Twenty-five mayors participated in the local dialogues, and governors of 39 States and 2 territories issued proclamations in support of dialogues on race and/or participated in events related to Statewide Days of Dialogue, which began on April 30, 1998. Board members and Initiative staff fanned out across the country to give strength and momentum to the day. Over a 3-day period, Board members and Initiative staff had a presence at more than 100 events in every region of the country. (See Appendix F for a listing of Statewide Days of Dialogue events.)

In forums...or in city councils and county governments, the voices of American Indians are very often neglected, simply because they're too few in number and they're too spread out.

Dr. Matthew Snipp, Advisory Board meeting on race and poverty, San Jose, California, February 11, 1998

We can't redo history, but we can more accurately reflect America's history in our schools' textbooks.

Mike Her Many Horses, Executive Director, Oglala Lakota Nation, meeting with the Dakota Territories Tribal Chairmen's Association, Washington, D.C., May 20, 1998

In recognition of the special legal and political status of tribal governments in the United States and to ensure that American Indians and Alaska Natives had an opportunity to participate in the conversation, Board members made a special effort to meet with and hear from tribal leaders. (See Appendix C for listing of specific meetings.) Two common issues were raised at almost every meeting:

- American Indians and Alaska Natives face a unique challenge from racism and ignorance in the United States; tribes are not respected as governments because non-Indians do not understand the fundamental principle of sovereignty and how tribal governments fit into the Federal system.

- Participants expressed disappointment and concern that there was no American Indian or Alaska Native Board member. American Indians often lack representation on councils and boards and often are not part of important discussions and policymaking decisions.

In addition, many tribal leaders expressed concern that in many instances the United States Government fails to work with tribes on a government-to-government basis. Other frequently expressed sentiments included the concern that "one America" would be interpreted as a modern form of assimilation. U.S. Government policy toward American Indians and Alaska Natives has always been one of assimilation versus integration. Indian country fiercely defends the right to be self-governing and to maintain their own languages, cultures, religions, ways of life, and traditional practices. Lastly, American Indians and Alaska Natives expressed concern that they are an invisible community in America, viewed as the "vanishing race" because of their depiction by Hollywood, their relatively small population, the remote location of their reservations, the lack of understanding that tribes are governments, and the way school books do not accurately reflect the history of American Indians and Alaska Natives.

A GUIDE TO DIALOGUE

Board members supported the creation of a guide to assist in furthering discussion about race issues. In March 1998, the Initiative and the Community Relations Service of the U.S. Department of Justice collaborated with six nonprofit organizations[8] specializing in race dialogues to draft and publish the *One America Dialogue Guide*, a thorough and authoritative guide to conducting discussions on race. (See Appendix G for excerpts from the *Guide*.) More than 6,000 *Guides* have been distributed to individuals and groups eager to conduct meaningful discussions on race, and it is available on the Initiative Web site (www.whitehouse.gov/Initiatives/OneAmerica/america.html).

The *Guide* has proved to be extremely valuable and should continue to be distributed. The President should make direct appeals to public and private institutional leaders in a public information campaign about the usefulness of the *Guide* in sparking dialogue. The Administration should secure long-term commitments from organizations that reach communities that do not normally discuss race to use and distribute the *Guide*. Lastly, the Administration should develop a strategy to increase the number of people skilled in facilitating racial dialogue.

We have made a significant start in sparking the dialogue. We have observed successful efforts involving thousands of people in Columbia, South Carolina; Jackson, Mississippi; Winston-Salem, North Carolina; Hartford, Connecticut; Providence, Rhode Island; Los Angeles, California; Lincoln, Nebraska; Topeka, Kansas; Cleveland, Ohio; Santa Fe, New Mexico; Seattle, Washington; and in many other cities across the country. We hope that our efforts will have a ripple effect and eventually touch every person in America.

> *I spoke to 900 people in Seattle in which the grassroots groups from many parts of the city came together to talk about their work on various racial problems in their communities.*
>
> **John Hope Franklin on an example of a dialogue that he witnessed on April 13, 1998**

LEADERSHIP COUNTS

Without strong leadership, finding common ground across racial lines would be extremely difficult and slow. Leaders can encourage dialogue and bring about action that will help bridge racial divides. Because dialogue alone does not suffice, another prong of our strategy to achieve racial harmony was to identify a cadre of leaders who are committed to this work over time. We found many leaders and "local heroes" who, on their own initiative, were mobilizing colleagues to build racial bridges in their communities, at their workplaces, and in their houses of worship. We sought to build on these existing efforts and recruit new leaders.

Special attention was devoted to the religious and corporate sectors by organizing forums to engage leaders from these sectors. The religious sector brings the strength of its moral authority and history of commitment to racial healing efforts. The power of economic motivation makes the corporate sector a potentially invaluable partner in building one America.

THE ROLE OF RELIGIOUS LEADERS

Many religious leaders are already engaged in building bridges of racial reconciliation. At the same time, many members of the clergy could do much more for racial reconciliation. Some in the religious community have expressed regret at the clergy's lack of leadership and a desire for them to become more aggressive leaders in this regard. Most agreed that, for whatever reason, places of worship are among the least racially integrated institutions in our society.

Board member Reverend Dr. Suzan D. Johnson Cook took the lead in outreach efforts to the religious sector. On November 19, 1997, following the President's prayer breakfast, she convened a small group of religious leaders representing a variety of faiths to discuss the most effective ways to reach out to the religious community. These leaders agreed that holding forums for religious leaders to discuss race and faith would be useful.

In response to these leaders' suggestion, the Board held two forums for religious leaders. (See Appendix C for more information on the forums.) Locations were chosen because of the diversity of their faith communities. Those who attended were primarily local religious leaders, with a small representation of leaders from national religious organizations.

At these two forums, participants found common ground despite racial differences. Most importantly, many who attended agreed that they had a role to play in achieving racial harmony. The forums focused on three areas:

- **Examining the changing demography of the faith community.** Leaders explored how the demographics of their faith communities were changing dramatically and how they need to examine the significant implications these changes have for racial healing among their congregations.

- **Exploring the key elements to success of efforts to bridge racial divisions.** Many participants agreed that crucial elements for success include getting a significant number of white people to come to the table, providing more student and adult education programs, and offering forums for direct communication among community members.

- **Strengthening efforts of the faith community with regard to racial reconciliation activities.** Despite the active involvement of many members of the faith community, most participants agreed that much more can be done. At the forums, small group breakout sessions were used to develop plans for local efforts to narrow racial divisions.

An enormously compelling example of successful racial integration of a religious institution was found in Glide Memorial Church in San Francisco, which the members of the Advisory Board visited. The church is well known for its innovative is reflected in all aspects of its structure and programming.

> *And it is our hope and prayer...that through this Initiative and through the dialogue that we...can be headlights as we go into the new millennium, that we will let our light shine, that others will see the work that is before us.*
>
> **Reverend Dr. Suzan D. Johnson Cook, religious leaders forum, New Orleans, Louisiana, May 21, 1998**

There ministry, which seeks to address a wide range of human needs, including nutrition, health care, employment training, and spiritual nourishment through the arts and music. The church's ability to respond to diversity among its members should be continued outreach to the religious community. A small group of religious leaders should be convened who could engage people at the national, local, and tribal levels and call upon religious and spiritual leaders at all levels to use their moral authority more assertively. Our ability as a Nation to be a credible and effective moral leader around the globe rests largely on our ability to exercise moral leadership within our own borders.

THE ROLE OF CORPORATE LEADERS

Enlisting leaders in the corporate sector is vital. It is in the workplace where people most often come into contact with people from other races. Although corporate leaders do not always agree on the best approach to handling race in the workplace or on the extent of racial issues in their workplace, they repeatedly told us that diversity in the workplace was simply good business in a global economy.

The main vehicle for reaching leaders in the corporate sector was the convening of four forums in different parts of the country, hosted by Advisory Board member Bob Thomas. (See Appendix C for more information on these forums.) These forums offered opportunities to learn of the commitment many corporate and labor leaders have made to provide a fair and equitable work environment in firms, unions, and small businesses. Company executives also clearly expressed their understanding that their workforce needs to reflect the characteristics of the cities and towns they serve and in which they are located.

The three primary purposes for the forums were to:

- **Discuss the economic benefits of having a racially diverse workforce.** As *Miami Herald* publisher David Lawrence told the forum in Miami:

  > Our newspapers—and your businesses—need a workplace environment that encourages and enables all employees to achieve their full potential and, hence, produce the best results for our customers and constantly changing communities.

- **Identify and share best practices.** Diverse groups of panelists shared their companies' experiences in recruiting, hiring, training, promoting, and retaining minority employees. Panelists also discussed how their companies built a cohesive and productive racially diverse workforce. For example, during the January 1998 corporate and labor forum in

Phoenix, Arizona, a representative of Lucent Technologies described a range of programs their corporation supported, many of which are the product of collective bargaining. He referred to scholarship and training programs; diversity council networks and affinity groups; professional development programs; an employee assistance program to help employees with drug, alcohol, gambling, and family problems; and accountability measures. He also emphasized the vital importance of leadership from the top in both words and deeds and pointed to the diversity of the top leadership team at Lucent.

- **Strengthen networking between majority-owned and minority-owned companies.** Representatives of major corporations and minority suppliers and vendors explored ways to strengthen the relationships between large majority-owned companies and smaller minority-owned companies as an important element to promoting entrepreneurship in minority communities. This approach offers the promise of not only job development but also wealth creation, which ultimately provides the community with a more stable route to economic empowerment.

Finally, one of the many insights gained at these forums was the realization that many minority companies are small businesses and there are a number of small business issues that need to be addressed. Regardless of the stimulus, any substantive progress on improving governmental red tape issues for small business will help small companies owned by minorities (many of whom are women) or by white men and women.

The forums provided leaders in the corporate community with tangible evidence that harmonious, racially diverse workforces are usually more effective and creative at problem solving than homogeneous workforces. Although building a harmonious, racially diverse workforce takes time and effort, the experience of these corporate leaders shows that it pays off in productivity.

THE ROLE OF YOUNG LEADERS

In addition, we also engaged in specific outreach to young leaders. The quality of leadership that emerges from our young people will determine the future of America; they will ultimately decide whether we achieve our goals. Therefore, they must be at the top of our policy agenda.

Our outreach strategy comprised two phases. Phase one of this strategy, built on direct appeals from the President, Vice President, and First Lady, called for the direct involvement of young people interested in leading efforts in their communities. This included a letter from the President to

25,000 high school, college, and university student leaders and leaders from national and local youth organizations challenging them to become involved by promoting racial reconciliation in their communities.

Phase two involved the aggressive marketing of one America to young America. Board members personally spread the message to young people through participation in forums, conferences, seminars, One America Conversations, town hall meetings, and school visits.

The Student Council from Plum Senior High School in Plum, Pennsylvania, led an effort that resulted in their school, district, and borough declaring May 1, 1998, as "Youth Action for Diversity Day." Students held rallies and appeared on television, speaking openly about the value of diversity and the importance of the Race Initiative.

John Hope Franklin and William Winter participated in a children's dialogue on race, poverty, and community forum sponsored by the Children's Defense Fund as part of its 1998 annual national conference in Los Angeles. Nearly 100 high school and college students from diverse racial backgrounds explained how race has had an impact on their lives. They expressed their views on the origins of stereotypes and how they are perpetuated, gave detailed accounts of how they are often seen by their peers and others from a stereotypical perspective, and spoke about how stereotyping often leads to painful experiences such as racial and social isolation, social conflicts, and self-segregation. At the conclusion of the forum, the students committed themselves to promoting greater racial understanding among their peers and families by, for example, rejecting negative racial views held by family members and friends and increasing interaction with people of other races during social activities.

Angela Oh visited the Loredo Elementary School in Los Angeles in preparation for the December 17, 1997, Board meeting on K–12 education. In her discussion with the students—90 percent are Spanish speaking, and 10 percent are Asian Pacific American—she found that they were interested in learning languages other than their native language. There were Spanish speakers who wanted to learn Cantonese, and numerous students sought out Spanish language instruction. This seemed to stem from a fundamental desire to be able to communicate with, and among, diverse student groups in the school. In addition, she was impressed with the students' awareness of diversity when she joined a group of second graders who were reading the Spanish translation of the book *Amazing Grace*; they discussed the theme of exclusion raised in the story and wrote essays about the underlying feelings that they would have if they found themselves in the protagonist's role.

> *I don't think we need to become one culture. I think we just need to respect the differences of each culture.*
>
> **Megan, Children's Defense Fund conference, Orange County, California, March 26, 1998**

The youth outreach effort is a continuing process. The views of America's young people on race are different than those held by any generation preceding them. Board members were surprised and heartened to learn that young people are more willing than their elders to look at each other as equals and friends regardless of race. When they encounter racism, it frustrates and angers most of them. Young America is an untapped resource for achieving racial harmony. We must find ways to channel their considerable energies into positive action and turn instances of personal or group intolerance into proactive inclusiveness.

SUPPORTING COMMUNITY LEADERS

Community leaders—"local heroes" of all ages in all sectors—are key to racial healing and the achievement of racial harmony. They possess the type of commitment that cannot be manufactured and is needed to overcome the inevitable challenges they will face. These local heroes viewed the Initiative as a much-needed affirmation of the work they are doing, and they told Board members that the Initiative's presence and support has spurred many of them to do more.

On a daily basis, they are engaged in directing individual or institutional attention to racial divisions and disparities, channeling resources toward eliminating divisions and disparities, changing social norms toward promoting diversity and inclusion, advocating for change in social or institutional practices, and building coalitions across racial lines. This can be exciting, challenging, and rewarding work; too often, however, it can be difficult, frustrating, and dangerous as well. The quest for racial justice can be lonely, and these leaders need the following help and support:

- Active leaders need to know there are others across the country working toward the same goal. They need contact with other leaders, moral support from authority figures, and recognition for their efforts from respected institutions.

- Many potential leaders need affirmation to overcome fears of fighting the social norm, a norm that guides many to avoid dealing with difficult issues such as race and discrimination.

- Leaders in activities designed to affect racial attitudes need to be formally appreciated for what they do. Often, they are discouraged when their efforts are characterized as insignificant because they do not address specific important issues of disparities in educational attainment, economic opportunity, access to affordable housing and quality health care, and fairness of law enforcement. Addressing racial attitudes is an equally vital task because it affects the political and social climate in a

[I]t is absolutely delightful that the children at the elementary level don't know what color is. They understand diversity...they celebrate their differences. One young student said, 'And that makes us one. We all are the same inside.' And I got that very distinctly from the curriculum, from the expression of the parents, from the expression of the teachers...I was absolutely blown away by how intense these young fourth and fifth graders were in expressing why to them there is absolutely no difference between all of them, no matter what their name is and no matter what the color of their skin is.

Linda Chavez-Thompson on her visit to Bailey's Elementary School, a school of racial and ethnic diversity, Fairfax County, Virginia, December 17, 1997

manner that makes people more receptive to policies designed to narrow specific disparities.

- Many potential leaders want to provide leadership, but they do not know what to do or how to reach out to broad sectors of their community. They need advice and support from other leaders to help them in their efforts.

- Many active and potential leaders need to be reminded that fighting racism often is a personal and lifelong struggle. Although there is progress, the finish line is not yet in sight. We must have leaders in every generation who will speak to their peers with the passion and commitment necessary to bring each generation closer to the vision of one America.

- Many active and potential leaders could make good use of additional funds from governments, foundations, and corporations to assist with their activities, including wider mailings, facility rentals, dialogue materials, and travel to provide and obtain technical assistance.

PROMISING PRACTICES GIVE US HOPE[10]

Participation in common activities and working toward a common goal is among the best means to reduce racial tension and promote racial tolerance and acceptance. One of the Board's most gratifying discoveries was the vast number of existing efforts to improve race relations in communities throughout the country. These Promising Practices usually involve or result from dialogue and are products of strong leadership. (See Appendix H for a listing of the many organizations identified during the year; refer to the One America Web site at www.whitehouse.gov/Initiatives/OneAmerica/america.html for a full description of these Promising Practices.)

Sometimes, these Promising Practices are informal efforts and not institutionalized.[11] In other instances, organizers recognize that they would better help their communities if formal programs and organizations are created so others can join. Promising Practices represent not only one-time events but regular sustained efforts. They are examples that can be replicated and tailored to other communities.

Some of these efforts are large programs run by national organizations with affiliates around the country.[12] Others are small and often involve only a handful of people meeting regularly at a local diner.[13] These programs range from efforts to involve multiracial groups of people in common service projects[14] to programs that focus on creating settings that foster interracial dialogue[15] to programs that concentrate on expanding the opportunities of

> [W]hat our Initiative has done is prick the consciousness of America. The Promising Practices that we've seen have heightened my hope to show that America is more hopeful than not.
>
> **Reverend Dr. Suzan D. Johnson Cook, Washington, D.C., June 18, 1998**

historically disadvantaged groups and efforts to reduce racial disparities.[16] These efforts vary in scope, duration, and intensity of activity, but all are making some improvement in the racial climate.

The programs demonstrate what leaders can do when they commit themselves to making a change and finding common goals across racial lines. Promising Practices are a source of optimism; they demonstrate that people concerned about race relations can go beyond mere concern and take action to improve race relations.

Although we expected to find a wide variety of programs that could play a vital role in racial reconciliation, the vast range of existing programs was a surprise. Following are descriptions of some of the many efforts we discovered.

One program that is explicitly concerned with reducing minority communities' dependence on government through entrepreneurship is the Start-Up program in East Palo Alto, California, which Bob Thomas visited in conjunction with the February 11, 1998, Board meeting on race and poverty. Start-Up puts together aspiring business people from low-income communities with students from the Stanford Business School and provides grants. During his visit, Bob Thomas heard from East Palo Alto residents about their difficulties obtaining capital and the importance of Start-Up in assisting them to become entrepreneurs. General racial discrimination issues in starting up and sustaining a new business also were discussed.

John Hope Franklin and Linda Chavez-Thompson learned about the programs offered by Chicanos Por La Causa, Inc. (CPLC) when they visited the corporation in conjunction with the January 14, 1998, Board meeting in Phoenix, Arizona. CPLC is a community development corporation that offers educational and training services designed to promote the employment of members of the poor, largely Hispanic, South Phoenix community. For teen parents and expectant mothers, CPLC provides classes on child-rearing skills, health, nutrition, and occupational skills. For adults, it provides a comprehensive educational training and employment program, including an initial assessment, vocational counseling and training, employment and postemployment tracking, and support services.

Governor Kean was particularly impressed by Two Towns: One Community in Maplewood and South Orange, New Jersey, which develops home ownership strategies to promote racial diversity. It assists low-income disadvantaged residents in how to purchase a home. Services include how to finance a home, understanding the loan process, and what to ask when purchasing a home. The project goal is to improve the asset holdings of low-income residents and their economic stability.

One promising program, Communities Taking Charge (which we heard about at the Carnegie Endowment for International Peace meeting on immigrants and race), will begin this fall and is sponsored by the Los Angeles Human Relations Commission. The executive director described how it often is difficult to bring people together to understand that they share similar concerns and problems because Los Angeles consists of individuals from many different racial, ethnic, and cultural backgrounds. The program will place community organizers in racially and ethnically diverse communities to train and assist residents in how to support or create community-based infrastructures such as neighborhood councils and steering committees. These infrastructures are expected to encourage local leadership on issues that promote common neighborhood interest across racial and ethnic lines. Because this program is just starting, it has not been highlighted as a Promising Practice.

Other organizations such as the Healing Racism Institutes located in such areas as Little Rock, Arkansas, and Houston, Texas, focus on reexamining the social and psychological aspects of racism rather than on an action agenda. John Hope Franklin spoke with some of the leaders of this organization and learned more about their work examining the complexity and pervasiveness of racism and prejudice. They call themselves "recovering racists," drawing a close analogy between themselves and drug addicts. He heard about how the institutes help program participants change their lives to overcome racial barriers.

As these examples show, Promising Practices bring people together and allow them to find and share common goals and activities. Although dialogue serves as an important first step in achieving racial harmony, Promising Practices often go beyond dialogue to stimulate and support more active efforts to bridge racial divisions. These Promising Practices and the leadership that makes them work must be recognized and rewarded, nurtured and supported if one America is to become a reality.

This chapter has presented the core of the Board's work over the past year, serving as the "eyes and ears" of the President to understand the "the course our Nation is charting on issues of race relations and racial diversity."[17]

These activities and efforts focus on taking the pulse of the Nation on matters dealing with race and identifying viable means to address the complex problems of race that still divide our country. While we have much that unites us, the legacy of America's racial history, racial disparities, and discrimination continue to plague us in our ability to become one America.

It was moving meeting Captain Kwame Cooper of the Los Angeles Fire Department at his precinct in West Los Angeles and having him show us how he and his fellow firefighters were using their fire station as a community center for the kids in their precinct and how they were getting them to be members of their "Junior Firefighters" organization rather than joining a street gang.

William Winter, visiting the Community-Based Fire Protection Program, March 27, 1998

In the remaining chapters, we share many of the lessons we learned this year and how they led us to make recommendations about how to change public policies and programs as well as how to improve hearts and minds on the issue of race. These lessons also helped us understand how we can use dialogue, an ever growing cadre of informed and dedicated leaders, the sharing and replication of Promising Practices, and appropriate government policies and programs to become one America in the 21st century.

CHAPTER TWO—STRUGGLING WITH THE LEGACY OF RACE AND COLOR

Does race matter in America? During the Initiative year, this question arose over and over again. Time and again, the Advisory Board heard, "Yes, race matters." It became increasingly clear that America is still struggling with the impact of past policies, practices, and attitudes based on racial differences—what we are calling the legacy of race and color.

During the first meeting of the Advisory Board on July 14, 1997, Board members John Hope Franklin, Linda Chavez-Thompson, and Angela Oh began a discussion of the legacy of race and color, its implications for the future and achieving the goal of one America in the 21st century. Ms. Chavez Thompson initiated the discussion with her comment, "[T]he classic American dilemma has now become many dilemmas of race and ethnicity." Ms. Oh expressed her interest in having the conversation on race go beyond discussions of racism affecting blacks. She indicated: "We need to go beyond that because the world is about much more than that, and this [Initiative must look toward]…the next horizon." In response to Ms. Oh's comment, Advisory Board Chairman Dr. Franklin remarked:

> This country cut its eye teeth on racism in the black/white sphere…[The country] learned how to [impose its racist policies on]…other people at other times…because [it had] already become an expert in this area.
>
> And I think that gives us the kind of perspective we need. It's not to neglect [others]…but it's to try to understand how it all started and how we became so proficient and so expert in this area [of racism].

This brief discussion was perceived by many as a split in the Board over whether the Initiative's focus would be on the past or future and whether the President's Initiative on Race would be confined to what many called "the black-white paradigm." The Board did not share this characterization of the discussion as dissension. Neither did the Board subscribe to the view that this preliminary discussion signaled an intent to ignore the growing racial diversity of the American people.

As the year progressed, we had numerous opportunities to read, think, and talk about these issues. We heard from many experts and individuals about the significance of the legacy of race and color and the way that legacy is manifested in current attitudes and behavior by both individuals and institutions. We have never been in doubt about the necessity of looking to the past to understand how America's history of slavery and racial exploitation has helped to set the stage for the framework of racial hierarchy, discrimination, and domination with which we now contend as a Nation. Appreciating this deep, historical root is fundamental, in our view, to understanding how the race issue has become a seemingly intractable part of our social life. In turn, this understanding is the platform upon which we will learn how to manage more effectively the increasing diversity and complexity of our Nation's ethnic and cultural present and future. In the words of Dr. Franklin at our first meeting: "The beginning of wisdom is knowledge, and without knowledge of the past we cannot wisely chart our course for the future." Nor was there any doubt that in looking to the future, we would seek to include those who are neither black nor white in our work.

In this chapter, we share some of the insights gathered during monthly Board meetings and at other events to which individual Board members were invited. Among the lessons learned is this: The absence of both knowledge and understanding about the role race has played in our collective history continues to make it difficult to find solutions that will improve race relations, eliminate racial disparities, and create equal opportunities in American life.

This chapter is not intended to be a recitation of the full history of every minority group in this country that has been subjected to discrimination. Nor could it be. It is an attempt to point to some of the more egregious examples of a long and documented history of racism and systematic discrimination in this country. For it is our history of denying rights and benefits on the basis of race that condition our present and potentially our future. This must be understood, but it is beyond this Report to provide that lesson in the detail that is necessary. Our point is that our history has consequences, and we cannot begin to solve "the race problem" if we are ignorant of the historical backdrop.

If we fail to devise effective solutions, we will, in turn, undermine our future as the world's most internally strong and globally competitive society. Educating the Nation about our past and the role race has played in it is a necessary corollary to shaping solutions and policies that will guide the Nation to the next plateau in race relations—at which point race no longer results in disparate treatment or limited opportunities and differences are not only respected but celebrated. We understand that this challenge is a formidable one. We also recognize the potential cost of not going forward and are heartened by the obvious enthusiasm of the many Americans who have participated in dialogues and meetings stimulated by the Initiative.

UNDERSTANDING THE PAST TO MOVE TO A STRONGER FUTURE

At the dawn of a new century, America is once again at a crossroads on race. The eminent African American scholar W.E.B. DuBois noted decades ago that the main problem of the 20th century would be the color line.[18] Indeed, at the end of the 20th century, the color of one's skin still has a profound impact on the extent to which a person is fully included in American society and provided the equal opportunity and equal protection promised to all Americans in our chartering documents. The color of one's skin continues to affect an individual's opportunities to receive a good education, acquire the skills to get and maintain a good job, have access to adequate health care, and receive equal justice under the law. But now, more than ever, racial discrimination is not only about skin color and other physical characteristics associated with race, it is also about other aspects of our identity, such as ethnicity, national origin, language, accent, religion, and cultural customs. The challenge for America is to ensure that none of these factors continue to affect the quality of life choices so that we can finally treat each other with dignity and respect regardless of our differences.

The Board's work over the past year demonstrates that to meet this important challenge, it is necessary for all Americans to improve their understanding of the role of race in American history, including the history and contributions of all minority groups and the continuing effect of that history on race relations in America today. For example, few Americans realize that from 1934 to 1949, the Federal Housing Administration (FHA)[19] used clauses mandating segregation in any housing development that used FHA financing, even after the Supreme Court invalidated such clauses in 1948. Segregation clauses were permitted until 1962.[20] After that, racial segregation in housing originally financed by FHA remained entrenched based on custom and attitude. The concentration of public housing in cities is a similar example. Although discriminatory laws and policies may change over time, the long-term impact of these forces has been significant. Until all people regardless of race have equal opportunities, properly constructed and targeted programs such as race-conscious affirmative action are necessary tools that expand opportunity, increase diversity, as well as remedy past discrimination.

A critical component for a constructive and honest national dialogue about race and racism is a greater public awareness of the history of oppression, conquest, and private and government-sanctioned discrimination and their present-day consequences. Fundamental to this historical understanding is an appreciation of the ways in which the long history of slavery in this country has codified the system of racial hierarchy in which white privilege has been protected by custom and then by law. Even today many whites view African Americans and Latinos as less intelligent and more prone to violence than other ethnic groups.[21] In addition, Dr. James Jones, at the second Board meeting, commented:

> We are influenced by our past in ways that are not always obvious. It is too much to claim that four centuries of bigotry and bias, institutionalized deprivation, and cultural oppression were eliminated by an act of Congress....We have not by any means undone the legacy of racism.[22]

Knowledge of the history of suffering experienced by minorities and people of color must also be supplemented by an understanding of their many contributions to American society.

OUR HISTORY, OURSELVES: LOOKING AT AMERICA THROUGH THE EYES OF OTHERS

From the first contact between the indigenous peoples and colonists from Europe to the latest hate crime in the evening news, our Nation has grappled with the tensions caused by interaction between peoples of different cultures and races. Our system of government has evolved from one in which rights and privileges were accorded only to those men of European heritage, whose physical attribute of white skin and whose ownership of property connoted superiority and privilege, to one in which a purported bedrock principle is that *every* American, regardless of race, color, national origin, religion, disability, age, or gender, is entitled to equal protection under the law.

The path toward racial progress has had a difficult, sometimes bloody history: Our early treatment of American Indians and Alaska Natives, followed by the enslavement and subsequent segregation of African Americans and then the conquest and legal oppression of Mexican Americans and other Hispanics, the forced labor of Chinese Americans, the internment of Japanese Americans, and the harassment of religious minorities is a history of which many Americans are not fully aware and no American should be proud. Even the language we chose to characterize these actions is likely viewed as too conciliatory—or kind—by those affected groups.

However, as difficult as it may be to acknowledge the darker side of our history, we strongly acknowledge and appreciate that at every stage of the struggle to close the gap between the promise of our democratic principles and our policies and practices, Americans of every race worked side-by-side to move the Nation closer to the realization of that promise. From the abolitionists of the 18th and 19th centuries to the migrant workers of the West and Southwest to representatives and constituent members of the Leadership Conference on Civil Rights at the close of the 20th century—all have fought to retain and expand civil rights protections. No racial group in America has been absent in these pursuits. Nor can it be so in the future if we are to succeed.

As we look back, we can see more than struggle and discrimination. Along the uneven path to racial progress, we have also witnessed great courage and extraordinary leadership by ordinary Americans. These are ordinary men and women who have recognized that race is often at the center of our challenge to close the gap between who we are and who we aspire to be as a Nation. Our continuing challenge is to understand fully what the struggle was about—making real the promise of America for all—and to identify and harness the energy and commitment exhibited by earlier generations of ordinary Americans of all races at critical points in our history.

Any analysis or description of a group—particularly as large a group as a race of people—has its limits and exceptions. No group is monolithic. Nevertheless, based on existing research and on what we heard and learned, there are some statements and conclusions about people in specific racial groups and their experiences in America that are valid more often than not. It is in that context, here and throughout the Report, that we offer our observations.

We begin the next section with a brief discussion of the experiences of the country's native, original populations with the system of racial domination. This is followed with a discussion of slavery and its aftermath, a discussion of Latinos and Asian Pacific Americans, and, finally, a brief reference to white immigrant and ethnic groups. These synopses are not intended to substitute for the comprehensive, complex histories of misuse, oppression, conquest, and slavery that many groups have experienced as they have voluntarily or by force migrated to this country. It is designed to highlight the long legacy of mistreatment that is so easy to forget while permitting us to the discuss the many contributions and positive changes that have occurred as racial and ethnic groups have adapted to and been assimilated into our society. Although there is a story of America that as a country has made great progress in racial accommodation, it is, we believe, essential to recall the facts of racial domination.

The events discussed are not treated in a comprehensive manner. Rather, they are meant to be signposts of historical episodes that have greatly influenced our attitudes about race. The very complexity of our task in this limited context highlights the very real difficulties of those who wish to engage constructively in racial reconciliation.

THE AMERICAN INDIAN AND ALASKA NATIVE EXPERIENCE DEMONSTRATES THE COMPLEXITY OF RACIAL RELATIONSHIPS

Our understanding of America's racial history and its significance within the context of our larger history often is impeded by complex relationships and competing, sometimes contradictory, principles and values. The experience of American Indians and Alaska Natives is a powerful example of this complexity and contradiction.

We had a unique opportunity to meet with and learn from American Indian and Alaska Native tribal government leaders and members throughout the year.[23] Board member Bob Thomas recently made this observation about American Indians and Alaska Natives:

> Their history is unique, their relationship with our State and Federal governments is unique, and their current problems are unique. While not large in numbers, their situation tugs at the heart. I confess to being embarrassed this past year at my lack of knowledge of their overall situation. Embarrassed because I actually grew up and worked much of my life in geographic areas populated by Indian tribes, and I was oblivious to all but the common stereotypes. I suspect that most Americans are as equally oblivious, and believe a focused 'education' initiative [for] the American public is in order.[24]

On virtually every indicator of social or economic progress, the indigenous people of this Nation continue to suffer disproportionately in relation to any other group. They have the lowest family incomes, the lowest percentage of people ages 25–34 who receive a college degree, the highest unemployment rates, the highest percentage of people living below the poverty level, the highest accidental death rate, and the highest suicide rate.

American Indians and Alaska Natives have both a distinctive and extraordinarily complex status in the United States. They are the only minority population with a special relationship with the United States—one that has been developed over a 200-year period. It was crafted from an enormously varied set of indigenous societies, a massive European immigrant population, and the separate laws of each.[25] The more than 550 American Indian and Alaska Native tribes are home to people who are both U.S. citizens and members of tribes that are sovereign nations.

Sovereignty as an independent political entity means that, like any Nation, they have geographic, land-based boundaries. No other racial minority in this country has a land base of over 56 million acres in mostly reservation land held in trust in the continental United States, with an additional 40 million acres in Alaska. Like any other nation, the relationship of tribal governments with the Federal Government is defined by the United States Constitution; treaties; executive orders; congressional acts; Federal, State, and tribal court judgments; and programs administered by all Federal agencies.[26] Within reservation boundaries, American Indians are subject to tribal *and* Federal laws, but *not* the laws of contiguous States without tribal consent.[27]

The significance of sovereignty to American Indians and Alaska Natives cannot be overstated.[28] In a statement provided to the Board, tribal leaders of the Hualapai Indian Tribe described the importance of sovereignty and its relationship to race and racism:

> [We] wanted to touch on a few key points for an understanding of how racism manifests itself against Indian tribes....As Indian people, we have survived years of persecution—in what can only be understood today as a combination of racism and greed...we have survived as a Tribe. Our sovereign status is therefore not only a political status, recognized from the earliest days of European settlement in the United States, it is also key to our existence as Indians. Accordingly, the most virulent and destructive form of racism faced by Indian people today is the attack on our tribal sovereignty.[29]

Recently, Indian tribes have had to respond to questions about tribal sovereignty in the U.S. Congress. During the 105th Congress, Senate Bill 1691 was introduced that would provide, among other things, a waiver of tribal sovereign immunity.[30] One tribe, the Pueblo of Laguna, has described this legislation as today's versions of the forced marches and allotments of years past because it attacked the foundations of tribal sovereignty and tribal-Federal relations.[31] The resolution of this issue promises to strain relations between the U.S. Government and Indian nations.

Few Americans have had an opportunity to learn about the indigenous people of America in a way that extends beyond the most simplistic, widely perpetuated stereotypes of Indians. Based on the experiences of the Board members during the year, it appears that little, if any, correct information about tribal governments is taught in most schools. This lack of understanding is particularly problematic when it involves those who are responsible for developing and implementing government policies and programs—at the Federal, State, and local levels.

Race and racism affect American Indian and Alaska Native communities in ways similar to their effect on other non-white and Hispanic minorities in

America. Deeply entrenched notions of white supremacy held by European immigrants were applied to American Indians and Alaska Natives, who were regarded as inferior and "uncivilized." Therefore, access to opportunities has been limited, and American Indians and Alaska Natives have experienced exclusion and isolation from rights and privileges often taken for granted by most white citizens. They have become America's most invisible minority.

There have been some indicators of progress in redressing the shortfalls of history, such as President Clinton's 1994 reaffirmation of the Federal Government's commitments to operate within a government-to-government relationship with federally recognized American Indian and Alaska Native tribes, and to advance self-governance for such tribes. He also directed Federal agencies to build a more effective working relationship with tribes, consult with them openly and candidly, and fully consider their views prior to undertaking actions that may affect their well-being.[32]

AFRICAN AMERICANS AND THE UNIQUE LEGACY OF SLAVERY

Blacks have been subjected to long-term and systematic social and economic discrimination since their arrival on these shores. The African American experience is unique because of constitutionally sanctioned and governmentally enforced slavery and its legacy. However, discrimination directed against blacks began even before slavery was institutionalized. This discrimination reflected negative attitudes about race and color that were to remain in place from the 17th century to the present.

In many respects, the plight and history of blacks has commanded more attention than the history and treatment of other American racial minorities. This is true for a number of reasons. African Americans have constituted the largest American minority community for more than two centuries. An enormous body of thought was developed and propagated to justify their enslavement; out of this the negative stereotypes, myths, and superstitions about race were born. The only Civil War fought in the United States was over slavery and its economic importance to the Southern States.

For most blacks, the period following the Civil War and Reconstruction was a repudiation of the principles and values of the Constitution as they applied to Americans of African descent. Even as citizens, blacks were denied by law in the Southern States and by social custom in the North and West practically all the rights and privileges of American citizenship enjoyed by whites. This was accomplished in a systematic and complete way. In spite of the 13th, 14th, and 15th Amendments of the Constitution, the deeply ingrained ideology of white supremacy continued to impose upon black citizens the badge of inferiority and closed off most opportunities for them to assimilate as equals in American society.

Throughout the Initiative year, Board members frequently were asked if we would support a formal apology for slavery by either the President or Congress. Advocates for an apology maintained that this is a necessary step in the racial healing process for the country. We have given this issue considerable thought over the course of the year. We conclude that the question of an apology for slavery itself is much too narrow in light of the experience of blacks over the course of this Nation's history. Discrimination and racism directed against blacks have been unparalleled in terms of scope and intensity, not only during the period of slavery but also during the century following its demise. The period of slavery in this country represents a National tragedy from many perspectives.

Unless we take forceful steps to eliminate the consequences of this awful history of racism, they will continue to blight our Nation's future. The apology we must all make cannot be adequately expressed in words but in actions. We must make a collective commitment to eliminate the racial disparities in opportunity and treatment that characterize too many areas of our National life.[33]

PERPETUATION OF THE BADGE OF INFERIORITY

Latinos.[34] Every minority group in America has a distinct and unique historical experience with racism and oppression. The early connections of American Indians, Alaska Natives, African Americans, Asian Pacific Americans, and Puerto Ricans and other Latinos to the United States are fundamentally different. Latinos trace their presence in the United States to either conquest or immigration. In 1848, with the end of the United States' war against Mexico, thousands of people living on land that was formerly part of Mexico became subjects of the United States. Similarly, Puerto Ricans became part of the United States by conquest in 1898. Puerto Ricans, like Mexican Americans, were bound by their language and culture and, although Americans by conquest, remained native to their geographical homeland. All groups, however, experienced marginalization and discrimination in the United States.

Hispanics are currently the second largest minority group in the United States; more than 1 in 10 Americans, or 10.7 percent, are Hispanic. Latinos are also one of the fastest growing populations and are expected to become the largest "minority" group by 2005. Latinos are now roughly 12 percent of the labor force and are expected to become almost 40 percent of new labor force entrants.[35] About one in three Hispanics (30.3 percent) live in

> *From slavery to freedom, we have come a long way. But we are not all the way to freedom yet. It is not any one person's or faction's fault. Rather, it is the result of the deep and pervasive penetration of race into our collective psyche and social institutions.*
>
> **Dr. James Jones, Advisory Board meeting, Washington, D.C., September 30, 1997.**

poverty, compared with 29.9 percent of blacks and 11.2 percent of whites as of 1990.

There have been a number of fundamental historical events which have helped shape the course of the relationship of the white population in the U.S. to its Mexican American neighbors. Foremost among them was the war against Mexico in the 1840s. In 1848, at the conclusion of that war, the U.S. and Mexico signed the Treaty of Guadalupe Hidalgo,[36] in which the U.S. absorbed Texas, California, and the southwest. The U.S. occupied Mexico City in early 1848 and then ceded this territory for the modest payment of $15 million to Mexico. General Winfield Scott wrote at the time that during the war American soldiers "committed atrocities to make heaven weep and every American of Christian morals blush for his country."[37] The former secretary of state of the Republic of Texas commented:

> The two races, the Americans distinctively so called, and the Spanish Americans or Mexicans, are now brought by the war into inseparable contact. No treaties can henceforth dissever them; and the inferior must give way before the superior race.[38]

This experience of exclusion and discrimination has continued for other Hispanics who have come to the United States in large numbers since the late 1950s (Cubans) to the present record levels of immigration from Central American countries. It is critically important that the country be committed to including the historical experiences of Hispanics and other minorities within a comprehensive framework of our Nation's history if we are ever able achieve one America.[39] This is especially true with Latinos; according to the Census Bureau, they will become the largest minority group in America in the next century.

Asian Pacific Americans—The Perpetual Foreigners.[40] The treatment of Asian Pacific Americans as non-white, non-European immigrants was similar to that of other non-white minority groups. For example, Native Hawaiians, following the conquest of the Hawaiian Islands in 1893, experienced the same type of racial and cultural subordination that Puerto Ricans experienced.[41] Only in the past few years have the Native Hawaiian people gained recognition as a significant force in reclaiming their place in negotiations over such issues as land rights, cultural preservation, health care, and education in their native geographical homeland.

Although most Americans believe that Asian Pacific Americans are new to this country and have only recently affected the Nation's conversation and debate on race, Asian Pacific Americans have been shaping the discussion since the last half of the 19th century. Those who were immigrants were often thought of as a source of cheap labor. Discriminatory laws and informal sanctions during those early years limited the economic opportunities of Asian Pacific Americans and excluded them from certain occupations.[42] They were also prevented from establishing families and owning land in the early 1900s. The first Asian Pacific American immigrants thus were relegated to jobs as agricultural and factory laborers or owners of small businesses such as laundries, restaurants, and grocery stores that required little capital and few English language skills.

While discriminatory laws have limited economic opportunities for Asian Pacific Americans, America's long history of limiting the ability of Asian immigrants to become citizens and obtain the full benefits of citizenship has had an even more significant impact.[43] These laws limiting citizenship and naturalization worked in tandem with seemingly neutral laws such as those that prohibited aliens from owning land to discriminate against Asian Pacific Americans. The internment of Japanese Americans was the most extreme of the discriminatory laws passed that treated Asian Pacific Americans as outsiders and foreigners who should be questioned about their loyalty.[44] Even today new immigrants, many from other regions of Asia, such as the Phillippines, Vietnam, Laos, and Cambodia continue to feel the legacy of discriminatory laws against Asian Pacific Americans because they continue to be perceived and treated as foreigners.

Each of the minority groups discussed above share in common a history of legally mandated and socially and economically imposed subordination to white European Americans and their descendants. Such subordination has had powerful consequences for us as a Nation, which are manifested in the racial disparities discussed in Chapter Four.

However, our interaction with thousands of Americans of all races during the year has taught us that the blatant and egregious forms of prejudice and discrimination that were routine even three decades ago are not as frequent in contemporary society. Racial discrimination is still a fact of life—although it often is subtle. What clearly remain are significant barriers to opportunity. Barriers such as racially isolated and underfunded schools and deeply embedded racial stereotypes about the capacity, motivation, and ability of minorities have their roots deep in the past but have the capacity to shape our future unless we act as a community to eliminate them. Many Americans are searching for answers on how to achieve that result.

THE WHITE IMMIGRANT EXPERIENCE

Another experience that is important to the building of America is that of the white immigrant and the impact of ethnic difference on one's ability to assimilate into American society. For immigrants from countries such as

Ireland or Poland, the process of assimilation often was fraught initially with discrimination in employment and disenfranchisement at the polls. After these groups gained some empowerment through the political process, social acceptance followed. For other groups with strong religious identification, such as those who were Jewish or Catholic, some degree of social exclusion, discrimination, and disenfranchisement was common, with social acceptance slower to follow. More recent immigrants, many of them Muslim, are only now undergoing the immigrant experience, and old world antagonisms fueled by new world rivalries slow the prospects for inclusion and acceptance of these groups.

The point is that any group that enters a new country has had to face a barrage of barriers, whether language or religion or unfamiliar customs. The greatness of the American experience has been the opportunity for immigrants from every other country to become active participants in our political process. However, we also recognize that race and color have added significantly to the difficulty of some groups to gain acceptance as Americans with full rights of citizenship.

AMERICANS HOLD CONFLICTING VIEWS ON RACE AND RACIAL PROGRESS

While most minorities and people of color recognize the role of the legacy of race and color in their experiences, many whites do not. The Board found that the story of race at the end of the 20th century and into the 21st century is a story of conflicting viewpoints. Americans—whites, minorities, and people of color—hold differing views of race, seeing racial progress so differently that an outsider could easily believe that whites and most minorities and people of color see the world through different lenses. Whites and minorities and people of color also view the role of government in extremely divergent ways, especially with respect to the government's role in redressing discrimination.

Another element of contradiction, if not conflict, is the way in which America functions as a Nation of great optimism, tolerance, and inspiration focused on creating a more stable and diverse community, although discrimination, racial and ethnic oppression, and a smaller number of instances of outright racial evil persist. We are a country in racial transition; some of us welcome the change, others are unaware of or fear the change and its ramifications, while a few cling to an older order in which racism is so comfortably ingrained that it is simply characterized as "the way it is."

DIFFERING ATTITUDES

According to numerous polls and surveys that we reviewed, most whites believe that much of the problem of racial intolerance in this country has been solved and that further investigation is unwarranted and inappropriate. Polls also show that most Americans have a distorted view of who we are as a Nation and are intolerant of some racial groups other than their own.[45] A poll released by the *Washington Post,* Kaiser Family Foundation, and Harvard University revealed surprisingly uninformed views on the racial composition of America and the negative views that each minority group holds toward one another.[46] A 1997 Gallup poll pointed out, "From the white perspective, there are fewer race problems, less discrimination, and abundance of opportunity for blacks, and only minimal personal prejudice."[47] Another 1995 poll by the *Washington Post* revealed that only 36 percent of whites believe that "past and present discrimination is a major reason for the economic and social problems" facing blacks.[48]

A contradictory image of race in this country is clearly held by a large majority of blacks and Hispanics.[49] Numerous civil rights cases and social science reports carefully document this stark difference in viewpoints. Legal analyst Richard Delgado offered an explanation: "White people rarely see acts of blatant or subtle racism, while minority people experience them all the time."[50] Research by psychologists echoes that conclusion:

> [W]e [white Americans] tend to see racism as not a problem and particularly not a problem for us....However, from the perspective...of the people of color...[t]hey experience the consequences of...subtle biases on a daily basis. [T]hey see a discrepancy between what we say overtly, which is about fairness, and justice, and equality, and the subtle biases that pervade our society, and the way whites behave....[C]reat[ing] a situation of distrust, where they don't believe whites and where they tend to see this bias everywhere.[51]

Evidence presented to the Board makes it clear that many whites, in general, are unaware of how color is a disadvantage to most members of other groups.[52] For example, at the September Board meeting, Dr. Lawrence Bobo of Harvard University observed:

> In many ways, the centerpiece of the modern racial divide comes in the evidence of sharply divergent beliefs about the current level, effect, and very nature of discrimination blacks and Latinos, and many Asian Americans as well, feel it and perceive it in most domains of life. Many whites acknowledge that some discrimination remains, yet tend to downplay its contemporary impor-

tance....However, minorities not only perceive more discrimination, they see it as more institutional in character.[53]

A number of experts raised the sensitive issue of "white privilege"— institutional advantages based on historic factors that have given an advantage to white Americans. To understand fully the legacy of race and color with which we are grappling, we as a Nation need to understand that whites tend to benefit, either unknowingly or consciously, from this country's history of white privilege. Examples include being able to purchase an automobile at a price lower than that available to a comparable minority or person of color;[54] not being followed through department stores by clerks or detectives who seemingly follow almost all young Hispanic and black men; being offered prompt service while minorities and people of color are often still refused service or made to wait.[55] White privilege can impact all aspects of life, as Dr. James Jones stated: "While whites are generally privileged or at least given the benefit of the doubt, too often persons of color are simply doubted."[56] One of the lessons of our experience is the significant degree of unawareness by whites today of the extent of stereotypes, discrimination, and racism. One of our conclusions is the importance of educating all people of the continuing existence of prejudice and privilege. These invisible benefits need to be acknowledged by all as a vital and consequential feature of our society.

Moving in the Right Direction

If there has been a constant theme in our meetings over the year, it is this: Persistent racial disparities and discrimination remain.[57] *Changing America: Indicators of Social and Economic Well-Being by Race and Hispanic Origin*, a report compiled by the White House Council of Economic Advisers, is being released in conjunction with this Report. These indicators of social and economic well-being by race present evidence that although progress has been made, significant racial disparities and discrimination continue despite more than 30 years of civil rights laws and some progress directly attributable to affirmative action and other programs.

Those who argue that there has been no change, however, and that racism is an unchanging fixture in American life are, in our observation, incorrect. Research revealed steadily improving racial attitudes, especially among whites, over the past four decades. It is fair to say that there is a deep-rooted national consensus on the ideals of racial equality and integration, even if that consensus falters on the best means to achieve those ideals. For example, local police and the Federal Bureau of Investigation aggressively pursued the investigation of the murder of James Byrd[58] and death threats

> *"When I pump gas at a Circle K, and I don't have to worry about getting green carded, that's white privilege. When I get in trouble with the law, and...not having to fear getting knocked up beside the head by a police officer at the station, that's white privilege. When I have the expectation of graduating from a decent college and moving on to a decent well-paying job and seeing that as part of my birth right, that's white privilege.*
>
> **Joel Olson, Community Forum, Phoenix, Arizona, January 14, 1998.**

to 60 University of California at Irvine students with Asian surnames,[59] and there was a recent conviction obtained in the 30-year-old cases involving Klan-related murders of Medgar Evers and Vernon Dahmer.

Many tangible examples of racial progress exist, from the integration of the military to the numbers of minority-elected officials compared with 30 years ago, from the freedom of minorities and people of color to use public accommodations to the reduction of racial hostility when minorities and people of color seek to rent or buy homes, from the growing minority middle-class to the significant increase in interracial marriages. Discriminatory treatment still persists, but it is often, although not always, more subtle and less overtly hostile.

Too few of us have a real, or less than superficial, understanding of the forces that have resulted in the racial disparities that exist in educational and economic opportunity. Nor do we have a full or clear understanding of the way societal institutions currently manifest the vestiges of past discrimination and racist behavior. Many believe that racial discrimination is a thing of the past—the distant past at that. Yet, many also sincerely believe that racial inequality and racial disparities in education and employment are the result of lack of capacity, individual failing, poor family values, the influence of an environment in which personal responsibility is absent, or just plain bad luck. Although all of those factors may play a role with respect to specific individuals, the fact that minorities and people of color experience certain life conditions far more negatively than non-minority citizens offers powerful evidence that the consequences of a long history of discrimination, prejudice, and unequal treatment have not been adequately addressed in our society.

It is essential that we recognize the continuing impact of our history on today's world. We must be equally aware of the increasingly diverse Nation in which we live—which we discuss in Chapter Three—so that proposals for addressing discrimination and disparities reflect the issues and needs of a changing society.

CHAPTER THREE—THE CHANGING FACE OF AMERICA

With few exceptions, the challenges and issues that the Advisory Board confronted in its meetings, dialogues on race, reports, and correspondence, while often complex, were not new. What has changed and will continue to change is the extent of our racial and ethnic diversity.

Thirty-three years ago, in 1965, President Johnson wrote in the foreword to a journal exploring the state of race relations:

> Nothing is of greater significance to the welfare and vitality of this Nation than the movement to secure equal rights....No one who understands the complexity of this task is likely to promote simple means by which it may be accomplished. [The]...effects of deprivation [are interlocking]—in education, in housing, in employment, in citizenship, in the entire range of human endeavor by which personality is formed.
>
> If we are to have peace at home, if we are to speak with one honest voice in the world—indeed, if our country is to live with its conscience—we must affect every dimension of the [black American's] life for the better.[60]

President Johnson and society's focus then was almost exclusively black-white. Sixteen years later, in 1981, President Johnson's 1965 statement about the plight of blacks was cited again in the same journal.[61] However, in addition to confirming its continued relevance, the journal's editor noted that the issues raised by the President had grown even more insistent and complex. Importantly, the discussion in 1981[62] was expanded to include not only blacks but also American Indians and Alaska Natives, Mexican Americans, and Puerto Ricans; "four peoples—the 'victims' of conquest—men and women who did not choose America, who have long suffered exclusion and discrimination because of their origins, live overwhelmingly in conditions substantially different from those common to other groups in the United States."[63]

In 1998, although we have made a great deal of progress, Americans are still divided by racial and cultural barriers.[64] Our challenge is to see the barriers that remain as opportunities for learning, not as obstacles to common interests. We believe it is a challenge that can be met.

To be successful, however, we as a Nation first need to understand the changing face of America and the implications of the changes on how we think about race and race-related issues and how we improve race relations and become one American community in the new millennium. Trends indicate that as we move into the 21st century, we can anticipate an even more significant shift in the racial and ethnic profile of the American population, making reconciliation even more urgent.

A NATION IN RACIAL TRANSITION

From before its founding, through its expansion and colonization, and through immigration, this Nation has always had a diverse mix of races, cultures, and ethnic groups. This diversity is greater now than at any time in our history. America's native populations alone include more than 550 American Indian and Alaska Native tribes with distinct cultures, speaking more than 150 different languages—only a fraction of whom the Board was able to reach during its tenure. The Hispanic population comprises individuals of different cultures, national origins, and color. For example, people with family roots in Spain, Cuba, Mexico, the Dominican Republic, Argentina, and other Central and South American countries (e.g., Honduras, Columbia, Peru, and El Salvador) are considered Hispanic. Similarly, the Asian Pacific American category covers a large number of ethnic groups who also have distinct languages. Indians, Pakistanis, and Sri Lankans from South Asia are grouped together with Chinese, Japanese, and Koreans from East Asia. Also included in this group are Southeast Asians (such as Vietnamese, Hmongs, and Laotians) as well as Pacific Islanders (such as Fijians, Samoans, and Guamanians).

The black population is equally diverse. Although a majority of African Americans are native born, an increasing number of people who are considered blacks are immigrants from Africa and the West Indies. Of course, this heterogeneity within racial groups is not a new phenomenon. Whites have always included people of diverse ethnic, language, and national backgrounds. Europeans from different regions as well as people from the Middle East are classified as white for the purposes of data collection but obviously represent distinct groups.

During our meeting in September 1997, we heard from demographers who described the current United States population and the expected future racial composition of the population in the next 50 years. Today, as of the 1990 Census, the face of America is almost 73 percent white, 11 percent Hispanic, 12 percent black, 4 percent Asian Pacific American, and 1 percent American Indian and Alaska Native.

Census projections indicate that in the 21st century, America's racial landscape will continue to shift. In 2050, the population in the United States is projected to be approximately 53 percent white, 25 percent Hispanic, 14 percent black, 8 percent Asian Pacific American, and 1 percent American Indian and Alaska Native. (See "Racial/Ethnic Composition of the Population" at the end of the document.) Almost two-thirds of the U.S. population growth over the next 50 years most likely will come from immigrants, their children, and their grandchildren.[65] Both Census Bureau and Immigration Naturalization Service (INS) statistics reveal that the overwhelming majority (almost three-fourths) of the new immigrants to the United States are Hispanic or Asian Pacific Islander.

According to recent Census Bureau reports, the United States now has, for the first time, more Hispanic children under age 18 than it does black children.[66] Hispanic children have grown from only 8 percent of the population in 1980 to 15 percent in 1998.[67] The Census Bureau estimates that by the year 2020, 20 percent of all children under 18 years of age will be of Hispanic origin, while black children will constitute 17 percent of this age group.[68] Another example of dramatic demographic change is that of Asian Pacific Americans, which was less than 1 percent of the total U.S. population in 1970. The Census Bureau estimates that this population will grow to 8 percent in 2050, representing the greatest percentage change of any racial group for that period.[69]

RACIAL DESIGNATIONS ARE GROWING MORE COMPLEX

The country's growing diversity will be influenced by the increasing number of intermarriages. Americans are marrying persons of different races at increasing rates. While second-generation immigrants often intermarry, third-generation intermarriage is even more frequent.

U.S. Census 1990 data for people ages 25–34 indicate that almost 32 percent of native-born Hispanic husbands and 31 percent of native-born Hispanic wives had white spouses. Thirty-six percent of native-born Asian Pacific American men married white women, and 45 percent of Asian Pacific American women espoused white men. A majority of American Indian and Alaska Native men and women married white spouses and had the highest rates of intermarriage. In the 25–34 age group, 8 percent of black men and 4 percent of black women married individuals of another race.[70] The percentage of whites intermarrying was smaller than that of blacks.[71]

In our view, rates of intermarriage are important for two reasons. They measure social interaction between persons of different races *and* they complicate the way the offspring of these marriages may identify themselves by race. The U.S. Census has only recently allowed individuals to identify themselves by race using more than one racial category. It remains to be seen how offspring of racial intermarriage will identify themselves.[72] This uncertainty casts doubt on whether the demographic changes predicted by the U.S. Census, based on the trends of previous years, will be fully realized. Indeed, the concepts of race and the language we use to discuss our diversity today may change as fast and dramatically as our diversity itself.

There are no easy metaphors or key slogans to describe what we are becoming. In the travels of the Board and through discussions with people across the Nation, it was apparent that people struggle to attach a new metaphor to the changing demography. The metaphors of a "melting pot" and "mosaic" are inadequate given what we know today. The melting pot suggests a loss of identity, and mosaic suggests that people will never come together but instead will maintain rigid separation. Instead, we are becoming a new society, based on a fresh mixture of immigrants, racial groups, religions, and cultures, in search of a new language of diversity that is inclusive and will build trust.

SEARCHING FOR A NEW LANGUAGE OF DIVERSITY

The changing face of America has serious implications for how we will talk about race in the future. We know, as Dr. James Jones stated during an early Board meeting, that race is a "social, not a biological construct," and that "race is a term whose use and impact is far more consequential to those who have been targets of hostile actions than those who have perpetuated them or been the incidental beneficiaries of their consequences."[73]

There is no simple way to say what race or racial groupings mean in America because they mean very different things to those who are in and those who are out of the target "racial" group. At a Board meeting in San Jose, California, we were criticized for not including European-Americans. When two Board members who are white indicated that they were descendants of Europeans, the critic denied that they were capable of speaking for European Americans, but when questioned was unable to explain with clarity why he felt that was so.

We have seen in our own lifetimes how social changes can influence the way we understand and talk about race. For example, most Americans have learned that it is inappropriate to use the terms "Colored" or "Negro" to refer to blacks or "Oriental" to refer to Asian Pacific Americans. It is also no longer an acceptable social norm to use derogatory racial epithets or caricatures, even though, regrettably, a few people continue to use them.

Further, many individuals want to identify themselves differently than society does. They bear the brunt of criticism by those who believe those individuals want to deny affiliation with particular racial groups. For example, Tiger Woods, the dynamic young golfer and the youngest player to win the prestigious Masters tournament, recognizes the contributions of both his mother's (Asian) and father's (black and American Indian) ancestors to his racial identification and has been criticized for searching for an alternative label for himself.[74]

Racial groupings may be inadequate because individuals are uncomfortable with the breadth of the categories. For instance, many Americans of Asian Indian descent are uncomfortable with the use of the category Asian Pacific American to describe themselves or are uncertain if the term encompasses them. Cubans do not have the same culture as immigrants from Spain or El Salvador. Similarly, blacks who are immigrants from Caribbean countries or who have strong roots in the Caribbean are often more comfortable being described as Caribbean American than African American. In many cases, Arab Americans chafe at being labeled white, because this characterization ignores that Arab Americans are a diverse group of people.[75] Even many members of white ethnic groups view the use of their ethnic origin in describing themselves (e.g., Italian Americans or Irish Americans) as an important aspect of who they are. Racial categories, although useful and necessary to track discrimination, often get in the way of both a clear analysis of facts and a clear-headed dialogue about what individual cultures offer to the community and country as a whole.

The country has moved toward new, as yet unsolidified, ways of thinking and talking about race and ethnicity. Yet there are still troublesome examples of racist activity: racially motivated hate crimes, the continued use of American Indians as mascots,[76] and intimidation by white supremacist groups. The shifting characteristics of racial and ethnic groupings and their deeper meanings make it hard to have a concrete conversation about what race means to any one group.

DETERMINING THE FACTS OF RACIAL DIVERSITY

In trying to develop a framework for the study and discussion of race during the year, Board members were aware of a number of reports and studies on the root causes of racial prejudice and its consequences. Two notable studies, Swedish sociologist Gunnar Myrdal's *An American Dilemma*[77] and the Kerner Commission's *Report of the National Advisory Commission on Civil Disorders*[78] described the history and systematic racial discrimination suffered by blacks. The Kerner Commission's dire prediction that we are a "Nation moving towards two societies, one black, one white—separate and unequal"[79] chronicled the deliberate exclusion of Americans of African descent from full participation in American society. During the early months of the Initiative, despite our best efforts to broaden discussions and examinations of race, they seemed to veer almost inevitably to black-white issues. Until recently, most of the data gathered on race by government agencies compared black and white disparities. Searches on the Internet for data about racial categories and issues produce volumes on blacks and increasingly more on Latinos. But finding good sources of trend data beyond the black-white paradigm and recent data beyond Latinos is difficult. The major analytical reports on race in the past have focused primarily on blacks.

America's history of research obscures today's racial realities and issues. In his critique of the continuing and almost exclusive reference to the black-white paradigm in discussions of race, Professor George Sanchez of the University of Southern California made the following observation:

> The history of white on black racism blinds Americans from recognizing any other forms of interracial tensions. Racism against Asian Pacific Americans and Latin Americans is dismissed as either "natural byproducts" of immigrants' assimilation or as extensions of the white-black dichotomy. Moreover, when African Americans perform acts of racism, they are quickly ignored or recast except as a threat to the white dominated society.[80]

America's racial conflict can no longer be confined to a discussion of white versus black. The concerns of Professor Sanchez must be included more often in the conversation on race and in the discussion of solutions. We can approach these issues more constructively if we acknowledge that the success of the modern civil rights movement is considered by many to have been a powerful influence on this country's consciousness about race, and it also helped to encourage more advocacy and activism among other minority communities.[81] However, a more important factor influencing the expansion of the dialogue is the growing complexity and changing demographics of race since the 1960s.

IMPROVE DATA COLLECTION

To understand fully the challenges we face in the 21st century, it is essential to improve reporting on America's less visible racial groups: American Indians, Alaska Natives, Native Hawaiians, and all of the subgroups that make up the big umbrella categories of Asian Pacific Americans and Hispanics. Board members often heard anecdotes about individuals feeling "left out" of the discussion because we failed to make appropriate distinctions and references. For example, the experiences of most Vietnamese Americans are different from those of Korean Americans or Japanese Americans. Yet, all fall under the category "Asian Pacific American."

Puerto Ricans have experiences that are distinct from Cubans. Guatemalan Americans have a history different from Mexican Americans. In this case, all are Latinos or Hispanics in the demographic tables.

Steps are being taken to close the data gap. For the first time, a fact book has been published that documents differences in well-being by race and ethnicity in seven broad categories: population, education, labor markets, economic status, health, crime and criminal justice, and housing and neighborhoods. The book *Changing America: Indicators of Social and Economic Well-Being by Race and Hispanic Origin* was produced by the Council of Economic Advisers in consultation with the Federal statistical agencies in response to the Initiative. The information provides a benchmark for measuring future progress and highlights priorities for reducing disparities across racial and ethnic lines. It is only the first effort to identify such indicators; we hope they will be improved in the next few years. As we discuss in Chapter Five, these indicators can serve as the basis for a periodic report card on racial progress.

In addition, the National Research Council, the research arm of the National Academy of Sciences, will convene a conference in October 1998 to examine past and emerging trends for different racial and ethnic groups in key areas, including health, education, employment, and the administration of justice. Researchers will submit papers summarizing social science evidence on these trends for whites, blacks, American Indians, Alaska Natives, Hispanics, Asian Pacific Americans, and others, and how the trends have been affected by public policy. The conference also will identify key gaps in research and data that need to be filled to promote a clear understanding of race-related issues.[82]

The story of race in America is a story of transition. That we have changed and will continue to change is inevitable—how we make this transition is the story to be written and is within our control. Armed with more complete data, good will, and resources, we will be better able to identify problems, focus on our challenges, and establish our policy priorities. We also will be better equipped to learn and talk about our diversity in school, at work, and at home. We have good reason to know about all of America's faces because wherever we came from, and however long ago, we are moving into the 21st century together.

The next chapter is an assessment of the challenges we face and must meet if we are to sustain the forward movement of recent years in resolving the "problems of the color line" in America. Those challenges are not new, but they are more complex. As we have described, the face of America has changed and will change even more dramatically in the next half century.

We believe the recommendations that follow represent a downpayment on our future success as a multiracial, internally strong, and globally competitive democracy.

CHAPTER FOUR—BRIDGING THE GAP

Significant progress has been made in expanding the promise of America to members of minority groups.[83] By the same token, the legacy of race and color continues to limit opportunities. The life chances of minorities and people of color in the United States are constrained by this legacy and by continued discrimination and racial disparities[84] that are often the result of discrimination.

Summarized here are some of the key facts and background information presented at Advisory Board meetings, which show that persistent barriers to full inclusion in American society exist in education, employment, economic opportunity, criminal justice, and health care. We also reiterate many of the recommendations we made to the President throughout the year.[85] We are grateful that the Administration has already begun to implement some of these key recommendations and is reviewing and considering others. Several of the recommendations are longer term solutions that will require further study by the President and other public and private sector officials.

One of our fundamental beliefs is that the creation of greater opportunities and the reduction of racial disparities in the important facets of American life will lead us to a more just society.

CIVIL RIGHTS ENFORCEMENT

Data as well as anecdotal information demonstrate that discrimination on the basis of race, color, and national origin is active and the source of harmful consequences to men, women, and children who are its targets. Discrimination contributes to alienation and further impedes our ability to live, work, and grow together as one America, free from prejudicial, stereotypical behavior. Much of this discriminatory behavior is illegal and can be pursued in courts by individuals or the Federal Government under existing civil rights laws.

However, major impediments block effective civil rights enforcement. Two of the most significant barriers are the lack of data about some minority groups and underfunding of civil rights enforcement agencies. Data and research on discrimination have not been systematically developed and maintained for minority communities other than for African Americans and, more recently, Hispanics. Systematically developed and maintained data on discrimination are lacking for Asian Pacific Americans, American

Indians (including Alaska Natives and Native Hawaiians), and others protected by law from racial discrimination.[86]

In addition, since roughly 1982, Federal civil rights enforcement agencies have lost considerable ground. Their budgets and staffing have been notably reduced while many of their responsibilities have increased, which has necessarily limited their ability to aggressively and effectively enforce civil rights laws. Recent funding increases have not kept pace with inflation, the volume of cases or the need for careful compliance investigations.[87]

Budget and staffing reductions make it particularly difficult for these agencies to devote sufficient time and attention to training staff and provide federally funded recipients with technical assistance to recognize and prevent discrimination. This is especially true for the increasingly subtle and complex forms of contemporary discrimination, which have largely supplanted more blatant forms of discrimination typically found before and immediately after the enactment of the major civil rights laws in the 1960s.

RECOMMENDATIONS

- **Strengthen civil rights enforcement throughout the United States.** The President has proposed an $86-million increase in funding for civil rights enforcement in fiscal year (FY) 1999, which is the largest increase in nearly two decades. We urge the President to build on the Administration's FY 1999 budget proposal and propose additional funding increases in FY 2000. The President should enable and require Federal enforcement agencies to create partnerships with States and localities that enforce laws comparable to those that operate at the Federal level. The goal would be to strengthen agencies' capabilities to effectively enforce the civil rights laws.

- **Improve data collection on racial and ethnic discrimination.** The Federal Government should improve its ability to collect, analyze, and disseminate reliable data on the nature and extent of discrimination based on race and national origin, but not to the exclusion of data collection on other protected classifications (e.g., gender, age). A well-designed and coordinated process of generating relevant indicators should become part of a regular report on the extent of discrimination in such areas as education, health care, employment, housing, and the administration of justice. Such a report would not only assist policymakers but also would increase cooperation among the various Federal agencies involved in civil rights enforcement and education. The information also will aid the public by identifying trends. Further, these reports and indicators can be enhanced with data for local areas.

> *I've come to see poverty and race as two separate issues, and those who have opportunity still get affected by race and those who don't have opportunity still get affected by race.*
>
> **Bob Thomas, Advisory Board meeting, Washington, D.C., June 18, 1998**

Central to our concern is the need to significantly improve the level of information about *all* minority groups and the discrimination they face.

- **Strengthen laws and enforcement against hate crimes.** We must take action to eliminate hate crimes. In 1996, more than 10,000 hate crime offenses were reported, the vast majority of which were based on racial and ethnic bias.[88] Hate crimes are far more destructive than other criminal acts, for each offense has many victims. "A hate crime victimizes not only the immediate target but every member of the group that the immediate target represents."[89]

The White House Hate Crimes Conference yielded important proposed solutions concerning how to better address hate crime, including enhancing data collection on hate crimes, strengthening hate crime laws, increasing hate crime prosecutions by assigning additional FBI agents and prosecutors to work on enforcement, establishing local working groups to develop best practices to address hate crimes, and developing educational materials to prevent hate crimes by teaching young people the importance of tolerance and respect. We strongly endorse these efforts and urge continued vigilance to prevent and punish hate crimes.

EDUCATION AND RACE[90]

All children in America should have the opportunity to obtain a high-quality education in an environment that inspires the desire to learn and grow. Education will provide future generations of Americans the ability to compete effectively in the information-age economy. Education will guide Americans to recognize that the racial differences among our people can be a source of strength. Education will allow every individual to move beyond his or her own personal experiences and understand that the most important values we hold as a Nation require informed, active participation of the public at large.

> *Unless we educate leaders from and for all segments of our society, a society that is changing dramatically in our time, becoming more multiethnic, more multicultural, unless we educate leaders for all segments of our society who have learned to work together, we will have failed in one of our most important obligations.*
>
> **Nannerl Keohane, President of Duke University, Advisory Board meeting on diversity in higher education, College Park, Maryland, November 19, 1997**

Our concern is that educational opportunities and public resources are being restricted to those who live disproportionately in areas of concentrated poverty. Concentrated poverty means they face a confluence of interlocking disadvantage. The disadvantages include ineffective schools, where low expectations and low standards are the norm; substandard and crumbling school facilities and housing; inadequate public transportation; and poorly financed social services. More importantly, the restrictions are being felt most deeply among poor children, minority children, and children of color. The data concerning teacher preparation, early childhood learning, high school achievement, college admission, and school learning environments suggest that there are several steps that both the Federal and local governments can take to broaden opportunities and level the playing field. There also is room for community-based organizations to help create a channel for research, public education, and access to services. In addition, innovative partnerships with private businesses should be considered since many private companies share a concern that the future workforce of the Nation be prepared not only to function, but also to compete in the information-age economy. To the extent that the Government can encourage partnerships that reflect collaboration across racial and ethnic lines, such partnerships should be supported through Government programs and other privately funded programs. We must debunk the myth that increasing the national commitment to education means increasing national control over education rather than strengthening the partnership between State, local, and tribal governments.

Two challenges are of primary importance. The first is overcoming racial disparities in educational opportunity and attainment by providing all our children with the highest quality education beginning in the earliest years and extending throughout the education pipeline. Data show that substantial racial disparities exist. (Students of color are less likely to have access to such educational opportunities and resources as preschool programs, high-quality teachers, challenging curriculums, high standards, up-to-date technology, and modern facilities.[91] For example, a recent study shows that 42 percent of schools with more than 50-percent minority enrollment reported at least one inadequate building, compared with 29 percent of schools with 5 percent or less minority enrollment.[92]

Second, we must seek to educate all our children in high-quality, integrated schools where they have the opportunity to learn together in ways that can break down negative stereotypes and improve race relations. Segregation remains a problem both in and among our schools, and the situation appears to be getting worse.[93]

These goals of high-quality schools and integration are not mutually exclusive. They are complementary goals. Simply put, high-quality, integrated schools provide a more complete educational experience for all students than high-quality segregated schools. Conversely, ineffective, racially isolated schools in high-poverty areas present our greatest obstacle to the two goals set out above. State finance systems often shortchange these schools where educational need is greatest—directing funds away from poor neighborhoods to those that are more affluent. In addition, teachers with more experience opt to teach in more affluent neighborhoods. To a great extent, we know what to do to promote educational equity and excellence; we just have to have the commitment and courage as a Nation to do it. If we are successful here, fundamental change will follow.

RECOMMENDATIONS

- **Enhance early childhood learning.** Emerging evidence indicates that a child's development in the earliest years is crucial to his or her development throughout life. However, data indicate that racial disparities persist in terms of early childhood learning. For example, 1996 data show that 89 percent of white children ages 3–5 were read to 3 or more times per week compared with 76 percent of black children and 65 percent of Hispanic children. White children were also more likely to have visited a library in the past month.[94] The Federal government should take action to help eliminate such disparities and enhance early childhood learning opportunities for children of all races.[95] Such efforts could include providing training and services for parents, who must be every child's first teachers, and expanding support for such programs as Head Start, Early Head Start, and Even Start.

- **Strengthen teacher preparation and equity.** There is strong consensus that high-quality teachers are our most valuable educational resource, and the need for high-quality teachers is increasing; an estimated 2 million new teachers will be hired in the next decade. However, although many of our Nation's teachers are exceptional public servants who deserve great respect and support, there also is a consensus that high-quality teachers are too scarce a resource, especially in high-poverty, high-minority communities. Many teachers in such communities are teaching without certification and/or without a college major or minor in their primary fields.[96] If we are serious about ensuring that all children have access to high-quality education and high standards, the Nation must make a national priority the task of increasing the number of high-quality teachers with high expectation for all students.

  The Federal Government should take action to strengthen teacher preparation and professional development, to promote equity by encouraging high-quality teachers to teach in underserved communities, and to ensure that teachers promote high expectation for students of all races. Such efforts could include encouraging States to strengthen teacher certification requirements and holding colleges and universities accountable for producing teachers who meet certification requirements. They also could include creating incentives to both attract top students to teaching and encourage certified teachers to teach in underserved communities. Teachers who perform well should be rewarded, teachers who perform poorly should receive additional training, and the government should work with unions to establish procedures to counsel ineffective teachers out of the profession. The President's proposed Initiative to Get Good Teachers to Underserved Areas, which would provide $350 million to recruit new teachers to teach in low-income schools and create grants for colleges and universities to improve teacher preparation, is an important step. A larger, more comprehensive effort is necessary.

- **Promote school construction.** Students cannot learn effectively in overcrowded schools with crumbling walls, old wiring, inadequate heat, and/or no air conditioning. Poor facilities hinder teaching and learning, limit access to technology, and dampen students' expectations and feelings of self-worth. It is estimated that building and renovating our public schools to adequately serve all students will cost more than $100 billion.[97] The Federal Government should take action in partnership with State, local, and tribal governments, the private sector, and the nonprofit sector to address this need. The President's proposed School Construction and Modernization Initiative, which would provide Federal tax credits to pay interest on $22 billion in bonds to renovate schools, is crucial, but it should be expanded by committing direct Federal funds and requiring State matching funds, similar to Federal funding for highway construction. School construction must be made a national priority.

- **Promote movement from K–12 to higher education.** As with elementary and secondary school education, full and equal access to higher education is essential. However, data show that racial disparities persist in movement from secondary school through higher education.[98] (See "Persons Aged 25 to 29 with a Four-Year College Degree or Higher" at the end of the document.) Furthermore, in those States in which affirmative action has been made or declared unlawful, data show a substantial decrease in the numbers of students of color accepted at the most prestigious institutions.[99]

Efforts must be taken to ensure equal opportunity in higher education and to strengthen the pipeline from K–12 through higher education. Such efforts should include support for partnerships between college and K–12 schools that increase expectations by exposing students to future educational opportunities. Programs also should help students meet those expectations by providing vital support services, such as mentoring and counseling, to improve academic achievement levels and reduce dropout rates.[100] Preliminary research shows that such programs work. The President's proposed High Hopes Initiative, which would create partnerships between colleges and schools in low-income communities to administer such programs, is directly on point and could be expanded in several ways, such as continuing the student support services throughout college. Other efforts could include increasing the availability of advanced placement courses in high-poverty, high-minority school districts and providing financial support, such as loans or grants, for college test preparation courses.

- **Promote the benefits of diversity in K–12 and higher education.** Emerging evidence shows that diversity in the education context, including racial diversity, is essential to provide all students with a complete educational experience. To varying degrees in the K–12 and higher education contexts, diversity can promote many benefits that accrue to all students and society, including: improve teaching and learning by providing a range of perspectives that enrich the learning environment; strengthen students' critical-thinking skills by challenging their existing perspectives; teach students how to interact comfortably with people different than themselves and thereby how to function as good citizens and neighbors; improve students' preparation for employment by teaching them the value of different perspectives, how to function in diverse business settings, and how to communicate effectively in our increasingly diverse domestic marketplace and the expanding global marketplace; and foster the advancement of knowledge by spurring study in new areas of concern.

  To realize these benefits, we need to promote diversity in our academic institutions and create environments that offer opportunities for students to learn from and about persons who are different than themselves. The Federal Government should work with the education community to articulate and publicize these benefits of diversity. Such efforts should include ensuring that tracking in primary and secondary schools is not implemented in ways that improperly resegregate students and working with higher education leaders to share best practices that can promote the educational benefits of diversity.

- **Provide education and skills training to overcome increasing income inequality that negatively affects lower skilled and less educated immigrants.**[101] The high rates of Hispanic high school drop-outs (some of whom are immigrants or children of immigrants) suggest that in addition to improved educational quality for poor children and children of color, there is a clear need for continued English-language training to ensure that limited-English proficient students can perform and compete in the educational system. High-quality bilingual education programs have significant educational value because limited-English proficient students can keep up with other subjects while

> *Where you don't have trained teachers, where you don't have good teachers particularly in the lower grades, children don't succeed.*
>
> **Thomas Kean, Advisory Board meeting, Washington, D.C., June 18, 1998**

learning English. Bilingual education programs must be flexible. They should be implemented with the needs of communities and their members as top priorities. However, as a Nation, we have done an inadequate job of explaining the need for and the best characteristics of bilingual training for adults and children. We therefore recommend that the Department of Education improve research in this area to assess the value of well-implemented programs and to share promising models from different communities.

- **Implement the comprehensive American Indian and Alaska Native education policy.** To meet the particular needs of American Indian and Alaska Native students, we urge that the Administration ensures the effective implementation of the comprehensive Federal American Indian and Alaska Native education policy outlined in Executive Order 13096. This policy includes strategies for improving and expanding educational opportunities for American Indian and Alaska Native students.

RACE AND POVERTY

We heard much debate over whether "the issue" is race or poverty. Based on our experiences, we believe it is both. Socioeconomic factors alone cannot account for all disparities in achievement, status, and opportunity because racial discrimination continues to play a major role in limiting opportunities.

DISPARITIES IN LIVING STANDARDS CONTINUE

We know that building one America requires that we overcome racial disparities—particularly those relevant to educational attainment and opportunity and participation of minorities in the economy—whether they are caused by socioeconomic or racial factors or both. The fact that these racial disparities are significant and continue to exist even in a time of relative prosperity is more troubling than whether the cause is race or poverty.

In the 1950s, the poverty rate of blacks was nearing 60 percent, while the white poverty rate was less than 20 percent. Although this gap declined substantially by the mid-1990s, it did not disappear (see "Poverty Rates for Individuals" at the end of the document). Moreover, the gap is significant not only for blacks but also for American Indians and Alaska Natives, Hispanics, and Asian Pacific Americans as well. According to 1996 statistics, 11 percent of whites, 14.5 percent of Asian Pacific Americans, 28 percent of blacks, 29 percent of Hispanics, and 51 percent of American Indians who live on reservations[102] live in poverty. Despite the higher relative rates of

[I]t's very rewarding to see how strongly the American people believe in the power of education. There are many reasons we have this kind of faith and knowledge in learning, and this view is no doubt premised on the understanding that in today's world, there can be no equity without education.

U.S. Secretary of Education Richard W. Riley, Advisory Board meeting, Annandale High School, Fairfax, Virginia, December 17, 1997

There's no way that you could... explain adequately the concentration of minorities in ghettos and slums and among the poor population without dealing with race.

William Julius Wilson, Advisory Board meeting on race and poverty, San Jose, California, February 11, 1998

poverty for minority groups, it also is useful to recall—as many easily forget—that in terms of actual numbers nearly half of all the poor people in the United States are white.[103]

CONCENTRATED POVERTY AND RACE

Poverty is not only a matter of individuals and families living with insufficient income. Large portions of America's cities and some rural communities experience pockets or patterns of "concentrated poverty" in which 30 to 40 percent or more of the residents are poor. These neighborhoods are typically stigmatized by dilapidated housing, vacant units with broken or boarded-up windows, ineffective and crumbling public schools, inadequate or limited public and private transportation, and despair. These inner-city "ghettos" and "barrios" are often many miles from suburban and emerging job centers (i.e., minorities are disproportionately segregated or isolated in these areas of concentrated poverty).[104] Demographic research clearly indicates that racial discrimination and segregation tend to cause and compound the problem of spatially concentrated poverty in our country.[105]

Today, we have a deeper appreciation for the complex relationship of race and poverty within the web of such public policy issues as welfare, housing, transportation, childcare, employment, and actionable discrimination. Due to the difficulty in untangling the various causes of poverty from overarching race issues, the solutions to these problems are complicated and present enormous public policy challenges for the Administration and State, local, and tribal governments.

RECOMMENDATIONS

- **Examine income inequality.** The President should initiate discussions among senior policymakers and congressional leaders, as well as among leaders in the private sector, on the existence of long-term patterns of income inequality. These discussions would flesh out potential means to reduce these patterns that so notably limit the country's ability to reduce systemic poverty and concomitant racial disadvantage.

- **Support supplements for small business administration programs.** Tax credits and other benefits that permit corporations to provide philanthropic support for micro-credit development programs should be strongly encouraged. Such financing is critically important; many, if not all, of the clients for such programs have damaged or limited credit histories that prevent them from seeking funding from regular lending institutions or from the Small Business Administration.

- **Use the current economic boom to provide necessary job training and to increase the minimum wage.** It is important to take advantage of the current economic boom to aggressively reach out to educate, train, and place as many people as possible in positions in the new economy. These additional efforts would supplement the welfare-to-work transition and should also include a commitment to a higher minimum wage.

- **Evaluate anti-poverty program effectiveness.** The Board recommended the establishment of a White House task force involving Federal agencies engaged in addressing various aspects of the anti-poverty problem. The task force would evaluate which of these current or lapsed programs have proven useful in reducing poverty on a sustained basis. The task force should use available data to assess whether programs are equally effective for all minority groups. If they are not, the task force should seek the reasons they are not succeeding. This cross-agency evaluation would assess how to improve coordination and integration of local level programs so that tools managed by different agencies have a better, cumulative impact.

WELFARE REFORM AND RACE: AN ISSUE IN NEED OF MONITORING

In 1996, President Clinton signed sweeping welfare reform legislation (the Personal Responsibility and Work Opportunity Reconciliation Act of 1996) aimed at moving persons receiving public assistance from welfare rolls onto payrolls. The White House also launched the Welfare-to-Work Partnership, an independent, nonpartisan effort by companies nationwide to hire welfare recipients. Welfare rolls have fallen 37 percent since the President took office in 1993 and 27 percent since the enactment of welfare reform in 1996. In 1 year, 135,000 former welfare recipients were hired. Today, the percentage of the U.S. population on welfare—3.3 percent—is at its lowest level since 1969. A large part of this decline is due to the robust conditions of the economy. What is not clear is what will happen to this decline in welfare rolls if the economy stagnates or enters a recession.

The fact that most States are still designing and implementing welfare-to-work programs means that there are few good studies or data on how well welfare reform is working and whether there are any disparate impacts on minorities and people of color. Clearly a healthy labor market helps enormously but it may not help all minorities and people of color equally. A recent Brookings Institution study, for example, reports that the inner cities, compared with their rural and suburban areas, were much slower in reducing their welfare caseloads. Cities with larger numbers of distressed, minority neighborhoods had even slower rates of caseload decline. Some studies suggest that even when caseloads are reduced, the family members do not necessarily find jobs that pay a living wage.[106]

There is also worry that because minorities typically spend more time living in poverty than whites that they will remain longer on welfare caseloads, resulting in higher minority representation in the total program. Poverty data (SIPP and PSID) reveal that white households typically have shorter durations living in poverty and spend less time drawing down welfare benefits than black or Hispanic households. In addition, recent evidence finds that as welfare rolls continue to plunge, "White recipients are leaving the system much faster than black and Hispanic recipients, pushing the minority share of the caseload to the highest level on record." This is in part due to important differences in education: While 64 percent of Hispanic recipients lacked a high school education, this was true of only 33 percent of whites and 40 percent of blacks.[107] It is therefore critical that attention be paid to the impact of welfare reform on minority families and communities to ensure that the program is administered fairly.[108]

RACE AND ECONOMIC INEQUALITY

The Advisory Board believes that disparities in economic opportunity, like education disparities, have the potential to deeply fracture America. Although education is important for raising income and living standards, education alone cannot eliminate income disparities among racial groups. The gap in earnings among racial groups persists at all educational levels.[109] Although there has been considerable progress by minorities and people of color who have moved into the middle class during the past 40 years, significant disparity remains between the earnings capacity, economic prosperity, and wealth of whites and most minority groups.[110] (See "Median Usual Weekly Earnings of Male Full-Time Workers," "Median Usual Weekly Earnings of Female Full-Time Workers," "Median Family Income," and "Labor Force Participation Rates of Persons Aged 25 to 54" at the end of the document.)

Many of the experts and community members heard from over the year presented tangible and gripping evidence of racially discriminatory treatment; they shared, in many instances, personal accounts and written complaints of discrimination. They alleged discrimination in employment, pay, housing, consumer markets, credit markets, and public accommodations.[111]

> [E]ducation alone... has not been fully or completely effective in closing the earnings gap between minority workers and whites.
>
> **Linda Chavez-Thompson, Advisory Board meeting, Washington, D.C., June 18, 1998**

EMPLOYMENT AND LABOR MARKETS

In many communities, the lack of available work opportunities and the adequacy of wages are especially acute problems. As Professor William Julius Wilson argued, the structural transformation of our economy has meant, and will continue to mean, decreased demand for certain types of unskilled workers and the lack of access to jobs for many inner-city residents who live in "jobless ghettos."[112] These major social and economic dislocations and restructuring cut minorities off from job networks, making it almost impossible for them to find employment.

Moreover, a recent synthesis of evidence suggests that minorities—blacks and Hispanics—are on average likely to be denied employment at least 20 to 25 percent of the time.[113] The use of employment "testers" to establish clear evidence of job bias, a technique that is gaining wide attention, is a useful and cost-effective tool to uncover systemic hiring discrimination. In one instance, a Hispanic tester was paired with a comparably qualified white tester. When the Hispanic tester applied for a receptionist position in a Washington suburb, she was told the company was not taking additional applications. The white tester called shortly after and was given an appointment for the next day. In another case, a black tester was offered $6.50 an hour for a sale's assistant position in a department store, while a white tester was offered $1 an hour more.[114]

Professor Jose Roberto Juarez also illustrated the continuing problem with hiring discrimination in his presentation in Phoenix:

> [E]mployers are looking for a variety of skills. But some of those skills can themselves sometimes be a subterfuge for discrimination. So that when we talk about an employer who says, "well, the reason that I hired this particular person is because they had better people skills." They were better able to relate to the other employees in the workforce.
>
> Quite often that means, gee, the white guy got along a whole lot better with all the other white guys and if we had this Chicano, she was going to make us all uncomfortable and so that's why we didn't hire her. And, of course, the employer isn't saying the last part of that, but that is, in fact, what may be happening. Not always. And I think it is very important to recognize that there are a number of different factors that are operating here.[115]

Discrimination in the workplace is not limited to hiring practices; discrimination in promotions also affects employment status and opportunities. Minorities and people of color who are well qualified for promotion to higher positions often find that the path to future advancement is blocked by a "glass ceiling," namely informal practices or procedures that inhibit minority advancement once they are hired.[116] In addition to the glass ceiling phenomenon, at the Board's meeting in Phoenix, Arizona, Dr. Paul Ong discussed other barriers to promotion and advancement within the workplace. He stated, "Disproportionately, Asian Pacific Islanders end up managing R&D [research and development] projects and not managing the business....[R]esearch indicates that there's a certain amount of steering that's going on."[117]

Another major indicator of disparities in economic and employment status is the unemployment rate (see "Unemployment Rates of Persons Aged 16 and Over" at the end of the document). Since the mid-1950s, the black unemployment rate has been roughly double that of whites and has increased more for non-whites in recessions than for whites. Indeed, the average rate of unemployment for blacks was more than 10 percent for roughly two decades and fell below that point for the first time in 1997.[118] Hispanics also have had a higher rate of unemployment than whites at 7 percent.[119] Much of this disparity persists even when differences in educational attainment are considered. Moreover, discrimination in hiring and few job opportunities in low-income communities contribute to higher rates of unemployment among minority workers. The following recommendations represent approaches that we believe to be essential in eliminating racial disparities and promoting a strong, vibrant economy in which every American can participate.

RECOMMENDATIONS

- **Increase the minimum wage for low-wage workers and their families.** Current economic growth has been a major stimulus to reducing the number of poor people in general and the unemployed poor in particular. The worry, of course, is that if labor markets again slacken, many newly hired workers will once again be separated from the economic mainstream. In addition, all too many jobs—while employing an individual full time—will not lift that individual out of poverty.[120] As stated earlier, the Nation should take advantage of the current economic boom to reach out to the working poor. A higher minimum wage that ensures a decent living for low-wage workers and their families is needed.[121] More permanent, full-time jobs paying a living wage must be created to increase living standards and reduce poverty among minority workers. In addition, the President should promote innovative partnerships between the public and private sectors to explore increasing the minimum wage, developing job training and

[T]wenty years ago I read...that when somebody worked at a minimum wage, you could pull a family of three out of poverty... Under the current new minimum wage, you can work full-time and you will still be $2,000 short and below the poverty line.

Jose Padilla, Director of California Rural Legal Assistance, Advisory Board meeting on race and poverty, San Jose, California, February 11, 1998

placement programs, and using the workforce emerging from our welfare rolls.

- **Improve racial data collection.** To more effectively target those communities requiring intervention to improve the economic and employment status of their members, private and public institutions must receive accurate and adequate data about existing disparities and opportunity gaps. Federal agencies that currently gather information about racial disparities should cooperate to improve data collection by race. The annual data gathered by the Current Population Surveys should provide a starting point. Every effort should be made to create statistically meaningful population samples, even if this means oversampling certain populations, including Asian Pacific Americans, American Indians and Alaska Natives, and Hispanics.[122]

- **Evaluate the effectiveness of job-training programs designed to reach minority and immigrant communities.** The President should direct the Departments of Labor and Health and Human Services to evaluate and identify elements that appear to predict successful job placement. This evaluation should also identify elements of the training programs that address the specific needs of these populations so they can be replicated. In addition, the Labor Department should collaborate with other agencies to create a strategic plan to address the anticipated growth in the Hispanic and Asian Pacific American populations. These populations are projected to more than double and triple respectively, in the next 50 years. There are enormous opportunities to diversify job-training programs that promote the use of this emerging workforce in innovative international public and private sector collaborations.

- **Commission a broad study to examine American Indian and Alaska Native economic development.** We urge the President to address the growing concern among American Indians and Alaska Natives about their ability to engage in community economic development programs and to address technology infrastructure needs in Indian country. The President has already asked the Small Business Administration, the Department of Interior, and the Department of Commerce to provide a report on the development of a plan to coordinate existing economic development initiatives that includes private sector involvement.[123] Other agencies with relevant programs should be encouraged to build on this effort.

> *[O]ne of the things that we'd like to see is more and more companies investing in their workers that they have on training and education programs to provide them upward mobility....*
>
> **Linda Chavez-Thompson, Advisory Board meeting, Washington, D.C., June 18, 1998**

> *If you're African American, if you're Latino, can you get a loan?. . . We are denied access to basic home loans; we cannot get basic banking services... We can't get educational loans...and business loans. . .*
>
> **Dr. Denise Fairchild, President of Community Development Technologies Center, Advisory Board meeting on race and poverty, San Jose, California, February 11, 1998**

> *[H]ousing markets don't simply distribute housing. Housing markets distribute anything that is correlated with where you live. So housing markets distribute education, housing markets distribute safety, housing markets distribute the insurance rates you pay, the peer groups your kids associate with, the environment that a family experiences.*
>
> **Professor Douglas Massey, San Jose, California, Advisory Board meeting, February 11, 1998**

- **Support organized labor and its outreach efforts to minority and immigrant workers.** Organized labor has demonstrated its ability to protect job security, reduce wage disparities, and provide necessary benefits to working people. It is important that there be increased recognition of the benefits of collective bargaining and the role of unions in ensuring employment equity. At the same time, the Board encourages organized labor to continue its outreach to minority and immigrant workers who commonly face exploitation in the workplace.

RACE AND HOUSING MARKETS

Active forms of racial discrimination in housing continue to infect our housing markets. That discrimination—whether in renting an apartment, buying a home, or obtaining a mortgage—is among the key causes of racial segregation and isolation of poor minority families. Housing, more than almost any other factor in life, helps shape who we are as individuals and affects our future life chances. The denial of a fair chance to own a home is a denial of access to the most basic American dream. Home ownership has been shown to be an essential first step in the American dream's promise of accumulating assets and wealth.[124]

We must address this lack of opportunity for home ownership through better mortgage loan products, better training of industry personnel on fair lending requirements, counseling of clients about their rights and the risks associated with predatory lending behavior, and the continued creativity of government-sponsored entities Fannie Mae and Freddie Mac.[125]

The Board learned at the Newark, New Jersey, meeting on housing issues that although there are fewer virulent and blatant acts of racial and national origin discrimination, currently blacks and Hispanics are likely to be discriminated against roughly half of the time when they go to look for a home or apartment.[126]

In both 1977 and 1989, the U.S. Department of Housing and Urban Development (HUD) funded national audits of discrimination in both the rental and sales markets. The studies examined a wide range of behavior associated with renting or purchasing a home. These two studies reveal a "gross" measure of discrimination in which black or Hispanic auditors experienced some form of differential treatment about 50 percent of the time. The more conservative net figure is that discrimination occurs 25 percent of the time. The Fair Housing Council of Greater Washington reported that in 1997, discrimination occurred 35 percent of the time a black or Hispanic tester tried to rent an apartment; higher levels occurred in suburban jurisdictions.[127]

Many poor minority residents live in segregated, isolated, and stigmatized neighborhoods. Racial segregation, limited job opportunities, and discrimination continue to serve as a basis for persistent minority poverty. As a result, efforts to remove these barriers to prosperity are important, although not easy, and will require commitment from government, business, the nonprofit community, and local communities.[128]

All of the evidence we received about housing and housing markets was not gloomy. The results of recent research on the practices of some mortgage lenders in various parts of the country indicate that they are trying hard to increase their lending to minority and low-income neighborhoods. These innovations involve lenders advertising and promoting their loan products in areas they usually do not serve, offering more flexible underwriting, and helping higher risk borrowers to ensure that they can maintain their mortgage and avoid risk of default. There is reason for "tempered optimism" that increasing numbers of lenders are helping to change our housing finance system so that it more aggressively assists minority and poorer communities.[129]

RECOMMENDATIONS

- **Continue to use testing to develop evidence of continuing discrimination.** Federally funded testing programs have played an important role in combating overt and subtle forms of disparate treatment. The Board supports HUD's decision to double housing-complaints processing by the year 2000 and urges continued attention to increasing the fair housing enforcement budget and related education and outreach efforts within the department.

- **Highlight housing integration efforts.** Through the efforts of innovative lenders and strengthened fair housing enforcement operations, a number of communities throughout the United States have become racially and ethnically diverse and integrated. In the President's report to the American people, some of these housing integration efforts should be highlighted. Many of these efforts promote integration through non-race based outreach strategies.

- **Support the increase and targeting of Federal funds for urban revitalization.** Housing development funding is an essential ingredient for the rebirth of many older, inner-city communities. We agree with the conclusion of the recently released report by The Milton S. Eisenhower Foundation, *The Millennium Breach: Rich, Poorer and Racially Apart,* in which the foundation recommends that Federal funds match private funds to support private nonprofit organizations to rebuild the

> *[W]e really need to look about housing more—about building community and not just shelter...Many of our inner city neighborhoods are going through tremendous change, economically and demographically.*
>
> **Gordon Chin, Executive Director of the Chinatown Community Development Center, Advisory Board meeting on race and poverty, San Jose, California, February 11, 1998**

core of inner-city neighborhoods, many of which are home to minority and low-income families.[130] We also recommend continued support for the type of targeting in HUD's HOME Investment partnership program and the Loan Guarantee Program, which permits funding of nonprofit developers who wish to rehabilitate older housing units or construct new housing. We further recommend an increase in overall levels of funding to meet the needs of such programs.

- **Support community development corporations.** The Board is convinced that local neighborhood community development corporations offer key, sensible, cost-effective, and locally legitimate programs that can improve conditions in minority communities in our inner cities. The Local Initiatives Support Corporation is one such program that has identified Promising Practices in this area. These are the types of programs that we recommend be highlighted in the President's report to the American people as important and successful community efforts to improve race relations by reducing racial isolation and the barrier of racial stereotyping that exist in both white and non-white communities.

- **Promote American Indian and Alaska Native access to affordable housing.** The President should direct HUD to facilitate a meeting between tribal government representatives and major lending and investment companies so that discussions concerning the development of financial products and strategies to build home equity and individual savings can take place.[131]

STEREOTYPES AND RACE

The issue of racial stereotypes is a core element of discrimination and the racial divisions and misunderstandings that stand as barriers to one America. The task of combating racial stereotypes is a formidable one, because these stereotypes are taught to us so early in life and are reinforced by so many different societal sources that they find a way to seep into our subconscious minds, even though we might be committed to racial equality. Because many of us have deeply ingrained beliefs that associate some racial groups with positive qualities and others with negative ones, our behavior toward people in other groups (as well as toward our own group) are often not based on the content of a person's character but rather the color of their skin.

Thus, we are all affected by racial stereotypes, though in different ways and at different times. Virtually everyone can think of a time when they have been seen through the prism of a negative racial stereotype, and most people have also experienced the benefits of additional trust or warmth when someone associates our racial group with positive qualities. Perhaps because the issue of stereotypes is so intensely personal and simultaneously so important to race relations between groups, the discussions held by the Advisory Board on this subject were sometimes very emotional, but ultimately quite enlightening.

The challenge is to accept that people cannot help but be influenced by society's pervasive racial stereotypes, and to commit to paying attention to how such stereotypes can insidiously affect the behavior of ourselves, our loved ones, and our institutions. Both public and private institutions and individuals should challenge policymakers and institutional leaders to examine, understand, and implement measures to change the role that racial stereotypes play in policy development, institutional practices, and our view of our own racial identity and that of others.

RECOMMENDATIONS

- **Hold a presidential event on stereotypes and what can be done about them.** As the Nation's leader, the President is in a unique position to underscore the link between racial discord in society and the stereotypes that lurk in the very private realm of our hearts and minds. A Presidential event—whether a speech, fireside chat, or other format—would need to include a call to action. This call to action would remind people that all of us—especially local leaders—are in a position to advocate for changes in the ways that stereotypes become unconsciously institutionalized into virtually every organization in society.

- **Institutionalize the Administration's promotion of racial dialogue.** In a variety of ways, the Race Initiative promotes involvement in small group racial dialogue. In addition to helping Americans learn more about racial issues, these efforts help reduce stereotypes by creating interdependencies and a common mission between people of different racial groups. The President should continue his commitment to racial dialogue so that it is institutionalized.

- **Convene a high-level meeting on the problem of racial stereotypes with leaders from the media.** The primary purpose of the meeting would not be to assign blame, but rather to focus Presidential and public attention on the role of the media in both helping and hindering societal progress on the issue of negative stereotypes. During the meeting, the President could encourage participants to pursue a number of strategies so that the media could play a more positive role.

RACE, CRIME, AND THE ADMINISTRATION OF JUSTICE[132]

Racial disparities exist in both the realities and perceptions of crime and the administration of justice. Minorities and people of color often absorb a disproportionate amount of the social, economic, and personal costs of crime. These groups want and need strong law enforcement. Building one America requires building a criminal justice system that serves and treats Americans of all races fully and fairly. To do so, we must build trust in our criminal justice system and reduce crime by and against minorities and people of color.

Substantial challenges remain to achieving these criminal justice goals. First, criminal victimization rates are significantly greater for minorities and people of color than for whites, especially with regard to violent crime.[133] Second, studies indicate that minorities and people of color have less confidence and trust in law enforcement than whites.[134] Several factors probably contribute to this mistrust. According to participants in our May meeting, these factors include negative interactions between minorities and people of color and law enforcement personnel (which may range from unjustified police stops to improper use of force), racial disparities in the administration of justice (including disparities in incarceration rates, sentencing, and imposition of the death penalty), and the lack of diversity among law enforcement personnel (e.g., police, prosecutors, and judges).

RACIAL PROFILING

Of particular concern is the use of racial profiling in law enforcement. Racial profiling refers to the use of race by law enforcement as one factor in identifying criminal suspects. Some in law enforcement may see racial profiling as a necessary, legitimate practice given limited law enforcement resources and evidence of racial disparities in criminal behavior. Some commentators urged the Board to note that racial profiling is based in part on the higher incidence of criminal activity by some minority offenders. But racial profiling also imposes costs on innocent persons, perpetuates and reinforces stereotypes, creates situations that can lead to physical confrontations, and contributes to tensions between persons of color and the criminal justice system. During the May meeting, Dr. William Wilbanks spoke about this issue with the following example:

> [T]o argue that we should consider age, sex or race when we know, for example, in terms of arrest rates that the level of offending may be 1,000 [times] greater for a young black male than an elderly white female....In my eyes if [you're] a police officer you're sug-

gested to say, 'Well, that's irrelevant. I'll just look at everybody alike.' People don't operate that way.

I think what you have to do is not let the police officer operate in a vacuum....He needs somebody in the department to say, "Look. Here are the problems with profiles. If you see, for example, only young black males, you're never going to find any elderly white females on I-95. They get a free pass."...You need to educate that officer. Right now, we're leaving him alone with this decision because we don't want to deal with the issue.[135]

But racial profiling also imposes costs on innocent persons, perpetuates and reinforces stereotypes, creates situations that can lead to physical confrontations, and contributes to tensions. Furthermore, scholars and practitioners at our May meeting universally agreed that racial stereotypes are being used in ways that inappropriately target minorities and people of color and that law enforcement personnel must receive training to avoid acting based on racial stereotypes.

For example, at our May meeting, we discussed a study of Maryland State Troopers and the rates at which they searched motorists of different races for drugs following traffic stops along Interstate 95. Evidence suggests that black motorists composed approximately 17 percent of all motorists and of those violating traffic laws in 1995, but they composed 77 percent of those searched for drugs by Maryland police following traffic stops (409 of 533 searches).[136] Why were black motorists searched so much more often? Mr. Stone explained it at our May meeting as follows:

The police explain that blacks are more likely to be carrying contraband. And the statistics show this to be true: [T]he police found contraband in 33 percent of the searches of black motorists, and in 22 percent of the searches of white motorists. But the mischief in this practice is quickly exposed. Blacks had a 50 percent higher chance of being found with contraband, but were searched more than 400 percent more often. The result is that 274 innocent black motorists were searched, while only 76 innocent white motorists were searched. The profiles apparently used by the Maryland State Troopers make 17 percent of the motorists pay 76 percent of the price of law enforcement strategy, solely because of their race.[137]

DIFFERENTIAL RATES OF ARREST, CONVICTION, AND SENTENCING

Data show that disparities exist throughout the criminal justice process. For example, a majority of all Federal, State, and local prison and jail inmates are non-white. Data show that blacks compose approximately 50 percent of

State and Federal prison inmates, four times their proportion in society, and Hispanics compose approximately 15 percent.[138] These disparities are probably due in part to underlying disparities in criminal behavior. But evidence shows that these disparities also are due in part to discrimination in the administration of justice and to policies and practices that have an unjustified disparate impact on minorities and people of color.

The most controversial example of a policy with an unjustified disparate impact is the present 100:1 disparity in sentencing for possession of crack versus powder cocaine, which was discussed at length at our May meeting. Under current Federal law, possession of 5 grams of crack cocaine triggers a 5-year mandatory minimum sentence; it takes possession of 500 grams of powder cocaine to trigger the same sentence. This 100:1 ratio has been widely criticized, in part because of the resulting racial disparity in drug sentencing—black defendants are 86 percent of those convicted for crack cocaine offenses (compared to 35 percent of those convicted for powder cocaine offenses).[139]

Several efforts at eliminating racial stereotypes and discrimination and reducing crime in communities of color have shown signs of success; they include community policing strategies, which have the potential to improve relations between law enforcement and communities of color, enhance confidence and trust in law enforcement, and reduce crime. During the past year, the President announced several initiatives designed to further these goals, including an initiative to provide $160 million in additional COPS grants to underserved areas. These grants would fund 620 new community policing officers in 18 cities with the greatest need, many of which are communities of minorities and people of color. In addition, the President proposed a $182 million initiative to strengthen law enforcement in Indian country.

RECOMMENDATIONS

- **Expand data collection and analysis.** As in other subject areas, one point that clearly emerged from our readings and discussions was the lack of existing data for some racial groups with regard to issues of criminal justice. For several reasons, much existing criminal justice data are restricted to blacks and whites, with little data available on issues affecting Hispanics, Asian Pacific Americans, or American Indians and Alaska Natives. The Administration should develop appropriate mechanisms to collect and analyze more complete criminal justice data for all racial and ethnic groups, so that issues of race can be better assessed and addressed.

- **Consider restricting the use of racial profiling.** We understand that the U.S. Department of Justice is examining the issue of racial profiling. We strongly endorse this effort and recommend that the President and the Attorney General consider restricting and developing alternatives to racial profiling in Federal law enforcement and encourage State and local governments to do the same. Such actions would send a powerful message that the Federal government does not sanction the disparate application of policing powers by race.

- **Eliminate racial stereotypes and diversify law enforcement.** The Administration should develop and support efforts to combat stereotypes through intense training and education for law enforcement personnel. Furthermore, it is crucial to promote diversity throughout the criminal justice system by increasing the number of minorities and people of color serving as police, prosecutors, judges, and other criminal justice practitioners.

- **Reduce or eliminate drug sentencing disparities.** Although there may be some justification for the different treatment of crack versus powder cocaine offenders, all participants in our May 19 meeting agreed that the present 100:1 sentencing disparity is morally and intellectually indefensible. The Administration has recommended reducing the disparity to 10:1 by raising the amount of crack cocaine and lowering the amount of powder cocaine that triggers a minimum sentence. We strongly support this action.

- **Promote comprehensive efforts to keep young people out of the criminal justice system.** Many communities of minorities and people of color face conditions of concentrated disadvantage, including high poverty, low-performing schools, high unemployment, low-quality health care, and absence of stable families. These conditions are linked to high rates of crime, including juvenile crime. Reducing crime and keeping young people out of the criminal justice system probably requires a comprehensive approach to law enforcement—one that involves all sectors of the community and includes education, economic, and criminal justice programs. We support several Administration efforts to prevent and address youth crime in communities of color, including the enhancement of afterschool programs and support for community partnerships. The Administration should further support coordinated efforts to address issues of concentrated disadvantage and keep young people out of the criminal justice system.

- **Continue to enhance community policing and related strategies.** As discussed above, community policing strategies have the potential to improve relations between law enforcement and communities of color, enhance confidence in law enforcement, and reduce crime. The Federal government should continue to support community policing efforts in communities of color.

- **Support initiatives that improve access to courts.** The Administration should support initiatives to increase understanding of the way our criminal justice system operates and improve access to our courts. At a minimum, all judicial systems should provide limited-English proficient users to access both the criminal and civil courts in their communities. Strategies that may be implemented include providing grants to community-based organizations for outreach and public education, providing training for law enforcement personnel (including judges) about the changing demographics in the communities they serve, and making available court-certified interpreters.

- **Support American Indian and Alaska Native law enforcement.** There is strong consensus that more resources are needed to adequately support the unique needs of criminal justice in Indian country, which has its own tribal court system. We were pleased that the President's FY 1999 budget proposal includes more than $180 million to strengthen law enforcement in Indian country. The Federal government should continue to take action to strengthen tribal law enforcement and justice systems in a manner that respects tribal sovereignty and preserves traditional tribal justice practices.

RACE AND HEALTH

The gaps in longevity and health care access for minorities and people of color are well documented and merit Presidential attention. On the most basic measure of fairness, America should not be a society where babies of different racial backgrounds have significantly different life expectancies. If our Nation is committed to the proposition that all people are created equal, our most basic indicators of life and health should reflect this principle.

The continuing gap in health care access undermines the vision of one America. A higher portion of minorities and people of color than whites are medically uninsured and/or live in medically underserved areas. Purposeful or even unintended discrimination by health care providers can result in unnecessary suffering and/or death. Providers often do not understand the ways that cultural influences affect them and their patients as they deliver medical services. At the same time that we confront these formidable challenges, the medical establishment is disproportionately white and becoming more so. For example, the percentage of first-year medical students who are black, Latino, or American Indian is dropping, even as these groups' percentage of the total population is growing.[140] These trends and their negative effect on the lives and health of minorities and people of color are barriers in our path.

STRUCTURAL INEQUITIES

Difficulties accessing the health care system are largely related to disparities in employment, income, and wealth; these difficulties often mean that minorities and people of color receive medical treatment less frequently and in the later stages of health problems than whites. Such inequities in access affect rates of sickness, disease, suffering, lower life expectancy, and death among different racial groups.[141] Furthermore, studies indicate that racial disparities in health and health care are interrelated and often persist even when controlling for socioeconomic status. In addition, because of poverty, minorities are more likely to be insured by Medicaid, which often affects the terms of care provided to them by managed care organizations, and they are more likely than whites to live in areas that are medically underserved.[142]

DISCRIMINATION BY PROVIDERS

Racial issues also may affect relationships between health care providers and patients of color in ways that lower the quality of health care. Health care providers, like other persons, are subject to racial stereotypes and may lack the language skills to serve fully patients of color. Health care providers—doctors, nurses, clinical attendants, and others—can either purposefully or unintentionally discriminate against patients based on stereotypes. This can result in differences in care, such as medical treatment being denied or delayed without reason and being inadequate, prescribed unnecessarily, or cursory.

CULTURAL COMPETENCY OF PROVIDERS

In addition to structural inequities and provider discrimination, racial disparities in health care access also are affected by differences in language

Fear of INS consequences stops many [immigrants in the Asian American community] from seeking care they are entitled to....There are not enough community health workers, trusted peers to help them navigate the troubled waters....Many Asians prefer practitioners of Eastern alternative medicines, like herbalists, acupuncturists, or chi gung specialists. However, even the best insurance doesn't reimburse for these services. If Asians do have to go to a hospital, interpreter services are missing. It's a common practice to tell patients to bring their own interpreter and that person is often their child.

Meizhu Liu, Health Care for All, statement at U.S. Department of Health and Human Services Town Meeting on race and health, Boston, Massachusetts, July 10, 1998

and/or culture between the provider and the patient. Providers need to be more culturally competent so they can deliver effective medical care to people from different cultures. In many health care settings, patients are confronted with providers who do not recognize or respect their patients' culturally influenced values and beliefs, which often affect their attitude toward the provider's advice. Often, these cultural differences undermine the necessary cooperation between providers and clients, which results in less effective medical services. To some extent, cultural competency also means addressing the barriers in language between providers and clients, not merely working around them or soliciting the assistance of untrained (and sometimes non-adult) interpreters. However, it is important to recognize that cultural competence is relevant not only when providers and clients speak different languages, but also when they both speak the same language but come from different cultural backgrounds.

The President's recently announced effort to eliminate longstanding racial disparities in infant mortality, cancer screening and management, heart disease, AIDS, and immunizations by 2010 is a bold and significant step, yet the Board believes that more must be done to eliminate disparities in other key areas of health care and access.

RECOMMENDATIONS

- **Continue advocating for broad-based expansions in health insurance coverage.** We recommend that the President continue his vigorous efforts to expand medical insurance coverage to all Americans. To the extent that he is successful, his efforts to expand coverage generally will help close racial disparities because minorities and people of color tend to be disproportionately represented in demographic groups with limited or no insurance. For example, universal health insurance coverage could be thought of as disproportionately helping Latinos, blacks, and American Indians and Alaska Natives, since these groups are overrepresented in the ranks of the uninsured.

- **Continue advocacy of increased health care access for underserved groups.** Programs aimed specifically at increasing health care access of underserved groups also have the potential for closing health disparities in minority communities. For example, because minority groups make up a higher portion of the child population than the adult population, a successful effort to increase children's access to health care would likely help close the gaps in access between whites and minorities and people of color. The Children's Health Insurance Program (CHIP) is an excellent example of a strategically targeted effort that will close the gap in racial disparities in health care access. In addition to supporting full funding for CHIP, we encourage consideration of other efforts to target specific populations with major gaps in health care access. For example, a similarly targeted effort toward public housing tenants or migrant farm workers would have a similar effect.

- **Continue pushing Congress for full funding of the race and ethnic health disparities initiative.** The President announced a new Federal initiative to eliminate racial health disparities by 2010. The health initiative includes several innovative components, such as the outreach campaign led by the Surgeon General; a national conference co-hosted by the U.S. Department of Health and Human Services (HHS) and Grantmakers in Health (an educational organization); and a commitment to develop national health goals for 2010 in cooperation with public health groups, medical and minority organizations, and the private sector. This year's commitment to full funding should be regarded as an important foundation for the future. As the program grows in future years, the Administration should consider including efforts to gather data on local health disparities. A number of panelists told us that having better community-based data about racial disparities in health would greatly assist their efforts to bring greater local resources to bear on minority health concerns.

- **Increase funding for existing programs targeted to underserved and minority populations.** In addition to broadening the health initiative to eliminate disparities, there are opportunities to strengthen programs that are dedicated to helping the underserved increase their access to health care. To close racial disparities in health care access, we recommend significant increases in funding for the Indian Health Service, community heath centers, the National Health Service Corps, and other HHS programs with a track record of placing health care providers in underserved areas.

- **Enhance financial and regulatory mechanisms to promote culturally competent care.** There are some existing controls that influence the delivery of health services that may affect efforts to provide culturally competent care. We recommend that the appropriate agencies review the Medicaid reimbursement procedures and community health clinic funding mechanisms with the specific goal of changing regulations that unduly impede the expansion and increased understanding of culturally competent services.

- **Emphasize importance of cultural competence to institutions training health care providers.** HHS should strongly encourage

medical training institutions and accrediting associations to require that
students receive some training in cultural competency.

IMMIGRANTS AND RACE

In response to the President's call for a national dialogue, the Carnegie Endowment for International Peace and the Georgetown University Law
Center jointly sponsored a meeting, in which Board members participated,
exploring immigration and race. A historical and a contemporary context
for thinking about how immigrants help transform the race discussion beyond the black/white paradigm was provided and examples of promising
programs were presented. There also was a general round table discussion
by scholars, researchers, journalists, Government officials, and representatives from community organizations.

At this meeting, evidence was presented to show that race is the source of a fundamental rift in American society that affects many—but not all—immigrants and their experience with discrimination. At times, press stories suggest that issues surrounding immigrants' social, economic, and political position in America can aggravate already existing racial tensions. However, as several conference panelists noted, race, and not immigration, is the fundamental source of division in this society. Historically and currently, immigrant adjustment and degrees of "Americaness" have been measured using whiteness as a yardstick. Skin color, more than culture or language, influences the way immigrants and their offspring become incorporated into our society. Sociologists call this a process of "segmented assimilation" in which immigrants who are white or identify as white have different and better opportunities than do immigrants of color, such as Haitians, Jamaicans, and non-white Hispanics.[143]

Many of the panelists, who have worked with or studied different immigrant and racial groups, described varying magnitudes of color-based discrimination and levels of prejudice against them. For example, West Indian, Haitian, and African immigrants are more likely to be identified or treated like blacks[144] and concomitantly experience comparable levels of discrimination and exclusion. Thus color, usually more than ethnicity, plays a major role in how these immigrant groups are perceived.

The panelists noted, however, that there are also clear examples and evidence that stereotypes, alien status, language, and other factors can create boundaries for Asian and Latino immigrants leading to a perception of their status as "outsiders."[145] Their racial and ethnic distinctiveness sometimes results in significant discrimination in areas such as employment, housing, and education. In the case of Arab Americans, many of whom are Christian, the uninformed public image of them as all being Muslim subjects them to religious as well as racial discrimination. Stereotyping also comes into play, as many Arab Americans are mislabeled as members of terrorist organizations because of presumed political sympathies.

RECOMMENDATIONS

While we did not seek explicit policy recommendations from the panelists, we make the following recommendations on strategies to include immigrants of color into the American community and foster a greater degree of community cohesion. These fall into three main categories: (1) policies that orient newcomers to U.S. society and history; (2) policies that foster empathy and respect among groups; and (3) policies that support educational advancement, which were discussed in the recommendations for education section earlier in this chapter.

> *Not all Arabs are Muslims. In fact, there are about 16 [million] Arab Christians in the Middle East and about 2 million have immigrated to the United States....When we talk about Arabs...[a]re we talking about a race, a language, a culture, or a religion? [I]n the Unites States, we see they are all collapsed together. The Arab and the Muslim have become...not only the other, not only the potential terrorist who is a threat to the way of life...rather than our daydream— the Arab and the Muslim have become the enemy.*
>
> **Yvonne Haddad of the Center for Muslim and Christian Understanding, Carnegie Endowment for International Peace meeting, Washington, D.C., July 13, 1998**

- **Anti-discrimination measures must be strongly enforced on behalf of every racial and ethnic minority group.** Active enforcement of existing civil rights laws needs to continue to provide safeguards to all affected people. It is therefore important for the civil rights agencies to increase their sensitivity to newer forms of mistreatment and to develop education and outreach campaigns, in multiple languages, that inform newly arrived immigrants and citizens of foreign birth of their civil rights. This is a fundamental and, we believe, uncontroversial part of the American ideal. Congress needs to think seriously about fully funding the President's proposed FY 1999 civil rights budget requests, as many immigrants and other minorities and people of color continue to experience significant discrimination.

- **Promote programs, for both immigrants and those born in the United States, that would promote a clear understanding of the rights and duties of citizenship.** These types of programs would help to promote national identity and cohesion. We recommend that our educational institutions pay increased attention to the education needed by newcomers so that they may learn U.S. history and values while, concurrently, ensuring that native born citizens will learn to appreciate America's ideals of welcoming and integrating immigrants. This education should also include a discussion of the periods in which we did not live up to those ideals and rejected or attempted to exclude certain immigrant groups because they were not "like us." While we are not suggesting national curriculum standards for citizenship training, we believe that the Federal government can play a significant role in promoting a vision of our shared values based on history and our hopes for the future. We therefore recommend that, as part of the Millennium celebration and beyond, the President appoint a group of prominent advisors to establish a broad-based study to provide the Nation a civic lesson that will strengthen us all.

- **Support local level immigrant-inclusion initiatives.** We urge that Federal agencies champion local government programs that foster collaborative efforts to cross racial, ethnic, and immigrant group boundaries in pursuit of common goals. Some of these policies should be targeted at newcomers while others should be more general; all communities should be encouraged to try to foster their own version of these efforts. A mediation and community building function, as exemplified by the Community Relations Service (CRS) in the U.S. Department of Justice, is an essential means to reduce and possibly eliminate forms of racial and ethnic group tension that have and will, unfortunately, arise again in many communities. We therefore recommend that the functions of the CRS in community tension reduction on issues of race and immigration be reconsidered as a major, critical part of program operations at the national level until State and local governments are better able to offer the independent, mediation services. At a minimum, CRS' funding for the next 5 years should be increased significantly.

In June 1997, the President committed this Race Initiative to a study, dialogue, and action agenda. He indicated that he did not want the Board to wait until the end of the Initiative year to recommend action steps. The President intended, and has acted, to implement many of the proposals described in this chapter, which the Board submitted to him throughout the year. The other recommendations are being reviewed and considered further by the President and his staff.

In the following chapter, we describe the essential elements of a long-term strategy for continuing the work of the Race Initiative. We also briefly discuss critical issues that we did not have the opportunity to examine fully and recommend that they be given serious attention and rigorous review as we continue to build one America.

CHAPTER FIVE—FORGING A NEW FUTURE

The recommendations in this Report to the President are intended to preserve the integrity of the principles that lie at the core of our democracy: justice, equality, dignity, respect, and inclusion. It is with these principles in mind that the Advisory Board acted on behalf of the President in this year-long effort. At times, we were met with doubt, distrust, and even disbelief. The negative reactions often seemed to draw more attention than the positive responses to our work. However, in most instances, our efforts were met with both enthusiasm and appreciation for the leadership and the willingness of the President to undertake this unprecedented initiative.

Our task in the final analysis is to cause more people to look in the mirror and have them understand that the ultimate answer to the American dilemma, as defined more than a generation ago by Gunnar Myrdal, lies in their willingness to accept people for who they are, and not on the basis of what they look like, and to accord every other human being dignity and respect that is his or her God-given right.

**Gov. William Winter,
July 14, 1997**

Literally tens of thousands of Americans shared in dialogues to weave our different, and common, experiences together so that paths toward deeper understanding might emerge. While many of the conversations allowed for greater insight and a shared sense of commitment to find ways to advance race relations, some conversations ended without resolution. But that is the nature of dialogue—a process that invites differing points of view and is open to possibilities yet unrecognized. Regardless of the outcome, we learned that there exists a genuine recognition by many people that the challenges presented by racial and ethnic divides in the country must be met.

This Nation has the capacity to meet these challenges affirmatively and the capacity required to incorporate positively the growing racial and ethnic diversity of its people into the planning for our future well-being and prosperity. We have the capacity to communicate with each other faster and over greater distances using the latest electronic technologies. Factual information about our history, race, and race relations can be accessed with ease, making possible a more constructive dialogue.

The Board further recognizes that the key to our ability to coordinate this communications and problem-solving effort is our capacity to harness the emerging technological advances to ensure that all Americans may participate fully in this unprecedented undertaking.

MAPPING THE ROAD TO RACIAL JUSTICE AND EQUALITY

If we are to succeed in the mission to create a more just Nation, the Initiative's work must continue. Not only must it continue in name, but it must continue in the spirit with which it began. This year's effort has been vital to laying the foundation for the larger task. We now describe the essential elements we believe must be considered in developing a meaningful long-term strategy to advance race relations in the 21st century. These elements include the following:

- A permanent structure to continue the work of the Initiative.

- A public education program using a multimedia approach.

- A Presidential "Call to Action" to leaders in community, corporate, religious, and government sectors.

- A focus on youth.

All Americans can and should have a role in building on the vision for one America in the 21st century. As part of our final observations and recommendations, we have identified 10 ways that people can participate in this national effort to strengthen our communities and bring all Americans closer together. The final observations that follow address the need for an approach that can capitalize on the work accomplished this year.

THE PRESIDENT'S COUNCIL FOR ONE AMERICA: CONTINUING THE WORK OF THE ADVISORY BOARD

The goal of creating a more just and unified society requires continued leadership from the Office of the President. The momentum that has been created must be guided by the vision of the President as public discourse about race relations continues to expand and public policy recommendations are put into action. The need for such leadership can be most effectively asserted by establishing the President's Council for One America.[146]

Establishing this Council will demonstrate a long-term commitment to the mission of the President's Initiative on Race and will ensure that the work that lies ahead will be coordinated, focused, and productive. Creating a system of accountability in connection with these efforts is of concern to all those who have expressed interest in, and support for, the Initiative. In light of the fact that literally tens of thousands of people across the Nation have been involved in this first year of study and dialogue, with hundreds of programs having been identified as Promising Practices, the establishment of the Council will send a message that the Initiative has been a genuine beginning to a larger, more extensive and ambitious program with respect to the whole matter of race, racial reconciliation, and bridging racial divides.

No one viewed a 1-year timeframe as sufficient to begin this conversation, to study race relations, educate the Nation, take action, and achieve concrete, long-lasting results. The more extensive and ambitious program that should be created will be multifaceted and will preserve certain aspects of the initial effort. For instance, future plans should support opportunities for sustained dialogue at all levels, continue to identify leadership being demonstrated in local communities, expand research to include the experiences and analyses of increasingly diverse populations, and continue to educate the public about the facts and myths surrounding racial disparities and the value of our racial diversity.

One way of accomplishing these objectives is to publish a "White House Monograph on the State of Race Relations in America at the End of the 20th Century." We envision the monograph as a set of volumes containing work from a wide range of disciplines. What will make this effort valuable is that it will continue the dialogue and build on the social science research that is currently underway.[147] It will invite deeper examination about the possibilities of racial reconciliation and will permit the commitment and dedication of many individuals to contribute to the creation of an unprecedented, single piece of work. The White House Monograph could be presented to the American people at the end of this term, in the year 2000. It would be a unique, enduring, and unprecedented contribution to the body of literature concerning America's conversation about race relations at the turn of this century. It would also become the basis for public policymaking as we enter the 21st century.

The Council can be responsible for identifying contributing sources and coordinating the selection, reviewing, and editing of the articles to be included in the series. The final product will be of value to future generations of Americans who wish to study, understand, and gain insights about how race has influenced our history and the development of public policy and become a guide to future actions.

Although a substantial amount of the Council's work would be associated with the process of publishing the monograph, it would have several critical ongoing functions. The Council would coordinate and monitor the implementation of policies designed to increase opportunity, eliminate racial disparities, and would be authorized to propose policies that recognize the enormous impact that improving educational and economic opportunity will have on easing racial tensions. There is a tremendous need to continue dialogue about expanding opportunities because there are so many useful but underutilized strategies that can be pursued. The vital cross-sections among race, education, and economic status was emphasized by members of the public and experts who appeared before the Board during the year. Clearly, there is a need to support innovative and new research that takes into account our diverse population mix and the cost to the Nation of untapped and underutilized human resources because of discrimination and the vestiges of past discrimination.

Another primary function of the Council would be to promote and expand the work associated with Promising Practices, which includes the dialogue that is so critical to racial reconciliation. Many local efforts need assistance to find resources; to replicate, expand, or improve their programs; and to share their experiences with other communities. Moreover, the thirst for more and better dialogue about race must be met with a substantial effort to increase the number of people to conduct dialogues in other settings. The Council can play a valuable role by outlining a national plan that would expand racial reconciliation activities. Those activities would include identifying resources, providing a bridge to other Federal agencies, motivating community and sector leaders to become engaged, and helping to replicate successful models in different regions of the Nation. In pursuing the goal of expanding the number of people actively engaged in racial dialogue and other racial reconciliation activities, the Council can focus on creating greater opportunities to bring public, private, and nonprofit partnerships together. The desire to pursue more collaboration in this regard was heard frequently throughout the year.

Cabinet members, as well as public members who are not a part of the Administration, should be asked to serve. Bipartisan participation, similar to the model offered by the Glass Ceiling Commission,[148] should be sought in selecting public members. Public members would be drawn from a wide range of sectors, including but not limited to: local governance associations, philanthropy, faith-based organizations, private business, education, and advocacy groups.

The priority of the Council would differ dramatically from those of the Civil Rights Division at the U.S. Department of Justice, the Equal Employment Opportunity Commission, and the U.S. Commission on Civil Rights, those units that already study, monitor, and ensure compliance with our anti-discrimination laws. In contrast, the nature of the Council's work would be to expand on the process started in 1997–1998. This work includes coordinating the White House Monograph; working with the White House and other Federal agencies charged with implementing policies disproportionately affecting racial minorities and carrying out comprehensive civil rights policies; taking the next step with Promising Practices identified over the past year by convening a national meeting; responding to the continuing requests for information about what the Federal Government knows about race in America; and initiating opportunities for greater inclusion in the dialogue that was started. The unique role that the President's Council could play would almost certainly provide added value to the work already being done at the Federal level and would further stimulate the creation of new partnerships between government and non-governmental entities.

DEVELOPING A PUBLIC EDUCATION CAMPAIGN USING A MULTIMEDIA APPROACH

The role of print and electronic media in shaping public attitudes, beliefs, and opinions about race is enormous. Despite having only one formal opportunity to discuss media and racial stereotyping, the Board had the benefit of a study conducted by Robert M. Entman on media images of the major racial and ethnic groups in the United States.[149] Additionally, the Board heard repeatedly that more attention should be given to using media strategies in promoting greater understanding about racial diversity in America. Not only should there be a focus on news media, there should also be a focus on entertainment media, in which depictions of protagonists and situational vignettes can be developed in more inclusive and non-stereotypical ways.

A media campaign that has the capacity to effectively disseminate factual information and inspire creative expression should be explored. In addition, it is critical to develop a coordinated media campaign. Its focus should be to pay tribute to the many contributions of Americans from different racial and ethnic backgrounds to emphasize our common values and principles as a Nation and to highlight facts about our racial diversity.

A national "report card" on the progress we make toward improving race relations should be part of any media campaign. This effort could build on the publication of the Council of Economic Advisers'(CEA's) *Changing America,* on behalf of the Initiative. Many Federal agencies already gather information that illuminates areas where we have succeeded in reducing racial disparities and where improvement is needed. The report card will provide a single source for the data that demonstrates our progress. The data that are most compelling can be distributed and easily incorporated into local or regional campaigns involving public service announcements (PSAs), street flags/signs, airport terminal signs, and so forth. A separate strategy should be delivered to target our new citizens who, during their swearing-in ceremony, often view a film about becoming an American. That film should be updated to include a message about the strength of our nation being derived from our diversity and commitment to principles of our democracy. Presidential authority throughout this campaign, along with bipartisan support, would ensure a broad reach for this effort.

A CALL TO ACTION

The Board has only begun the process of advancing our commitment to embrace the multiracial and multicultural reality of our Nation. An essential part of any future plan must include, and perhaps even build on, leadership and commitment at the local level. A call to action should be sent from the President to the National Governors Association, U.S. Conference of Mayors, National League of Cities, and National Association of Counties. That call should seek input on how local governments can address the racial and ethnic divides in their communities. The local plans should include approaches that are being currently utilized, the identification of institutional efforts aimed at bridging the racial divide, and recommendations for appropriate Federal action to complement local action.

Because funding almost certainly will be one of the suggestions for appropriate Federal support, the call should incorporate a framework that invites recommendations that outline innovative ways in which grants or matching funds can be made available. Priority should be placed on promoting public/private/nonprofit partnerships that seek to close racial divides. The Council should consider designing a research project that documents and positively reinforces the different ways in which local governments have institutionalized their efforts to improve relationships across racial and cultural divides and, to the extent possible, measure the effectiveness of the different approaches.

As we have stated earlier, there is no single strategy, group, organization, political party, or religion that can single-handedly make racial reconciliation a reality. Creating a more just society must flow from the collaborative efforts of many and from the public will of our populace to give true meaning to the values we espouse. The Federal Government is in a position to promote coalitions that transcend racial and ethnic differences; to address complicated issues related to both our domestic and international obligations; to provide moral leadership concerning the need to find common ground among diverse people; and to facilitate collaboration between innumerable organizations, agencies, and individuals working in both the public and private sectors. This call to action should be expanded further to build on the outreach efforts to educational, corporate, and religious leaders described in Chapter One.

FOCUS ON YOUTH

Young people represent our greatest hope for realizing America's promise in the next century. The next step in this process should include a plan to address the many opportunities to work with youth. We urge the President to identify entities that have a commitment to youth leadership development, violence prevention, educational achievement, and the creative arts. Special attention should be given to making sure that the experiences of young people with disabilities, immigrant youth, and high-poverty populations are included.

OTHER CRITICAL ISSUES

Throughout this Report, we have made a series of recommendations on many important topics. In addition, there are many other difficult and challenging issues of race that we have been unable to address in the depth that is appropriate to their importance. These are the issues that we now discuss briefly to demonstrate why the dialogue begun by President Clinton must continue. Some of these issues arose during the course of our meetings. Other issues were raised by the public in correspondence received by the Initiative staff. Still others were identified by experts as issues that continue to divide Americans and on which common ground remains elusive.

CIVIL RIGHTS

Affirmative action retrenchment. As a number of polls have shown, Americans of all races agree that equal opportunity is an important principle of our democracy, but that agreement breaks down over what further actions, such as affirmative action, we should take to resolve the problem of discrimination.[150] Affirmative action, perhaps more than any other contemporary civil rights issue, continues to divide Americans. From its beginnings as an executive policy to level the economic and educational playing fields following civil rights legislation of the 1960s to its current status as a policy that generates resentment by many whites who believe their children are victims of reverse discrimination or by minorities who feel stigmatized by the policy, affirmative action has been controversial.

Public opinion polls show that a majority of Americans of all races still support affirmative action when it is described as a tool to reduce racial discrimination. Yet that support drops significantly when affirmative action is described as racial preferences or a racial spoils system. More recently, it has been used as a political wedge to polarize public opinion. The concept is rarely defined in neutral terms, thus generating inaccurate and misleading discussions of what type of affirmative action programs are still permissible under the U.S. Constitution.

Higher education affirmative action. Recently, the courts have sent conflicting messages on the permissibility of affirmative action in higher education. Since 1978, most colleges and universities have followed the Supreme Court's decision in *Regents of University of California* v. *Bakke* [151] in designing their affirmative action programs to increase minority admissions. Programs could use race as one factor to promote the educational benefits of racial diversity on campus. In 1996, however, the U.S. Court of Appeals for the Fifth Circuit ruled in *Hopwood* v. *Texas* [152] that the University of Texas School of Law could not use race as a factor in admissions to law school when white applicants with higher test scores than minority applicants were denied admission; the Supreme Court elected not to review this decision on appeal. Before California voters approved Proposition 209 in 1996, the Board of Regents for the University of California system had voted to end all race-based affirmative action programs in those colleges and universities. When asked to repeal legacy admissions to the State university system (i.e., students admitted because their parents were alumni), the Board of Regents refused to do so.

On the other hand, a Federal judge in Boston recently upheld an affirmative action plan at a popular magnet public school with a highly competitive admissions policy, which used racial diversity as one of its factors for admission to promote the educational benefits of diversity.[153] A disappointed white applicant's challenge to the University of Michigan affirmative action plan also is expected to further cloud the issue of how race may be used to enhance the educational experience. The Michigan case and other appeals will help clarify whether the *Bakke* decision is still good law. The Board is alarmed by the significant drop in black and Latino admissions in elite graduate programs in California and Texas and urges the development of a public education campaign to build a deeper understanding of the value of diversity in higher education.

Voters in the City of Houston voted this year to retain affirmative action by the city government when they voted for Proposition A; a judge in Texas ordered a new vote after a challenge to the language that was used in Proposition A. Voters in the State of Washington will vote later this year on whether to retain affirmative action by the State government. Similar challenges may be expected in other States. The U.S. Court of Appeals for the District of Columbia recently overturned an affirmative action policy maintained by the Federal Communications Commission to ensure racial diversity in the workforce of media outlets; an appeal is expected.[154] Many media firms responded by stating that they would voluntarily continue their affirmative action programs in light of that decision.

This is an area clearly in flux. Board members were repeatedly asked about our views on affirmative action. We support affirmative action as one of many vehicles to identify qualified minority candidates for admission into the Nation's colleges and universities. Affirmative action continues to be a critical and necessary tool for overcoming past discrimination, eliminating disparities in education, and moving us toward the goal of one America. During our November Board meeting, we discussed the value of diversity in higher education, recognizing affirmative action as one tool among many being implemented to promote such diversity on campus. In our corporate forums we discussed affirmative action in the context of employment and contracting practices. We found that many believed diversity in both the classroom and the workplace to be vital to America's future, especially given the growing racial diversity of the Nation. However, we found disagreements over the best ways to promote equal opportunity and to achieve more racial balance in higher education and the workplace.

Critics of affirmative action argue that 30 years of civil rights laws have leveled the playing field and that policies such as affirmative action are no longer needed.[155] Still others argue that non-racial factors such as class or poverty should be used instead of race. However, the data we have reviewed demonstrates that for far too many minorities, a level playing field remains a mirage. It is for these reasons and others that the Board supports the Administration's current policy regarding affirmative action.

In sum, affirmative action will continue to serve as a proxy for the Nation's continuing debate over equality and racial reconciliation. Leadership is needed to forge public consensus on affirmative action. The challenge is to develop public understanding of its value as a tool to achieve racial diversity and improve the public discourse on affirmative action programs. Significantly, a comprehensive study was recently published that presents empirical data on the long-term consequences of considering race in college and university admissions.[156] This represents an opportunity to dispel the myths and misinformation that often dominate the debate and make constructive dialogue difficult. This type of disciplined research must be encouraged in other areas as well. The President and the Council should support, encourage, and facilitate such efforts.

Federal sector employment. Since the 1960s, the Federal Government has had a more representative workforce than many sectors in private industry.[157] More recently, a number of Federal agencies have developed model programs for the recruitment, training, and promotion of their minority workers. They are experimenting with alternative dispute resolution methods to identify and resolve problems before they rise to the level of an Equal Employment Opportunity Commission complaint.[158] On the other hand, the high number of complaints of racial discrimination in Federal agencies suggest that the fact or perception of employment discrimination continues to hamper the career prospects of minority workers.[159] To the extent that additional resources for the Equal Employment Opportunity Commission would allow more prompt resolution of such complaints, the recommendations we have made previously will assist in this process. The Federal Government must ensure that it models the conduct we are encouraging other public and private employers to demonstrate. This issue requires serious consideration, study, and action.

Police misconduct. One of the more emotional issues we confronted during the year was police-community relations. From California to New York, from the Southwest to the Northwest, we heard far too many harrowing stories from minorities and people of color about police misconduct. At the same time, we recognize that the vast majority of police officers perform their jobs with dedication and a commitment to protect all citizens with equal vigor. However, actions by those officers who abuse the civil rights of minorities overshadow the positive actions of dedicated public servants and poison police-community relations. Too often, minorities and people of color view police officers as their enemies rather than as their protectors.

Clearly, this Administration's efforts to institutionalize community policing programs have been extremely helpful in improving relations between the police and minority communities, but more must be done. Police officers need to understand better the communities they serve, and community residents need an opportunity to get to know the police officers who pledge to serve and protect them. Police-community dialogues on a broader scale would help to build a sense of mutual respect and understanding and would help to isolate those police officers who dishonor their badges with their racist behavior.

Dialogue alone will not reverse years of mistrust and violent confrontations. Minorities and people of color demand that law enforcement agencies take more drastic disciplinary action against those officers who consistently violate their civil rights. If officers may routinely abuse minorities in their custody without fear of any real punishment for their actions, then this situation will continue to undermine efforts to improve police-community relations.

> *Almost every group we've gone to has said the media is a problem that has to be addressed. Children get more information from the media, unfortunately, than they do from schools.*
>
> **Gov. Kean,
> June 1998**

MEDIA AND STEREOTYPING

Negative racial stereotyping emerged as a central issue to reducing racial tensions and divisions in America. As the Kerner Commission recognized three decades ago, the media as an institution has both the power to exacerbate such stereotypes or to eradicate them through its work. That Commission exhorted the media to undertake an immediate self-examination of its coverage of the black community and the lack of racial diversity at every level of media. While the media has certainly improved the number of minority reporters, newscasters, producers, and filmmakers since then, a major problem still remains regarding the representation, coverage, and portrayal of minorities on the news, on television, in film, and in other forms of media.

A major study on race and media by a noted expert[160] on this issue made many important observations on the media's treatment of whites, blacks, Latinos, and Asian Pacific Americans that demand further attention, especially in light of the constraints of the First Amendment and the government's ability to address these concerns. We believe it is essential, however, to pursue strategies that could increase public understanding of the media's role in race relations and on racial attitudes.

Two other studies on media and race focused our attention on this area of inquiry. The Center for Living Democracy published a survey showing that the respondents felt that while the national media frequently contributed to the racial polarization in this country, those same media outlets were seldom initiators or supporters of interracial dialogue.[161] In March, 1998, Children NOW released its survey of 1,200 racially diverse children entitled *A Different World: Children's Perceptions of Race and Class in the Media,* in which young people demonstrated their sophisticated view of media images. These children indicated their desire to see all races portrayed "more often, more fairly, more realistically, and more positively."[162] If youngsters, who already watch more television than their elders and receive more political news and current events from television or the Internet than their elders, are not given the tools to distinguish between the transmitted images and reality, then the process of reconciliation will take much longer. These studies, taken together, demonstrate the importance of educating the public about the impact of the role of the media in race relations and on racial attitudes.

LACK OF ENVIRONMENTAL JUSTICE

Communities of color generally experience increased incidence of health threats associated with toxic pollution and other environmental sources of risk. A 1993 report by the Environmental Protection Agency (EPA) documented significant disparities in exposures to toxics and pollutants, particularly with respect to lead and air pollution.[163] These patterns of environmental risk are correlated with compelling data concerning public health threats to communities of color. For example, the occurrence of childhood asthma, which is closely linked to air quality, is almost twice as high for blacks and three times as high for Puerto Rican children as it is for whites.[164] Further research is needed to understand the precise role of environmental risks as distinct from other risk factors, such as access to health care, prevalence of tobacco use, or other health factors, in these communities.

Perceived and actual disparities in environmental conditions may be part of a more general exclusion from the governmental processes by which environmental priorities, policies, and standards are set. Pursuant to Executive Order 12898, Federal agencies have made a concerted effort to understand and address these types of disparities, and the White House Council on Environmental Quality (CEQ) has undertaken a series of meetings with communities to respond to the conditions that generate environmental justice concerns and develop better models of community participation in environmental decision making.

Angela Oh represented the Board at an environmental justice meeting on July 10–11, 1998, which was convened by CEQ and the Race Initiative. This meeting, which served as the main vehicle for the Board to learn about environmental justice issues, was held in South Central Los Angeles and focused on concerns in that community. It included presentations from community members as well as small-group meetings with senior policy officials from the U.S. Departments of Agriculture, Commerce, Housing and Urban Development, Interior, Justice, Transportation, and the Environmental Protection Agency.

Community leaders and citizens presented compelling examples of environmental justice concerns and demonstrated that there are often divergent views among the relevant government agencies and even within affected communities about the nature of the problem and the appropriate response. These debates highlight the need for better models for involving communities of color in the process of setting environmental and public health priorities, policies, and standards. In many cases, Federal jurisdiction to address these issues directly will be limited, but Federal leadership to compel State and local governments to pay attention to these issues will be essential.

EDUCATION

Bilingual education. During the past year, the State of California, which has the largest population of non-English speaking residents, voted to end bilingual education. To the extent that this issue becomes further politicized, other States with high immigrant populations may elect to follow California's lead. The Board heard from parents in a number of communities with large populations of students with limited-English language proficiency who were concerned about the ability of their children to receive an education if bilingual educations programs are curtailed.

In many instances, students from first generation immigrant homes still need help in acquiring the English language. Almost every survey conducted among immigrant families reveals that acquiring English is a high priority.[165] They understand that language proficiency is the key to success in America. Yet in too many political campaigns, voters are led to believe that immigrant families are reluctant to learn English. Bilingual education, when properly implemented, is a valuable tool that permits limited-English proficient students to study math, science, and other basic subjects in their native language. The Board is concerned that the rejection of bilingual education is another indicator of the growing backlash against newcomers to America and, as such, requires a closer examination of how to promote continued support for bilingual education.

This issue should not be about whether new immigrants should learn English. There is little disagreement about that. The issue is how they will learn it and whether we will leave it to the educators to determine the most effective way of teaching English to children of immigrants. Another way we can support English language acquisition is to provide more classes for immigrant adult students, given the long waiting lists for such classes.

Tracking. During our June 1998 meeting, the issue of tracking in public schools emerged as an important issue affecting race relations within multiracial school settings. This is the practice in which children are evaluated during the early years of elementary school in terms of their academic abilities and placed on an academic "track" such as gifted, average, or learning disabled. Parents of minority students believe that their children are not receiving fair evaluations of their abilities, but instead are disproportionately placed in lower tracks to the detriment of their children's academic careers. Some suspect that the ulterior motive behind tracking is not merely to teach children who are at the same level in separate classes (so that slower children do not hamper higher achieving students) but is really to maintain separate schools within integrated settings. This is an old problem that demands renewed attention and resolution.

> *The data tell us in almost every survey... that immigrants place among their highest priorities language acquisition...because they understand that you can't succeed in this society without mastering the English language.*
>
> **Angela Oh, Board meeting, June 1998**

Emerging technology issues. Technology can be enormously useful in bridging the gaps between disparate communities, but it can also widen them if we fail to acknowledge the gaps in access to new technologies. The information now available and the rapidity with which it can be transmitted across the country (and around the world) can facilitate dialogue on race. Chat rooms on the Internet that allow people to communicate without ever knowing each other's racial backgrounds are but one example of how new technologies can overcome negative stereotypes. At the same time, however, the ease of communication also makes it easy for those who would instigate racial hatred to spread their poison as well.[166]

Moreover, the speed with which information technologies are incorporated into every sector of American business and society suggests that the disadvantage minority children currently face will increase in the near future. Minority children who attend schools without computers already are behind their more fortunate counterparts before they even graduate from school. Being competent in math and sciences as well as knowing how to operate computers are just some of the skills high school graduates in the 21st century will be expected to possess. Those without such skills will be left behind in the information revolution.

The key to facilitating constructive dialogue, furthering education about race, and sharing Promising Practices in a coordinated, dynamic way is our capacity to harness these technological advances in communications. We recognize, however, that the issue of technology and race is one that clearly requires more study. We must develop ways to ensure that our new technology becomes an instrument to narrow racial disparities and unify people across racial lines rather than becoming another tool of racial division.

CONFLICTS BETWEEN PEOPLE OF COLOR

The perpetuation of negative racial stereotyping is not solely within the province of white America. The ability of the dominant society to translate negative racial attitudes into policies and behaviors that adversely affect minorities and people of color has been well documented. However, people of all races tend to feel prejudice toward and harbor negative racial stereotypes about people who are different from themselves. Focusing all of the attention on stereotypes held by whites and on racist behavior engaged in by certain elements of white America certainly tells only half of the story. Negative racial attitudes between members of different minority groups is just as damaging to racial harmony as that between whites and minorities. However, we will not be able to overcome these negative attitudes no matter whom they are directed against until we are willing to confront prejudice wherever it appears.

INTERNATIONAL HUMAN RIGHTS

Other countries that are grappling with the challenges posed by increasingly diverse populations are looking to our Nation for leadership. In 1994, the United States ratified the Convention on the Elimination of All Forms of Racial Discrimination ("CERD"), which embodies international standards against racial and ethnic discrimination that are consistent with American laws, values, and goals. Promoting respect for CERD's principles can strengthen America's global leadership and help eliminate racial discrimination on a global basis. The Council should look for opportunities to reference this recognition of the international dimensions of racial and ethnic non-discrimination in resolving domestic race relations problems.

BUILDING A NEW CONSENSUS

As we noted in Chapter Two, one of the barriers to improving race relations is our lack of knowledge about our collective past. As Board Chairman Dr. Franklin told us at our first meeting, "the beginning of wisdom is knowledge, and without knowledge of the past we cannot wisely chart our course for the future." A common base of knowledge is essential to genuine racial healing. We do not presume to tell teachers how to teach history, but we believe it is vital to our future that the history we teach accurately reflects our history from the perspective of all Americans, not just the majority population.

Teaching a more inclusive and comprehensive history is just one of the ways we may begin to become more comfortable about our Nation's growing diversity. Today, too many people fear the demographic changes that are occurring and too few people understand the strength that our diversity has always provided. On the other hand, minority communities continue to grapple with issues of inclusion or exclusion, which are often expressed in terms of identity politics that seem to reject the notion of common values and ideals. During this delicate period of redefining the American policy, we must exercise extra caution so that we may better understand and value our differences and understand that those differences do not signal disunity but instead reflect an enhanced strength.

REACHING BEYOND THE CHOIR

We were quite successful, we believe, in energizing people who are already involved in activities designed to bridge racial divisions—the so-called choir. We do not minimize this accomplishment, because we believe that even the choir needs reinforcement, recognition, and inspiration to sustain their efforts. At the same time, even stronger efforts must be made to reach beyond the choir to the vast majority of Americans who are people of goodwill, but who fail to recognize the importance to their individual lives and to the lives of their children of overcoming racial divisions and narrowing racial disparities. If America is to achieve her full potential and if our children are to have an opportunity to achieve the same standard of living we have achieved, we must, as Executive Director of the Race Initiative Judith Winston warned, "acknowledge the fact that most Americans are not, and do not consider themselves racist, but they have responses to people who are different than they on the basis of race, that suggest that they have internalized—we have internalized these racist concepts and stereotypes…we have to find a way of engaging people, helping people to become engaged in conversations that are not confrontational and that are constructive."

In the past 15 months, we have planted seeds of racial healing, seeds that can erase "the fault line of race." We have traveled to communities in every region of the country to discuss issues of race. While these issues are often laden with emotion, we have tried to move the discussion beyond the polarizing impact of debate to the unifying impact of reasoned dialogue.

For it is reasoned dialogue, and not divisive debate, that ultimately will ease the fault line caused by race and strengthen our resolve to work together to build an American community worthy of the principles and values we espouse.

Ten Things Every American Should Do to Promote Racial Reconciliation

One of the most striking findings from our work is that there are many Americans who are willing to accept that racial prejudice, privilege, and disparities are major problems confronting our Nation. Many of them told us that they would welcome concrete advice about what they should do. To fill that need, we offer a brief list of actions that individual Americans could take that would increase the momentum that will make us one America in the 21st century.

(1) **Make a commitment to become informed about people from other races and cultures.** Read a book, see a movie, watch a play, or attend a cultural event that will inform you and your family about the history and current lives of a group different than your own.

(2) **If it is not your inclination to think about race, commit at least 1 day each month to thinking about how issues of racial prejudice and privilege might be affecting each person you come in contact with that day.** The more that people think about how issues of race

But people of good will, those who wish to live in a community of racial peace and harmony, well understand that the road to racial peace is not without its problems and even pain. But the journey is worth taking, for in the end, we can forge institutions and adopt practices that will help us build communities, communities that are absent of fear, suspicion, and even paranoia, that all too often characterize our present communities.

John Hope Franklin, Advisory Board meeting, Washington, D.C., July 14, 1997

affect each person, the easier it will be for Americans to talk honestly about race and eliminate racial divisions and disparities.

(3) **In your life, make a conscious effort to get to know people of other races.** Also, if your religious community is more racially isolated than your local area, encourage it to form faith partnerships with racially different faith groups.

(4) **Make a point to raise your concerns about comments or actions that appear prejudicial, even if you are not the targets of these actions.** When people say or do things that are clearly racially biased, speak out against them, even if you are not the target. When people do things that you think *might be* influenced by prejudice, raise your concerns that the person or institution seriously consider the role that racial bias might play, even unconsciously.

(5) **Initiate a constructive dialogue on race within your workplace, school, neighborhood, or religious community.** The *One America Dialogue Guide* provides some useful ideas about how to construct a dialogue and lists some organizations that conduct dialogues and can help with facilitation.

(6) **Support institutions that promote racial inclusion.** Watch television programs and movies that offer racially diverse casts that reflect the real world instead of those perpetuating an inaccurately segregated view of America. Support companies and nonprofit organizations that demonstrate a commitment to racial inclusion in personnel and subcontracting. Write the institutions to let them know of your support for what they are doing.

(7) **Participate in a community project to reduce racial disparities in opportunity and well-being.** These projects can also be good ways of getting to know people from other backgrounds.

(8) **Insist that institutions that teach us about our community accurately reflect the diversity of our Nation.** Encourage our schools to provide festivals and celebrations that authentically celebrate the history, literature, and cultural contributions of the diverse groups that comprise the United States. Insist that our children's schools textbooks, curricula, and libraries provide a full understanding of the contributions of different racial groups and an accurate description of our historic and ongoing struggle for racial inclusion. Insist that our news sources—whether print, television, or radio—include racially diverse opinions, story ideas, analysis, and experts. Support ethnic studies pro-

grams in our colleges and universities so that people are educated and that critical dialogue about race is stimulated.

(9) **Visit other areas of the city, region, or country that allow you to experience parts of other cultures, beyond their food.** If you have an attitude that all people have histories, cultures, and contributions about which you could benefit from learning, it is usually not difficult to find someone who enjoys exposing others to their culture.

(10) **Advocate that groups you can influence (whether you work as a volunteer or employee) examine how they can increase their commitment to reducing racial disparities, lessening discrimination, and improving race relations.** Whether we are a member of a small community group or an executive of a large corporation, virtually everyone can attempt to influence a group to join the national effort to build one America.

ENDNOTES

[1] There has been some criticism of the use of the term "one America." Some have said the term is misleading and even worse, hypocritical. We urge that the term continue to be used. Because we are all proud of, and celebrate in word and song, the geographic diversity of our Nation's mountains, rivers, deserts, and plains, we should celebrate equally the diversity of our people. Black, white, red, brown, yellow, and multiracial people are as much a part of the landscape of this country as its geography. We are thankful for the resources and talents Americans provide and look with pride and appreciation upon the bounty of our human resources to match the bounty of our natural resources. We strive to be one America and call this America our America.

[2] Council of Economic Advisers, *Changing America: Indicators of Social and Economic Well-Being by Race and Hispanic Origin,* Washington, DC: Executive Office of the President, Council of Economic Advisers, 1998.

[3] The Constitutional Convention in 1787, the Lincoln-Douglas Debates in 1858, and the debates about civil rights in the 1960s are well-known race debates. More recently, debates about affirmative action have become frequent.

[4] Despite recognition of the failure of current language or terms of art to render fully the many issues with which we have wrestled, we must still rely on much of the inadequate language to present our findings. It is based on this qualification that, for purposes of this report, we use the term "minorities and people of color" to refer to the collective group of principal American minorities.

For purposes of uniformity, we use the race and ethnicity categories established in *Standards for Maintaining, Collecting, and Presenting Federal Data on Race and Ethnicity,* issued by the Office of Management and Budget (OMB) on October 30, 1997 (Federal Register Document 97–28653; 62 Fed. Reg. 58789). OMB developed these standards to provide a common language for uniformity and comparability in the collection and use of data on race and ethnicity by Federal agencies. The standards have five categories for race: American Indian or Alaska Native; Asian; black or African American; Native Hawaiian or Other Pacific Islander; white or non-Hispanic white; and Hispanic or Latino.

The Advisory Board will use the race and ethnicity categories set forth in the OMB directive with one exception: the broad category of Americans who trace their ancestry to any part of Asia or the Pacific Islands will be referred to by the Advisory Board as "Asian Pacific Americans."

[5] This apology occurred during a dialogue organized by the National Conference for Community and Justice (formerly the National Conference) on September 26, 1997, in Little Rock, Arkansas. The National Conference for Community and Justice organized these types of dialogues across the country.

[6] Du Bois, Paul Martin, and Jonathan J. Hutson, *Bridging the Racial Divide: A Report on Interracial Dialogue in America,* Brattleboro, VT: The Center for Living Democracy, 1997.

[7] While dialogue on race is vital, the call for a national conversation on race was not without challenge. The challenges the Board encountered included:

(1) How to define the conversation.

(2) How to engage in such a conversation without duplicating ongoing activities.

(3) How to reach those who do not traditionally see race as an issue of interest.

(4) How, with limited resources, to respond to the many requests for assistance in promoting the conversation in local communities.

(5) How to address the skeptics who argue that dialogue is of little value and action speaks louder than words.

[8] The organizations are Hope in the Cities, Richmond, Virginia; National Multicultural Institute, Washington, D.C.; YWCA, New York, New York; National Days of Dialogue, Washington, D.C.; Study Circles Resource Center, Pomfret, Connecticut; and National Conference on Community and Justice, New York, New York.

[9] Hoffman, Mary, and Caroline Binch, *Amazing Grace*, London, England: Magi Publications, 1995.

[10] In many fields, people use the term "best practices" to call attention to programs that should be models for others to replicate. The Board uses the term "Promising Practices," indicating that the Board has no predetermined understanding of what an ideal program should look like but that based on preliminary criteria, these efforts show promise. Because some of these efforts have been developed to address specific local issues, communities in different regions or locales should modify programs to suit their needs.

[11] For example, see Community Cousins, Encinitas, California.

[12] For example, see the National Multicultural Institute and the National Conference for Community and Justice, New York, New York.

[13] For example, see The Club, Kosciusko, Mississippi.

[14] For example, see Public Allies, Washington, D.C.

[15] For example, see Study Circles, Pomfret, Connecticut, and Multicultural Collaborative, Los Angeles, California.

[16] For example, see Bridging the Gap, Atlanta, Georgia; American Indian Science Technology Education Consortium, Las Vegas, New Mexico; and Higher Ground, Boston, Massachusetts.

[17] Executive Order 13050.

[18] "The problem of the twentieth century is the problem of the color line—the relation of the darker to the lighter races of men in Asia and Africa, in America and the islands of the sea." DuBois, W.E.B., *The Souls of Black Folk: Essays and Sketches*, New York: Blue Heron Press, 1953: 13. See also Franklin, John Hope, *The Color Line: Legacy for the Twenty-First Century*, Columbia, MO: University of Missouri Press, 1993. There is a voluminous library of material discussing the history and current practice of racism affecting African Americans. Among the suggested relevant texts are: Clayton, Obie, ed., *An American Dilemma Revisited: Race Relations in a Changing World*, New York: Russell Sage, 1996; Hacker, Andrew, *Two Nations: Black and White: Separate, Hostile and Unequal*, New York: Charles Scribner's, 1992; Oliver, Melvin, and Thomas Shapiro, *Black Wealth/White Wealth: A New Perspective on Racial Inequality*, New York: Routledge; Feagin, Joe, and Melvin Sikes, *Living with Racism: The Black Middle Class Experience*. Boston: Beacon Press, 1994; Gerald Jaynes and Robin Williams, *A Common Destiny: Blacks and American Society*, Washington, DC: National Academy Press, 1989; and Sniderman, Paul, and Thomas Piazza, *The Scar of Race*, Cambridge: Harvard University, 1993.

[19] The Federal Housing Administration (FHA) is a division of the U.S. Department of Housing and Urban Development. FHA was created in the 1930s as a means to bring stability and security to housing markets by providing foreclosure insurance to lenders. FHA offers 100-percent coverage against the loss of the principal loan amount and focuses on newly emerging and underserved markets. FHA helps make housing affordable for those unable to get assistance in the private mortgage market. See Bradford, Calvin, "The Two Faces of FHA: A Case of Government Supported Discrimination Against Minority and Racially Changing Communities," Chicago, IL: Chicago Fair Housing Alliance Policy Paper, March 1998.

[20] See *Shelley* v. *Kraemer*, 334 U.S. 1 (1948); and Norquist, John O., *The Wealth of Cities: Revitalizing the Centers of American Life,* Reading, MA: Perseus, 1998.

[21] See testimony of Larry Bobo, Advisory Board meeting on racial demographics, surveys, and attitudes on race, September 30, 1997.

[22] Dr. James Jones, Advisory Board meeting, September 30, 1997, Washington, D.C.

[23] "Indian tribe" means an American Indian or Alaska Native tribe, band, pueblo, village, or community that the Secretary of the Interior acknowledges to exist as an Indian tribe pursuant to the Federally Recognized Indian Tribe List Act of 1994, 24 U.S.C. Sec. 479a.

[24] Letter to the President from Bob Thomas, Advisory Board member, August 21, 1998, p. 4.

[25] Dorris, "The Grass Still Grows, the Rivers Still Flow," p. 43.

[26] See the U.S. Constitution, Article I, section 8, clause 3 (Indian Commerce Clause), which states, "The Congress shall have Power . . . to regulate Commerce with foreign Nations, and among the several States, and with the Indian Tribes."

[27] Ibid.

[28] Dorris, Michael A., "The Grass Still Grows, the Rivers Still Flow: Contemporary Native Americans," *Daedalus* (Spring 1981): 44. See also Vine, Deloria, Jr., *American Indian Policy in the 20th Century,* 1992, and *Red Earth, White Lies,* 1997; Fixico, Donald, *Rethinking American Indian History,* 1997; and "Statement of the Hualapai Indian Tribe on Racism, Stereotypes, and Recent Attacks on Tribal Sovereignty," remarks presented to the Advisory Board on March 23, 1998, Denver, Colorado, Office of the Chairman, Hualapai Nation.

[29] Written statement presented at a meeting with tribal leaders, Denver, Colorado, March 23, 1998.

[30] Indian Tribes, like other sovereigns, cannot be sued without an "unequivocally expressed" waiver of sovereign immunity (*Santa Clara Pueblo* v. *Martinez,* 436 U.S. 49, 1978). Additionally, S. 1691 would have fundamentally changed the way the Federal Government deals with Indian Tribes on torts, contracts, property rights, taxation, and civil rights—issues central to the concept of tribal sovereignty.

[31] Written statement of Pueblo of Laguna to the President's Initiative on Race, June 10, 1998.

[32] Executive Memorandum for the Heads of Executive Departments and Agencies, "Government-to-Government Relations with Native American Tribal Government," April 29, 1994; see also Annual Report of the Administration Working Group on American Indians and Alaska Natives, August 1996.

[33] See Chapter Four for the Advisory Board's recommendations on eliminating disparities in education, economic opportunity, the administration of justice, and health care. See also Chapter Five for how to expand this effort to other critical areas.

[34] The terms "Latino" and "Hispanic" are used interchangeably to describe residents of the United States who belong to Spanish-speaking ethnic groups (i.e., Mexican Americans, Puerto Ricans, Cuban Americans, Dominicans, South Americans, and Central Americans). Novas, Himilce, *Everything You Need to Know About Latino History,* New York: Penguin/Plume, 1994: 3.

[35] Yzaguirre, Raul, "A Hispanic Perspective on Employment Discrimination in the Federal Workplace," testimony before the Civil Service Subcommittee on Government Reform and Oversight, U.S. House of Representatives, September 10, 1997.

[36] Novas, *Everything You Need To Know About Latino History,* p. 83. "By a single stoke of the pen, Mexico lost 50 percent of its national territory, and the United States acquired a large group of new citizens who remained in their homeland and yet found themselves smack in the middle of a country whose laws, political and social institutions, and fundamentally WASP traditions were alien to them."

[37] Quoted in Takaki, Ronald, *A Different Mirror: A History of Multicultural America,* Boston: Little, Brown and Company, 1993: 175.

[38] Ibid, p. 176.

[39] For example, most Americans are unaware that the Supreme Court recognized that the racial segregation of Mexican American children in the public schools demonstrated one of the elements of a suspect classification of race in violation of the U.S. Constitution 2 weeks prior to the landmark case of *Brown* v. *Board of Education.* See *Hernandez* v. *Texas,* 347 U.S. 475 (1954) (case involving exclusion of persons of Mexican descent from the jury pool).

[40] The term "Asian Pacific American" is used in this report to describe residents of the United States who have origins in the Far East, Southeast Asia, South Asia, and Pacific Islands. See U.S. Commission on Civil Rights, *Civil Rights Issues Facing Asian Americans in the 1990s,* Washington, DC: U.S. Commission on Civil Rights, 1992: 1.

[41] Hawaii became a United States territory in 1893 and was annexed as a State in 1898. See U.S. Public Law 103–150. But see *Report on the Culture, Needs, and Concerns of Native Hawaiians,* Native Hawaiians Study Commission 102–104 (1983); David Stannard, *Before the Horror: The Population of Hawaii on the Eve of Western Contact* 20 (1989).

[42] For example, in 1852, California imposed a foreign miner's tax, in 1862, California passed a head tax of $2.50 per month on most Chinese residents, and in 1873, San Francisco passed an ordinance adding an additional tax targeted at Chinese laundries.

[43] Congress passed a law in 1790 limiting naturalization to "free white persons," and in 1870 Congress extended naturalization rights to African Americans, but not to Asian Pacific Americans.

[44] In 1942 President Roosevelt's Executive Order 9066 authorized the evacuation and relocation of Americans of Japanese descent to internment camps in isolated interior locations in the country. Individuals and families lost property and businesses because they generally were forced to relocate with less than 7 days notice. They were not officially released until 1945. In contrast, although America was also

at war with Germany and Italy, those of German or Italian descent were never evacuated or relocated.

45 For example, an October 1995 *Washington Post*, Kaiser Family Foundation, and Harvard University survey revealed that whites believe that the U.S. population is roughly 50 percent white; it is 74 percent. At the same time, blacks believe the country is roughly 45 percent white and 26 percent black; the black population is 11.8 percent. In the poll, 68 percent of blacks said that racism "is a big problem in our society today"; only 38 percent of whites agreed. Morin, Richard, "A Distorted Image of Minorities: Poll Suggests that What Whites Think They See May Affect Beliefs," *Washington Post*, October 8, 1995:1, 27, 28.

46 Brodie, Mollyann, "Four Americas: Government and Social Policy Through the Eyes of America's Multi-Racial and Multi-Ethnic Society," *Washington Post*, December 1995.

47 Gallup Poll Social Audit, *Black/White Relations in the United States 1997*, Princeton, NJ: The Gallup Organization, June 1997.

48 "Black/White Relations in the United States: 1997," Gallup Poll Social Audit, New York: The Gallup Organization, June 1997. See also Hochschild, Jennifer L., *Facing Up to the American Dream: Race, Class and the Soul of the Nation*, Princeton, NJ: Princeton University Press, 1995; and testimony of Dr. Lawrence Bobo, September 30, 1997.

49 We were able to find little survey data on the views of American Indians, Alaska Natives, and Asian Pacific Americans. Therefore, most of the polls that the Advisory Board reviewed were focused on the attitudes of blacks and whites.

50 Delgado, Richard, "Rodrigo's Eighth Chronicle: Black Crime, White Fears—On the Social Construction of Threat," *Virginia Law Review* (March 1994): 503–548.

51 Dr. John Dovidio, Advisory Board meeting, September 30, 1997, Washington, D.C.

52 Statement of Dr. Lawrence Bobo, Advisory Board meeting, September 30, 1997, Washington, D.C. See also Delgado, "Rodrigo's Eighth Chronicle," and Dovidio, Advisory Board Meeting.

53 Statement of Dr. Lawrence Bobo, Advisory Board meeting, September 30, 1997, Washington, D.C.

54 Ayres, Ian, and Peter Siegelman, "Race and Gender Discrimination in Bargaining for a New Car," *American Economic Review* 85 (June 1995): 304–321.

55 Feagin, Joe, and Melvin Sikes, *Living with Racism: The Black Middle-Class Experience*, Boston: Beacon Press, 1994; see also Scanlon, Kerry A., and Marc Bendick, "Racial and Ethnic Discrimination in Restaurant Franchising," testimony before the House Committee on Small Business, June 30, 1993.

56 Dr. James Jones, Advisory Board meeting, September 30, 1997, Washington, D.C.

57 By discrimination, we mean unfavorable treatment of a person solely on the basis of their membership in a protected class. These protected classes are defined under current U.S. civil rights laws; see Banton, Michael, *Discrimination*, Philadelphia: Open University Press, 1994.

58 In June 1998, James Byrd, an African American man, was tied to a truck and dragged, which resulted in his death and decapitation in Jasper, Texas.

[59] In September 1996, a former University of California at Irvine student sent threatening messages through e-mail and was the first to be prosecuted for a Federal hate crime committed in cyberspace. National Asian Pacific American Legal Consortium, *1996 Audit of Violence Against Asian Pacific Americans*, Washington, DC: National Asian Pacific American Legal Consortium, 1997: 17.

[60] Graubard, Stephen R., ed., "American Indians, Blacks, Chicanos, and Puerto Ricans," *Daedalus: Proceedings of the American Academy of Arts and Sciences* 110 (2) (Spring 1981): v, quoting President Johnson's 1965 statement.

[61] Ibid, v.

[62] In 1993, the U.S. Government finally acknowledged the illegal taking of the Nation of Hawaii in 1893. The conquest of that Nation and the annexation of the islands as a State produced the same kind of discrimination, disenfranchisement, and exclusion that American Indians, Alaska Natives, and Puerto Ricans experienced. The movement aimed at gaining Hawaiian sovereignty has emerged as a significant nexus between the mainland and Pacific Islander attitudes, beliefs, and opinions concerning race relations and culture.

[63] Graubard, "American Indians, Blacks, Chicanos, and Puerto Ricans," vii.

[64] We discuss these divides more fully in Chapter Four.

[65] Council of Economic Advisers, *Changing America: Indicators of Social and Economic Well-Being by Race and Hispanic Origin*, Washington, DC: Executive Office of the President, Council of Economic Advisers, 1998, 6; and U.S. Bureau of the Census, *Statistical Abstract of the United States: 1997*, Washington, DC: U.S. Bureau of the Census, 1997.

[66] See Bryson, Kenneth, "America's Children: Key Indicators of Well-Being, 1998," U.S. Bureau of the Census press release, July 16, 1998. Dr. George Vernez of The RAND Corporation has estimated that by the year 2005, persons who describe themselves as Hispanic will constitute the largest ethnic minority group in the United States. See also U.S. Bureau of the Census projections.

[67] Ibid.

[68] Ibid.

[69] Shepard, Paul, "Census May Allow for Mixed Races: Designation Worries Some Groups," *Detroit Free Press*, April 3, 1997.

[70] Lind, Michael, "The Beige and the Black," *New York Times Magazine*, August 16, 1998: 38 (citing data from Reynold Farley's analysis of the 1990 U.S. Census).

[71] See Council of Economic Advisers, *Changing America*, 10.

[72] On August 28, 1998, Advisory Board member Angela Oh discussed this issue with fathers of children who were biracial or multiracial and living in Hawaii. All the fathers who agreed to be a part of this conversation were white and self-identified as Hawaiian locals. When asked about how their offspring identify themselves, all the fathers acknowledged that their children did not identify themselves as white. Rather, they explained that identity was connected to whether someone was "local" or not. Despite this explanation, it appeared that being white is not considered to be a positive attribute in a State where whites are in a minority. One father illustrated this point with the following story: His son came home one day and expressed surprise that a friend from school had parents who forbid dating whites. The father asked his son how he felt about himself and his friend after learning about the prohibition. The son, looking directly at his white father,

responded with surprise that he was not white. Another father observed that when it comes to expressions of racial identity, like on the mainland, his son and other teenagers in the community identify with black sports professionals, musicians, rap, and hip hop music and dress.

73 Dr. James Jones, statement at the Advisory Board meeting, Washington, D.C., September 30, 1997.

74 Shepard, "Census May Allow for Mixed Races."

75 Shaheen, Jack G., *Arab and Muslim Stereotyping in American Popular Culture*, Washington, DC: Center for Muslim-Christian Understanding, The Edmund A. Walsh School of Foreign Service, Washington, DC: Georgetown University, 1997: 5-6.

76 "A mascot which is offensive or demeaning to groups of people should quite simply not be permitted. That principle is not subject to adjudication by referendum, any more than any fundamental human right is; unfairness, even to a small minority, cannot be sanctified by majority vote." Stanford University President Donald Kennedy, Stanford University News Service Press Release, October 1, 1980.

77 Myrdal, Gunnar, Richard Sterner, and Arnold Rose, *An American Dilemma: The Negro Problem and Modern Democracy*, New York: Harper and Brothers, 1944.

78 Kerner Commission, *Report of the National Advisory Commission on Civil Disorders*, New York: E.P. Dutton, 1968.

79 See the *Report of the National Advisory Commission on Civil Disorders* (Kerner Commission), March 1, 1968: 1.

80 Sanchez, George I., "Face the Nation: Race, Immigration, and the Rise of Nativism in Late Twentieth Century America," *International Migration Review* 31 (3) (Winter 1997): 1009–1030.

81 Efforts by organization such as the Rainbow Coalition and the Leadership Conference on Civil Rights are evidence of this point. See also Meyers, Samuel L., ed., *Civil Rights and Race Relations in the Post-Reagan-Bush Era*, New York: Praeger, 1997.

82 In addition, the White House Office of Science Technology Policy and the American Sociological Association sponsored a major conference on racial trends and patterns of causality in April 1998 to establish a state-of-the-art assessment of racial disparities and diversity in America. The conference was convened to assist the Race Initiative.

83 We base the discussion of disparities in this chapter on information provided to us during our Advisory Board meetings by experts in the field and other venues and by background reading done in preparation for these discussions. We do not purport to provide you with a definitive study of these issues but with a summary of the information on which we base our recommendations. We further suggest that additional efforts should be undertaken by the Administration to understand and communicate in a fuller and more definitive way the nature of the disparities that exist and how we, as a Nation, can most effectively eliminate them.

84 "Racial disparity" is defined as a systemic difference between racial groups in defined measurable areas such as employment rates, high school graduation rates, wage-earning differentials, and home ownership.

85 Although this is the Advisory Board's Report to the President, we thought it important for others who will read it to know that the Initiative year has been one devoted not only to dialogue and study, but to action as well.

[86] Federal civil rights laws also protect against discrimination on the basis of gender, disability, religion, and age.

[87] There were, for example, 2,850 full-time staff at the U.S. Equal Employment Opportunity Commission in 1990 at a time when the agency was receiving roughly 62,000 cases a year. In 1997, there were only 2,680 staff (170 fewer) at a time when the number of charges had risen to nearly 100,000. Similarly, the Office of Civil Rights at the U.S. Department of Education had 815 staff in 1990 to handle roughly 3,400 cases; in 1997, there were 134 fewer staff but more than 5,200 complaints. Even with the use of technology, more cannot be done effectively with so much less.

[88] Federal Bureau of Investigation, *Hate Crime Statistics 1996*, Washington, DC: U.S. Department of Justice, Federal Bureau of Investigation, Criminal Justice Information Services Division, 1998: 7.

[89] Bureau of Justice Assistance, *A Policymaker's Guide to Hate Crimes*, Washington, DC: U.S. Department of Justice, Bureau of Justice Assistance, 1997: x.

[90] For a good overview of racial disparities in educational opportunity, see Darling-Hammond, Linda, "Inequality and Access to Knowledge," in Handbook of Research on Multicultural Education, ed. James A. Banks and Cherry A. McGee Banks, New York: MacMillan Publishing Company, 1995: 465–483.

[91] Disparities in opportunity undoubtedly are linked to disparities in achievement. Students of color often trail white students in test scores, high school graduation rates, and college graduation rates. For example, although there is evidence of recent improvements in test scores for students of color, the National Assessment of Educational Progress (NAEP) average scaled-reading proficiency scores for 17-year-old black and Hispanic students in 1996 were less than the average scores for 13-year-old whites (265 versus 267 out of a possible 500, respectively; the average scores for white 17-year-olds was 294). Wirt, John, and Thomas Snyder, *The Condition of Education 1998*, Washington, DC: U.S. Department of Education, National Center for Education Statistics, 1998: indicator 16, chart 1; online publication http://nces.ed.gov/pubs98/condition98.

[92] U.S. General Accounting Office, *School Facilities: America's Schools Report Differing Conditions*, Washington, DC: U.S. General Accounting Office, June 1996.

[93] For example, a recent study reports that 34 percent of black students and 35 percent of Hispanic students attend schools with more than 90 percent minority enrollment. Orfield, Gary, Mark Bachmeier, David R. James, and Tamela Eitle, *Deepening Segregation in American Public Schools*, Cambridge, MA: Harvard Project on School Desegregation, April 1997: 11. Most dramatically, 88 percent of those schools with greater than 90 percent minority enrollment are predominantly poor (p. 19). These rates of segregation are worse than the rates of segregation from more than 15 years ago for blacks and 25 years ago for Hispanics (p. 11).

[94] See Council of Economic Advisers, "Participation in Literacy Activities with a Parent or Family Member by Children Aged Three to Five," *Changing America*, citing National Center for Education Statistics; see also Wirt and Snyder, *The Condition of Education 1998*, http://nces.ed.gov/pubs98/condition98.

[95] In 1997, for example, the President announced his Initiative to Reduce Class Sizes in Early Grades, which will provide $12.4 billion over 7 years to help reduce class size in grades 1–3 from a national average of 22 students to 18 students. This proposal will help overcome the modest racial disparities that exist in class size.

Data from 1993 show that the average class size has approximately one to three more students in schools where the majority of students are of color than in schools where students of color make up less than 10 percent of the student population. National Center for Education Statistics, *America's Teachers: Profile of a Profession, 1993–94,* Washington, DC: U.S. Department of Education, National Center for Education Statistics, 1997. In addition, this proposal will help improve learning for all students. Studies show that students learn more effectively when the class size is reduced and there is evidence that this return is greater for students of color than for white students. See, e.g., Word, Elizabeth, John Johnston, Helen Pate Bain, DeWayne Fulton, Jane Boyd Zaharias, Charles M. Achilles, Martha Nannette Lintz, John Folger, and Carolyn Breda, *The State of Tennessee's Student/Teacher Achievement Ratio (STAR) Project: Technical Report, 1985–1990,* 1990: 166–169.

[96] In 1993–94, for example, 39 percent of math teachers at public secondary schools with more than 50 percent minority enrollment were not math majors, compared with 25 percent of math teachers at schools with less than 5 percent minority enrollment. Wirt and Snyder, *The Condition of Education 1998,* supplemental table 58–2, http://nces.ed.gov/pubs98/condition98.

[97] U.S. General Accounting Office, *School Facilities: America's Schools Reports Differing Conditions.*

[98] For example, of those students who were in eighth grade in 1988 (and would graduate on time in 1992), 79 percent of Asian Pacific American students went on to some form of post-secondary education compared with 66 percent of whites, 53 percent of Hispanics, 52 percent of blacks, and 38 percent of American Indians and Alaska Natives. Mathtech Inc., *Factors Related to College Enrollment,* prepared for the U.S. Department of Education, Office of the Under Secretary, 1998: 16.

[99] For example, in 1998, according to university officials, the University of California at Berkeley had to reject more than 800 highly qualified black, Hispanic, American Indian, and Alaska Native applicants who had 4.0 or higher grade point average and scored 1200 or higher on the SAT. Sanchez, Rene, "With Ban on Preferences, UC Will Enroll 12% Fewer Blacks, Hispanics," *Washington Post,* May 21, 1998, A10.

[100] Although the percentage of white and black persons ages 25–29 who have completed high school are approaching parity at 88 percent and 86 percent, respectively, the percentage of Hispanics ages 25–29 who have completed high school remains considerably lower at 62 percent. Day, Jennifer, and Andrea Curry, *Educational Attainment in the United States: March 1997,* Washington, DC: U.S. Bureau of the Census, 1998: 3.

This high Hispanic dropout rate is explained in part by the increasing number of Hispanic immigrants in the population for whom the high school dropout rate for 18–21 year olds was 47 percent in 1990, but the dropout rate for native-born Hispanics remains high as well at 23 percent. Council of Economic Advisers, *Economic Report of the President,* Washington, DC: Executive Office of the President, Council of Economic Advisers, 1998: 134–135.

Data from 1990 also indicate that the percentage of American Indians and Alaska Natives age 25 and older who have completed high school is also lower at 66 percent. U.S. Bureau of the Census, *Population Profile of the United States, 1995,* Washington, DC: U.S. Bureau of the Census, 1995: 51.

The overall percentage of Asian Pacific Americans ages 25–29 with a high school diploma is 90 percent. Day and Curry, *Educational Attainment in the United States:*

March 1997, 3. That figure, however, masks substantial variation in graduation rates within the population, which ranged from approximately 31 percent for Hmong Americans to 88 percent for Japanese Americans in 1990. U.S. Bureau of the Census, *Population Profile of the United States, 1995,* 49.

[101] This recommendation in part is based on the meeting on immigrants and race, which is discussed later in this chapter.

[102] U.S. Bureau of the Census, "We the American People," September 1993, page 10, figure 18; see also *New York Times,* "Tribal Garden Helps to Ease Pain of Cutbacks in Welfare," August 23, 1998, 24.

[103] See also Dr. Manuel Pastor, Advisory Board meeting on race and poverty, February 11, 1998, San Jose, California. According to 1996 statistics, non-Hispanic whites constitute 45.1 percent of the Nation's poor while blacks constitute 26.5 percent and Hispanics 22.4 percent. Poverty and unemployment often affect approximately 40 to 50 percent of American Indians living on reservations or tribal lands and represents a major continuing source of frustration for all Federal agencies charged with delivering housing, development, and social services to Indian country.

Poverty data (SIPP and PSID) reveal that white households typically spend less time living in poverty and have shorter durations living in poverty then do blacks or Hispanics. White households also spend less time drawing benefits from AFDC.

In addition, recent evidence indicates that as welfare rolls continue to plunge, "white recipients are leaving the system much faster than black and Hispanic recipients, pushing the minority share of the caseload to the highest level on record." This is in part due to important differences in education: while 64 percent of Hispanic recipients lacked a high school education, this was true of only 33 percent of whites and 40 percent of blacks. DeParle, Jason, "Shrinking Welfare Rolls Leave Record High Share of Minorities: Fast Exodus of Whites Alters the Racial Balance," *New York Times,* July 27, 1998, A1, A12.

[104] Jargowsky, Paul. *Poverty and Place: Ghettos, Barrios, and the American City.* New York: Russell Sage Foundation, 1997.

[105] Massey, Douglas, and Nancy Denton. *American Apartheid: Segregation and the Making of the Underclass,* Cambridge, MA: Harvard University Press, 1993.

[106] Katz, Bruce, and Kate Carnevale, "The State of Welfare Caseloads in America's Cities," Washington, DC: The Brookings Institution, Center for Urban and Metropolitan Policy, 1998: 6.

[107] See DeParle, Jason, "Shrinking Welfare Rolls Leave Record High Share of Minorities: Fast Exodus of Whites Alters the Racial Balance," *New York Times,* July 27, 1998, A1, A12.

[108] Ellis, Virginia, and Ken Ellingwood, "Job Quest for Welfare Recipients Could Cost the Working Poor," *Los Angeles Times,* February 8, 1998, A1.

[109] A study by the Economic Policy Institute indicates that, in 1997, black males with a high school degree earned 80 percent compared to their white counterparts, and black males with a college degree earned only 77 percent what comparable white males earned. Mishel, Lawrence, Jared Bernstein, and John Schmitt, *The State of Working America 1998–1999,* Economic Policy Institute Series, Ithaca: Cornell, forthcoming 1999.

[110] The differences in the weekly earnings of whites, blacks, and Hispanics from the late 1960s to the present reveal two important issues: (1) the median wages, after adjusting for inflation, actually declined between the late 1970s and 1990s (but has risen somewhat in recent years) except for white women; and (2) whites still have higher average earnings than blacks or Hispanics. Council of Economic Advisers, *Changing America*, table on Median Family Income, p. 35. The earnings gap between whites and minority workers continues to persist, and is today greater than it was in 1979. In 1997, the weekly earnings of a typical black worker were only 77 percent of the earnings of a typical white worker, compared to 80 percent two decades earlier. (Bureau of Labor Statistics, Median Weekly Earnings Table, unpublished data.) The average family income of blacks, for example, has been less than 60 percent of that of whites for the years 1967–1997. Asian Pacific Americans have even higher average household incomes than whites. However, there are great differences among the ethnic groups in the Asian Pacific American and Hispanic categories. Council of Economic Advisers, *Changing America*, p. 35.

[111] Claudia Withers, Advisory Board meeting on race in the workplace, Phoenix, Arizona, January 14, 1998. Cross, H., et al., *Employer Hiring Practices: Different Treatment of Hispanic and Anglo Job Seekers.* Washington, DC: The Urban Institute, 1990 (discussion of an auditing project in the late 1980s in Chicago that showed clear signs of discrimination against Hispanics and immigrants).

In 1990, the Urban Institute conducted a major audit using matched pairs of comparably qualified job applicants who differed only in their race. This study concluded that black and Hispanic males were three times as likely as an equally qualified white male applicant to be turned down for a job. This report also states, "Hispanics were more likely to experience unfavorable treatment at the application and interview stages than were blacks," i.e., Hispanics appear to encounter even more discrimination in certain labor markets. Turner, Margery, Michael Fix, and Raymond Struyk, *Opportunities Diminished: Racial Discrimination and Hiring,* Urban Institute Report 91–9. Washington, DC: The Urban Institute Press, 1991: 56.

There are recognized limitations to some of this auditing research as discussed by Heckman, James, and Peter Siegelman, "The Urban Institute Audit Studies: Their Methods and Findings," in *Clear and Convincing Evidence,* Michael Fix and Raymond Struyk, eds., Washington, DC: Urban Institute Press, 1993.

[112] Wilson, William Julius, *When Work Disappears,* New York: Vintage Books, 1997.

[113] Fix, Michael, and Raymond Struyk, *Clear and Convincing Evidence: Measurement of Discrimination in America;* Bendick, Marc, "Measuring Employment Discrimination Through Controlled Experiments," *The Review of Black Political Economy,* Summer 1994: 25–48.

[114] Claudia Withers, Former Executive Director of the Fair Employment Council of Greater Washington, D.C., Advisory Board meeting on race in the workplace, Phoenix, Arizona, January 14, 1998; Bendick, Marc, "Measuring Employment Discrimination Through Controlled Experiments," 25–48.

[115] Jose Roberto Juarez, Statement at the Advisory Board meeting on race in the workplace, January 14, 1998, Phoenix, Arizona.

[116] The Glass Ceiling Report reveals that in 1989, 97 percent of top male executives were white. U.S. Census data from 1990 reveal that black men who hold professional degrees and top management positions earned only 79 percent of what white men earn. *Good for Business: Making Full Use of the Nation's Human Capital* A Fact-

Finding Report of the Federal Glass Ceiling Commission, Washington, DC: Federal Glass Ceiling Commission, March 1995: 12–13.

[117] Dr. Paul Ong, Advisory Board meeting on race in the workplace, January 14, 1998, Phoenix, Arizona.

[118] Council of Economic Advisers, *Changing America* 36.

[119] Ibid.

[120] Blacks and Hispanics are much more likely to work in jobs paying poverty-level wages, meaning that working full-time, year round will not lift a worker and his or her family out of poverty. Work should be a bridge out of poverty, but for many it is not. In fact, 30 percent of all workers were in jobs paying poverty-level wages in 1995. Minorities and people of color are much more likely than whites to work in poverty-wage jobs. Four in 10 blacks and almost half of all Hispanic workers were paid poverty-laid wages. Mishel, Lawrence, Jared Bernstein, and John Schmitt, *The State of Working America 1996–1997*, Economic Policy Institute Series, Armonk, NY: M.E. Sharpe, 1997.

[121] Furthermore, more and more jobs require nonstandard work arrangements, with little job security and no income stability. A non-standard work arrangement typically includes working without benefits, working irregular hours, working as a temporary employee or contractor, and working fewer than 40 hours a week, as well as other activities designed to adjust employment policies.

[122] Oversampling would occur over periodic intervals such as every 3 to 5 years so that national estimates could be produced for major sub-populations on critical areas of demographic and economic behavior. The Council of Economic Advisers has indicated, in *Changing America,* some of the types of data limitations which need to be addressed in such supplementary sampling.

[123] President Clinton's Memorandum for the Secretaries of Commerce, Housing and Urban Development, Interior, and Treasury, and the Administrator of the Small Business Administration, August 6, 1998.

[124] Research suggests the consequences of systemic denial of access to home equity and wealth accumulation that home ownership has brought to so many white Americans: "[w]hites possess nearly 12 times as much median net worth as blacks, or $43,800 versus $3,700. In even starker contrast . . . the average white household controls $6,999 in net financial assets while the average black household retains no . . . nest egg whatsoever." Oliver, Melvin, and Thomas Shapiro, *Black Wealth/White Wealth*, New York: Routledge, 1997:86.

[125] Fannie Mae is the Federal National Mortgage Insurance Corporation, which was founded in 1938 to ensure a consistent supply of mortgage funds for home buyers by investing in mortgages from the institutions which originate them. In 1996, Fannie Mae purchased or guaranteed $218 billion of home mortgages. Freddie Mac, the Federal Home Loan Mortgage Corporation, was founded in 1970 as a stockholder-owned corporation chartered by Congress to create a regular flow of funds to mortgage lenders and is comparable in size to Fannie Mae.

[126] Yinger, John, *Closed Doors, Opportunities Lost: The Continuing Costs of Housing Discrimination*, New York: Russell Sage Foundation, 1995; see also, Goering, John, and Ron Wienk, eds., *Mortgage Lending, Racial Discrimination, and Federal Policy,* Washington, DC: The Urban Institute Press, 1996.

[127] Fair Housing Council of Greater Washington, "The Fair Housing Index: An Audit of Race & National Origin Discrimination in the Greater Washington Real Estate Market: 1997," Washington, DC: The Fair Housing Council of Greater Washington, 1997. On credit market discrimination see Smith, S., and C. Cloud, "The Role of Private, Nonprofit Fair Housing Enforcement Organizations in Lending Testing," in *Mortgage Lending, Racial Discrimination, and Federal Policy.*

[128] See brief discussion of "Concentrated Poverty" 15 of this chapter.

[129] Dr. David Listokin, Advisory Board meeting on race and housing, April 23, 1998, Newark, New Jersey.

[130] The Milton S. Eisenhower Foundation and the Corporation for What Works, *The Millennium Breach: Richer, Poorer and Racially Apart,* Washington, DC: The Milton S. Eisenhower Foundation and the Corporation for What Works, 1998: 130–140.

[131] The Administration took a promising step to assist the American Indian community by holding the conference on August 5–6, 1998 "Building Economic Self-Determination in Indian Communities." in Washington, D.C. All American Indian tribes and Alaska Native community villages were invited to attend. The conference encouraged economic development on American Indian lands, provided accurate and current information about the Administration's commitment to American Indians, announced Federal policy developments focused on Indian country issues, and built bridges to different sectors of the American Indian community, tribal leaders, and tribal and non-tribal businesses.

[132] For a good overview of issues of race in crime and the administration of justice, see Sampson, Robert J., and Janet L. Lauritsen, "Racial and Ethnic Disparities in Crime and Criminal Justice in the United States," in Ethnicity, Crime, and Immigration, Michael Tonry, ed., 1997: 311–374.

[133] For example, at our May Advisory Board meeting, Christopher Stone, Director of the Vera Institute of Justice, reported that the homicide rate for white males is approximately 5 per 100,000, while the homicide rate for males of color is approximately 8 per 100,000 for Asian Pacific Americans, 18 for American Indians and Alaska Natives, 25 for Hispanics, and 58 for blacks. In general, 1994 victimization rates for violent and property crimes were approximately 65 per 1,000 for blacks, 63 for Hispanics, 52 for whites, and 49 for others (which includes Asian Pacific Americans and American Indians and Alaska Natives). Bureau of Justice Statistics, *Criminal Victimization in the United States, 1994,* Washington, DC: U.S. Department of Justice, Bureau of Justice Statistics, May 1997: viii.

[134] For example, in a 1995 Gallup poll only 40 percent of minorities and persons of color reported having confidence in the ability of police to protect them from violent crime, compared with 52 percent of whites. Bureau of Justice Statistics, *Sourcebook of Criminal Justice Statistics, 1996,* p. 129. Furthermore, in 1996, only 32 percent of minorities and persons of color rated the honesty and ethical standards of police as high or very high, compared to 51 percent of whites (p. 126.) (There is contrary data on issues of trust toward the criminal justice system, but most of the data we reviewed and discussions we held indicate that substantial disparities in trust persist.)

[135] Dr. William Wilbanks, Statement at Advisory Board meeting on race, crime and the administration of justice, Washington, DC, May 19, 1998.

[136] Russell Katheryn K., *The Color of Crime*: 41–42.; Christopher Stone, Advisory Board meeting on race, crime, and the administration of justice, Washington, DC, May 19, 1998.

[137] Christopher Stone, Advisory Board meeting on race, crime, and the administration of justice, Washington, DC, May 19, 1998.

[138] Bureau of Justice Statistics, *Correctional Populations in the United States, 1996*, Washington, DC: U.S. Department of Justice, Bureau of Justice Statistics (publication forthcoming). Weitzer, Ronald, "Racial Discrimination in the Criminal Justice System: Findings and Problems in the Literature," *Journal of Criminal Justice*, 24 (4), 1996: 316; *Prison and Jail Inmates at Midyear 1997*, Washington, DC: U.S. Department of Justice, Bureau of Justice Statistics, 1998: 6 (reporting that 42 percent of local jail inmates are black and 16 percent are Hispanic).

[139] Christopher Stone, Advisory Board meeting on race, crime, and the administration of justice, May 19, 1998.

[140] *Association of American Medical Colleges Databook: Statistical Information Related to Medical Education*, January 1998. People of color are underrepresented within the ranks of physicians, the most senior level of the health provider hierarchy. This underrepresentation has significant implications for health care access, largely because physicians of color are more likely to treat Medicaid or uninsured patients. For this and other reasons, it also appears that minority physicians are more likely to see patients of color than other physicians. (Komaromy, et al., *New England Journal of Medicine*, May 16, 1996) The gaps in minority enrollment in medical schools has a negative effect not only on health care for minorities and people of color but also on the racial inclusivity of the topics, methodologies, and patients involved in health research. The gaps are likely to continue and expand in the face of State and court "rollbacks" of affirmative action and continued deficiencies facing public education systems in our poorest communities.

[141] For example, in 1995, the black infant mortality rate was 15 per 1,000 births, more than twice the rates for whites, Hispanics, and Asian Pacific Americans, which are between 5 and 6 per 1,000 births. The infant mortality rate for American Indians and Alaska Natives is also higher at 9 per 1,000 births. *Changing America*, Council of Economic Advisers: 43, from *National Linked Files of Live Births and Infant Deaths*, National Center for Health Statistics, *1998 Health United States 1998 with Socioeconomic Status and Health Chartbook* and previous annual editions. Also, the alcohol and substance abuse in Indian country have harmed generations of American Indians and their communities, with the pattern continuing to this day. Statistics show that alcohol is an important risk factor associated with the top three killers of American Indian and Alaska Native youth—accidents, suicide, and homicide. Another example is the rate of AIDS among blacks over the age of 13, which is seven times the rate for whites. Black children contract AIDS at 19 times the rate of whites. Centers for Disease Control and Prevention, National Center for HIV, STD and TB Prevention, unpublished chart, 1996. Public health officials must pay more attention to these disparities and their effect on the physical and psychological health of the impacted communities.

[142] *Changing America*, Council of Economic Advisers, 43, from *National Linked Files of Live Births and Infant Deaths*, National Center for Health Statistics, *1998, Health United States 1998 with Socioeconomic Status and Health Chartbook* and previous annual editions. Although only 14 percent of white adults are medically uninsured, 21 per-

cent of African American adults and 35 percent of Hispanic adults are uninsured. National Center for Health Statistics, National Health Interview Survey, 1994–1995. Most Americans gain access to affordable health insurance through their employer or the employer of a family member. However, blacks and Hispanics are less likely to work in jobs with health insurance coverage. In 1996, 66 percent of whites in the private sector had employer-provided health insurance, while 60 percent of blacks and only 45 percent of Hispanics had employer-provided health insurance. Mishel, Lawrence, Jared Bernstein, and John Schmitt, *The State of Working America, 1998–1999*, Economic Policy Institute Series.

[143] See Portes, Alejandro, *The Economic Sociology of Immigration: Essays on Networks, Ethnicity, and Entrepreneurship*, New York: Russell Sage Foundation, 1995 (in which he discusses the segmented assimilation in which many immigrants of color are forced to select racial patterns of adaptation).

[144] Here, of course, we are using the term "black" as a social construct to refer to American blacks who are the descendants of slaves in the United States and not to skin color or relationship to the continent of Africa. See Portes, Alejandro, *The Economic Sociology of Immigration: Essays on Networks, Ethnicity, and Entrepreneurship*.

[145] See the work of Rumbaut, Ruben, "Assimilation and Its Discontents: Between Rhetoric and Reality," *International Migration Review*, 31, 1997: 923–960.

[146] We want to distinguish this entity from existing civil rights enforcement agencies and departments. The purpose of the Council would be to enhance the work of agencies such as the Equal Employment Opportunity Commission and the Office of Civil Rights in the U.S. Department of Justice and U.S. Department of Education. Moreover, the nature of the work of the Council would not conflict with that of the U.S. Commission on Civil Rights.

[147] On October 15–16, 1998, the National Academy of Sciences and the National Research Council are sponsoring a conference on racial trends in the United States that will provide a forum for discussion of the most important research and available facts on race.

[148] Federal Glass Ceiling Commission, *Good for Business: Making Full Use of the Nation's Human Capital: A Fact Finding Report of the Federal Glass Ceiling Commission*, Washington, DC: Federal Glass Ceiling Commission, 1995.

[149] This study examined the implicit and explicit messages transmitted by the media and how those images help to shape the attitudes, assumptions, anxieties, and hopes that people in each group have about themselves and those belonging to other groups. Entman, Robert, Barbara Hanson Langford, Debra Burns Melican, Irma Munoz, Simone Boayue, Anita Raman, Brian Kenner, and Charles Merrit, *Mass Media and Reconciliation*, a report to the Advisory Board and staff of The President's Initiative on Race, March 4, 1998.

[150] Brodie, Mollyann, "The Four Americas: Government and Social Policy Through the Eyes of America's Multi-racial and Multi-ethnic Society," *Washington Post*, Kaiser Family Foundation, and Harvard University, December 1995, 47; and Schuman, Howard, Charlotte Steeh, Lawrence Bobo, and Maria Krysan, *Racial Attitudes in America*, Cambridge, MA: Harvard University Press, 1997.

[151] 438 U.S. 265 (1978).

[152] 116 S.CT 2581 (1996).

153 *Wessman* v. *Boston School Committee, et al.*, CA No. 97–119231 (USDC, Mass), 1998.

154 See *Lutheran Church-Missouri Synod* v. *FCC*, 329 U.S. App. D.C. 382 (1998).

155 See Thernstrom, Stephan, and Abigail Thernstrom, *America in Black and White: One Nation Indivisible*, New York: Simon & Schuster, 1997.

156 Bowen, William G., and Derek Bok, *The Shape of the River*, Princeton, NJ: Princeton University Press, 1998.

157 National Association for the Advancement of Colored People, "Employment Discrimination and Abuses in the Federal Workplace," Washington, DC: NAACP Federal Sector Task Force, 1997.

158 The U.S. Department of Education has implemented a dispute resolution center for this purpose.

159 See Equal Employment Opportunity Commission, *EEOC Federal Sector Report on EEO Complaints, Processing, and Appeals by Federal Agencies for FY '96*, Washington, D.C.: Equal Employment Opportunity Commission, 1996.

160 Professor Robert Entman of North Carolina State University directed a study that resulted in the publication of *Mass Media and Reconciliation*, a report to the Advisory Board and staff of The President's Initiative on Race, March 4, 1998. Professor Entman makes several important observations:

a. While the continuing racial and ethnic prejudice and tension are not the media's fault or responsibility alone, there are a number of practices the media could change that would enhance racial and ethnic harmony.

b. Local newscasts treat black suspects and victims of crime differently than whites in the same categories and may cultivate an exaggerated sense of conflict between blacks and whites in the political arena.

c. With respect to network news images, all three non-white groups are underrepresented in roles as experts, while whites are significantly overrepresented as on-air reporters.

d. By not providing more contextual and fully balanced news presentations on racially relevant topics, the media is not educating the public on the continuing perplexities of democracy in a society of growing ethnic diversity.

e. With respect to ethnic images conveyed by the entertainment industry, real progress in including more black characters is offset by more subtle stereotyping, distancing, or exclusion of blacks, a pattern even more severe with respect to Latinos and Asian Pacific Americans by sheer neglect and near invisibility.

f. A public awareness campaign is needed to make the media's racial images and their impacts an important object of public attention and discourse.

161 Du Bois, Paul Martin, and Jonathan J. Hutson, *Bridging the Racial Divide: A Report on Interracial Dialogue in America*, Brattleboro, VT: The Center for Living Democracy, 1997.

162 Children NOW, *A Different World: Children's Perceptions of Race & Class in the Media*, 1998: 14. The results from the survey revealed that children were aware of negative images and stereotypes on the news and television but were more interested in shows that had more people of all races interacting with each other.

The children in this study all agreed that the news media tends to portray African Americans and Latinos more negatively than whites and Asian Pacific Americans, a finding consistent with the research detailed in the Entman study, *Mass Media and Reconciliation* (p. 12). They also agreed that authority roles on television programs (boss, cop, doctor, etc.) are usually played by whites, while the roles of criminals and maids and janitors are usually played by African Americans; Latino and Asian characters are never the dominant people in those roles (Entman et al., *Mass Media and Reconciliation*, p. 10.

[163] Environmental Protection Agency, *Environmental Equity: Reducing the Risks for All Communities*, vol. 1, Washington, DC: Environmental Protection Agency, June 1993.

[164] American Lung Association, "Lung Disease in Minorities 1998," Online publication, http://www.lungusa.org (April 21, 1998).

[165] Rumbaut, Ruben, "Coming of Age in Immigrant America," *Research Perspectives on Immigration*, Washington, DC: Carnegie Endowment for International Peace, July/August 1998; Transformations: the Post-Immigrant Generation in an Age of Diversity, unpublished paper presented at the Eastern Sociological Association meeting, Philadelphia, PA, March 21, 1998.

[166] Anti-Defamation League, *The Web of Hate: Extremists Exploit the Internet*, Washington, DC: Anti-Defamation League, 1996.

EXHIBITS

Racial/Ethnic Composition of the Population
Persons Aged 25 to 29 with a Four-Year College Degree or Higher
Poverty Rates for Individuals
Median Usual Weekly Earnings of Male Full-Time Workers
Median Usual Weekly Earnings of Female Full-Time Workers
Median Family Income
Labor Force Participation Rates of Persons Aged 25 to 54
Unemployment Rates of Persons Aged 16 and Over

Racial/Ethnic Composition of the Population

Source: Bureau of the Census

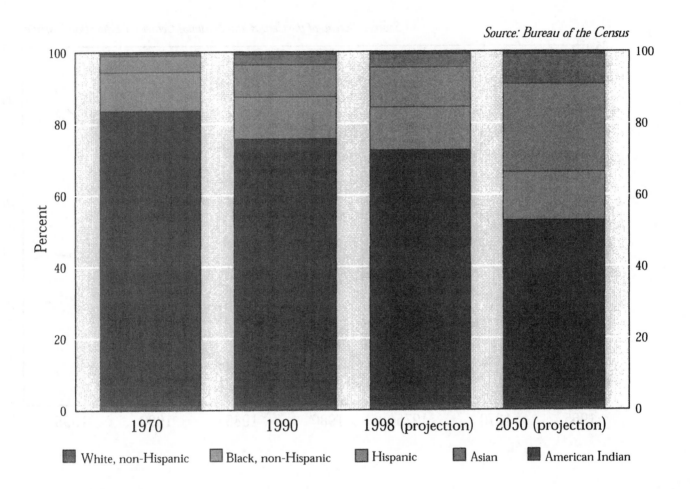

Note: Data for Asians exclude Hispanic Asians, and data for American Indians exclude Hispanic American Indians. In 1970, data for Asians are for Japanese, Chinese, Filipinos, Koreans, and Hawaiians.

Persons Aged 25 to 29 with a
Four-Year College Degree or Higher

Sources: Bureau of the Census and National Center for Education Statistics

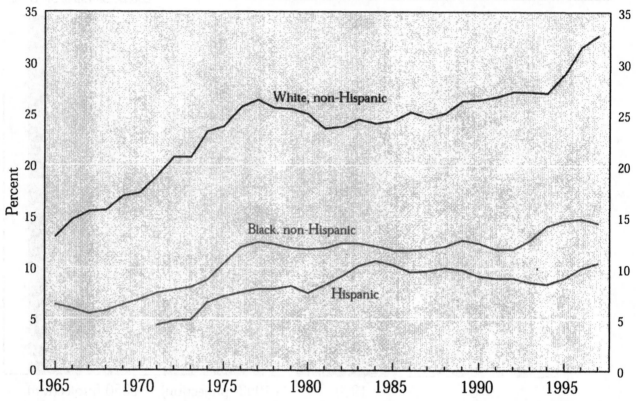

Note: Prior to 1971, data for whites include Hispanic whites, and data for blacks include Hispanic blacks. Data for non-Hispanic blacks and Hispanics are three-year centered averages. Prior to 1992, data are for persons having completed four or more years of college.

Poverty Rates for Individuals

Source: Bureau of the Census

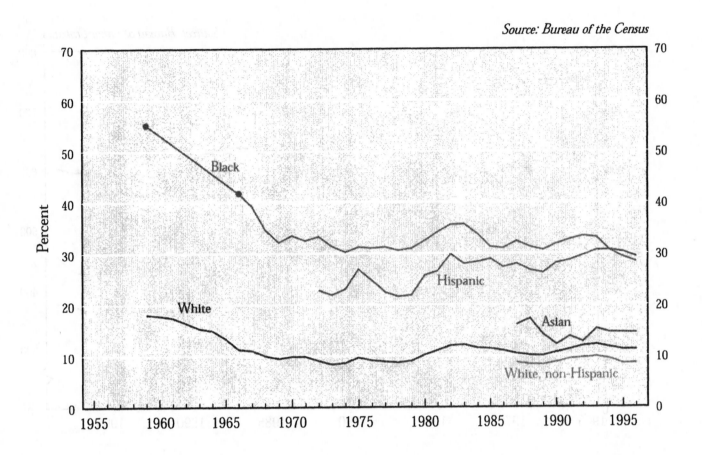

Note: *Straight line between dots indicates data are not available for intervening years.*

Median Usual Weekly Earnings of Male Full-Time Workers

Source: Bureau of Labor Statistics

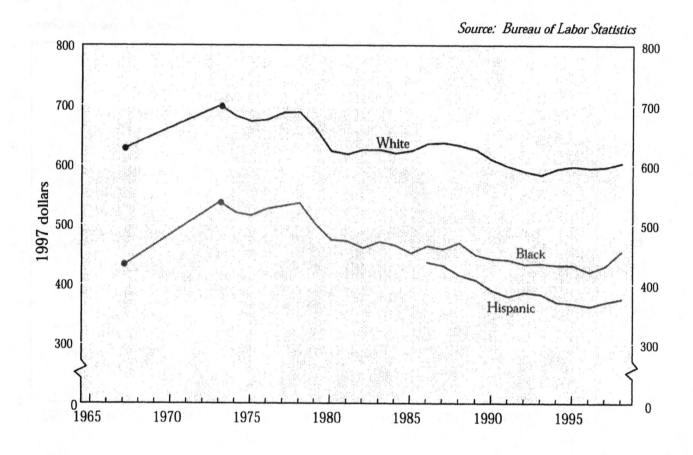

Note: *Straight line between dots indicates data are not available for intervening years. Prior to 1979, data for blacks include all non-whites. Data for 1998 are from the first two quarters.*

Median Usual Weekly Earnings of Female Full-Time Workers

Source: Bureau of Labor Statistics

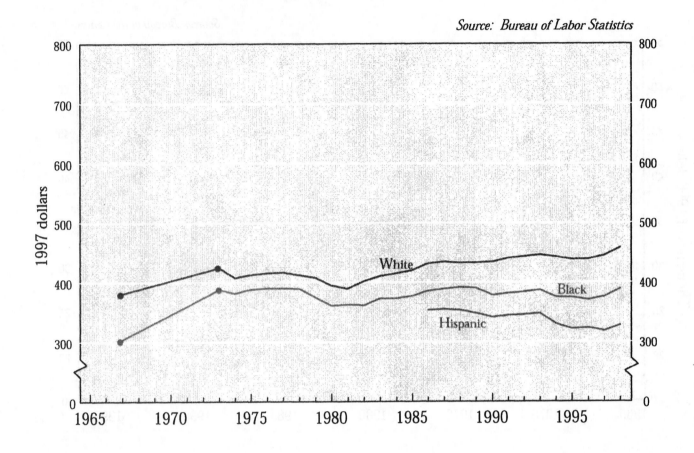

Note: Straight line between dots indicates data are not available for intervening years. Prior to 1979, data for blacks include all non-whites. Data for 1998 are from the first two quarters.

Median Family Income

Source: Bureau of the Census

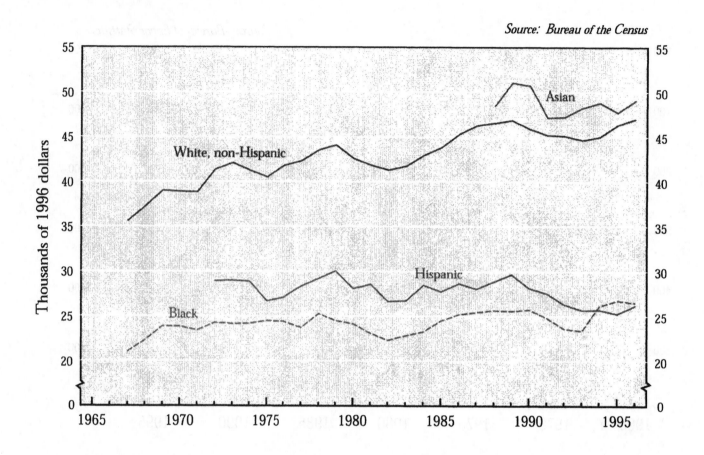

Thousands of 1996 dollars

White, non-Hispanic

Asian

Hispanic

Black

1965   1970   1975   1980   1985   1990   1995

Note: Prior to 1972, data for whites include Hispanic whites.

Labor Force Participation Rates of Persons Aged 25 to 54

Source: Bureau of Labor Statistics

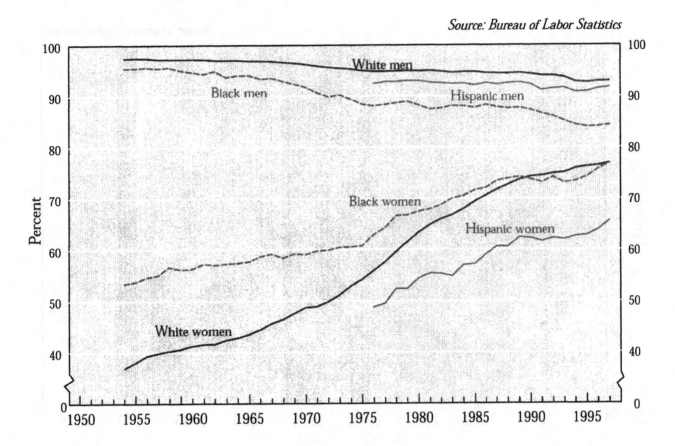

Note: Prior to 1972, data for blacks include all non-whites.

Unemployment Rates of Persons Aged 16 and Over

Source: Bureau of Labor Statistics

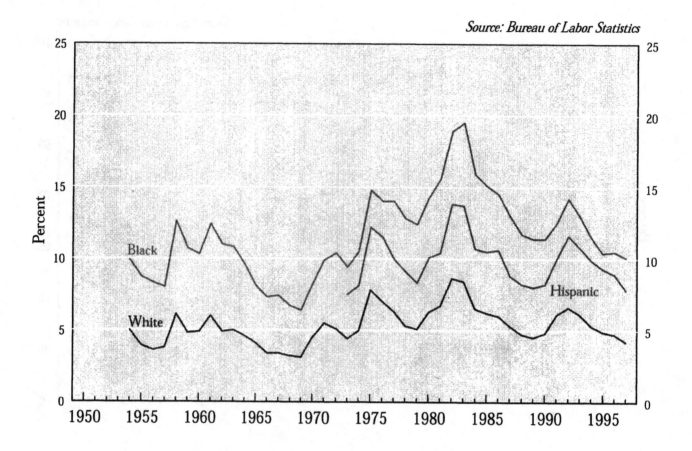

Note: *Data are annual averages of monthly unemployment rates. Prior to 1972, data for blacks include all non-whites.*

APPENDIXES

A. Executive Order 13050
   Commencement Address at the University of California–San Diego
   in La Jolla, California
B. The Advisory Board to The President's Initiative on Race
C. Advisory Board Meetings and Other Activities
   1. Advisory Board Meetings
   2. Corporate Leader Forums
   3. Religious Leader Forums
   4. Meetings With American Indian Tribal Governments
   5. Other Advisory Board Events and Activities
D. One America Conversations
E. Campus Week of Dialogue
F. Statewide Days of Dialogue
G. One America Dialogue Guide Excerpts
H. Promising Practices

Federal Register

Vol. 62, No. 116

Tuesday, June 17, 1997

Presidential Documents

Title 3—

The President

Executive Order 13050 of June 13, 1997

President's Advisory Board on Race

By the authority vested in me as President by the Constitution and the laws of the United States of America, including the Federal Advisory Committee Act, as amended (5 U.S.C. App.), and in order to establish a President's Advisory Board on Race, it is hereby ordered as follows:

Section 1. *Establishment.* (a) There is established the President's Advisory Board on Race. The Advisory Board shall comprise 7 members from outside the Federal Government to be appointed by the President. Members shall each have substantial experience and expertise in the areas to be considered by the Advisory Board. Members shall be representative of the diverse perspectives in the areas to be considered by the Advisory Board.

(b) The President shall designate a Chairperson from among the members of the Advisory Board.

Sec. 2. *Functions.* (a) The Advisory Board shall advise the President on matters involving race and racial reconciliation, including ways in which the President can:

(1) Promote a constructive national dialogue to confront and work through challenging issues that surround race;

(2) Increase the Nation's understanding of our recent history of race relations and the course our Nation is charting on issues of race relations and racial diversity;

(3) Bridge racial divides by encouraging leaders in communities throughout the Nation to develop and implement innovative approaches to calming racial tensions;

(4) Identify, develop, and implement solutions to problems in areas in which race has a substantial impact, such as education, economic opportunity, housing, health care, and the administration of justice.

(b) The Advisory Board also shall advise on such other matters as from time to time the President may refer to the Board.

(c) In carrying out its functions, the Advisory Board shall coordinate with the staff of the President's Initiative on Race.

Sec. 3. *Administration.* (a) To the extent permitted by law and subject to the availability of appropriations, the Department of Justice shall provide the financial and administrative support for the Advisory Board.

(b) The heads of executive agencies shall, to the extent permitted by law, provide to the Advisory Board such information as it may require for the purpose of carrying out its functions.

(c) The Chairperson may, from time to time, invite experts to submit information to the Advisory Board and may form subcommittees or working groups within the Advisory Board to review specific matters.

(d) Members of the Advisory Board shall serve without compensation but shall be allowed travel expenses, including per diem in lieu of subsistence, as authorized by law for persons serving intermittently in the Government service (5 U.S.C. 5701-5707).

Sec. 4. *General.* (a) Notwithstanding any other Executive order, the functions of the President under the Federal Advisory Committee Act, as amended, except that of reporting to the Congress, that are applicable to the Advisory Board shall be performed by the Attorney General, or his or her designee.

in accordance with guidelines that have been issued by the Administrator of General Services.

(b) The Advisory Board shall terminate on September 30, 1998, unless extended by the President prior to such date.

William T Clinton

THE WHITE HOUSE,
June 13, 1997.

[FR Doc. 97-16080
Filed 6-16-97; 12:17 pm]
Billing code 3195-01-P

Commencement Address at the University of California San Diego in La Jolla, California
June 14, 1997

Thank you very much. Thank you. Well, ladies and gentlemen, the first thing I would like to say is that Coleen spoke so well, and she said everything I meant to say—[*laughter*]—that I could do us all a great favor by simply associating myself with her remarks and sitting down.

I would also like to thank Dr. Anagnostopoulos for reminding us of the infamous capacity of faculty members to be contrary with one another. [*Laughter*] Until he said it, I hadn't realized that probably 90 percent of the Congress once were on university faculties. [*Laughter*]

Let me say to Chancellor Dynes and President Atkinson, to the distinguished regents and faculty members, to the students and their families and friends who are here today, I'm honored to be joined by a number of people who reflect the kind of America that Coleen Sabatini called for: Senator Barbara Boxer; and Senator Dan Akaka from Hawaii; your Congressman, Bob Filner; Congresswoman Maxine Waters, the chair of the Congressional Black Caucus; Congresswoman Patsy Mink; Congressman Jim Clyburn; Congressman John Lewis, a great hero of the civil rights movement; Congresswoman Juanita Millender-McDonald; Congressman Carlos Romero-Barceló from Puerto Rico; your Lieutenant Governor, Gray Davis; the Secretary of Transportation, Rodney Slater; of Labor, Alexis Herman; of Veterans Affairs, Jesse Brown; of Education, Dick Riley; our distinguished Ambassador to the United Nations, Bill Richardson; our distinguished Administrator of the Small Business Administration, Aida Alvarez, the first American of Puerto Rican descent ever to be in a Presidential Cabinet. I would like to ask them all to stand, along with the members of the White House staff who are here, including Thurgood Marshall, Jr., whose father has a college named for him at this great university. Would you please stand?

And I can't help but noting that there's another person here that deserves some special recognition—University of California at San Diego class of 1977—a Filipino-American woman who became the youngest captain of the Navy and my personal physician, Dr. Connie Mariano. Where is she?

Editor's note: This was not part of the original appendix A but has been added for historical context.

I want to thank you for offering our Nation a shining example of excellence rooted in the many backgrounds that make up this great land. You have blazed new paths in science and technology, explored the new horizons of the Pacific Rim and Latin America. This is a great university for the 21st century.

Today we celebrate your achievements at a truly golden moment for America. The cold war is over and freedom has now ascended around the globe, with more than half of the people in this old world living under governments of their own choosing for the very first time. Our economy is the healthiest in a generation and the strongest in the world, Our culture, our science, our technology promise unimagined advances and exciting new careers. Our social problems, from crime to poverty, are finally bending to our efforts.

Of course, there are still challenges for you out there. Beyond our borders, we must battle terrorism, organized crime and drug trafficking, the spread of weapons of mass destruction, the prospect of new diseases and environmental disaster. Here at home, we must ensure that every child has the chance you have had to develop your God-given capacities. We cannot wait for them to get in trouble to notice them. We must continue to fight the scourge of gangs and crime and drugs. We must prepare for the retirement of the baby boom generation so that we can reduce that child poverty rate that Coleen talked about. We must harness the forces of science and technology for the public good, the entire American public.

But I believe the greatest challenge we face, among all those that Coleen talked about, is also our greatest opportunity. Of all the questions of discrimination and prejudice that still exist in our society, the most perplexing one is the oldest, and in some ways today, the newest: the problem of race. Can we fulfill the promise of America by embracing all our citizens of all races, not just at a university where people have the benefit of enlightened teachers and the time to think and grow and get to know each other within the daily life of every American community? In short, can we become one America in the 21st century? I know, and I've said before, that money cannot buy this goal, power cannot compel it, technology cannot create it. This is something that can come only from the human spirit, the spirit we saw when the choir of many races sang as a gospel choir.

Today, the State of Hawaii, which has a Senator

and a Congresswoman present here, has no majority racial or ethnic group. It is a wonderful place of exuberance and friendship and patriotism. Within the next 3 years, here in California no single race or ethnic group will make up a majority of the State's population. Already, 5 of our largest school districts draw students from over 100 different racial and ethnic groups. At this campus, 12 Nobel Prize winners have taught or studied form 9 different countries. A half-century from now, when your own grandchildren are in college, there will be no majority race in America.

Now, we know what we will look like, but what will we be like? Can we be one America respecting, even celebrating our differences, but embracing even more what we have in common? Can we define what it means to be an American, not just in terms of the hyphen showing our ethnic origins but in terms of our primary allegiance to the values America stands for and values we really live by? Our hearts long to answer yes, but our history reminds us that it will be hard. The ideals that bind us together are as old as our Nation, but so are the forces that pull us apart. Our Founders sought to form a more perfect Union. The humility and hope of that phrase is the story of America, and it is our mission today.

Consider this: We were born with a Declaration of Independence which asserted that we were all created equal and a Constitution that enshrined slavery. We fought a bloody Civil War to abolish slavery and preserve the Union, but we remained a house divided and unequal by law for another century. We advanced across the continent in the name of freedom, yet in so doing we pushed Native Americans off their land, often crushing their culture and their livelihood. Our Statue of Liberty welcomes poor, tired, huddled masses of immigrants to our borders, but each new wave has felt the sting of discrimination. In World War II, Japanese-Americans fought valiantly for freedom in Europe, taking great casualties, while at home their families were herded into internment camps. The famed Tuskegee Airmen lost none of the bombers they guarded during the war, but their African-American heritage cost them a lot of rights when they came back home in peace.

Though minorities have more opportunities than ever today, we still see evidence of bigotry, from the desecration of houses of worship, whether they be churches, synagogues, or mosques, to demeaning talk in corporate suites. There is still much work to be done by you, members of the class of 1997. But those who say we cannot transform the problem of prejudice into the promise of unity forget how far we have come, and I cannot believe they have ever seen a crowd like you.

When I look at you, it is almost impossible for me

even to remember my own life. I grew up in the high drama of the cold war, in the patriotic South. Black and white southerners alike wore our Nation's uniform in defense of freedom against communism. They fought and died together, from Korea to Vietnam. But back home, I went to segregated schools, swam in segregated public pools, sat in all-white sections at the movies, and traveled through small towns in my State that still marked restrooms and water fountains "white" and "colored."

By the grace of God, I had a grandfather with just a grade school education but the heart of a true American, who taught me that it was wrong. And by the grace of God, there were brave African-Americans like Congressman John Lewis who risked their lives time and time again to make it right. And there were white Americans like Congressman Bob Filner, a freedom rider on the bus with John Lewis in the long, noble struggle for civil rights, who knew that it was a struggle to free white people, too.

To be sure, there is old, unfinished business between black and white Americans, but the classic American dilemma has now become many dilemmas of race and ethnicity. We see it in the tension between black and Hispanic customers and their Korean or Arab grocers; in a resurgent anti-Semitism even on some college campuses; in a hostility toward new immigrants from Asia to the Middle East to the former Communist countries to Latin America and the Caribbean, even those whose hard work and strong families have brought them success in the American way.

We see a disturbing tendency to wrongly attribute to entire groups, including the white majority, the objectionable conduct of a few members. If a black American commits a crime, condemn the act. But remember that most African-Americans are hard-working, law-abiding citizens. If a Latino gang member deals drugs, condemn the act. But remember the vast majority of Hispanics are responsible citizens who also deplore the scourge of drugs in our life. If white teenagers beat a young African-American boy almost to death just because of his race, for God's sake condemn the act. But remember the overwhelming majority of white people will find it just as hateful. If an Asian merchant discriminates against her customers of another minority group, call her on it. But remember, too, that many, many Asians have borne the burden of prejudice and do not want anyone else to feel it.

Remember too, in spite of the persistence of prejudice, we are more integrated than ever. More of us share neighborhoods and work and school and social activities, religious life, even love and marriage across racial lines than ever before. More of us enjoy each other's company and distinctive cultures than ever before. And more than ever, we understand the benefits of our racial, linguistic, and cultural diversity in a global society, where networks of commerce and communications draw us closer and bring rich rewards to those who truly understand life beyond their nation's borders. With just a twentieth of the world's population but a fifth of the world's income, we in America simply have to sell to the other 95 percent of the world's consumers just to maintain our standard of living. Because we are drawn from every culture on Earth, we are uniquely positioned to do it. Beyond commerce, the diverse backgrounds and talents of our citizens can help America to light the globe, showing nations deeply divided by race, religion, and tribe that there is a better way.

Finally, as you have shown us today, our diversity will enrich our lives in nonmaterial ways, deepening our understanding of human nature and human differences, making our communities more exciting, more enjoyable, more meaningful. That is why I have come here today to ask the American people to join me in a great national effort to perfect the promise of America for this new time as we seek to build our more perfect Union.

Now, when there is more cause for hope than fear, when we are not driven to it by some emergency or social cataclysm, now is the time we should learn together, talk together, and act together to build one America.

Let me say that I know that for many white Americans, this conversation may seem to exclude them or threaten them. That must not be so. I believe white Americans have just as much to gain as anybody else from being a part of this endeavor, much to gain from an America where we finally take responsibility for all our children so that they, at last, can be judged as Martin Luther King hoped, not by the color of their skin but by the content of their character.

What is it that we must do? For 4½ years now, I have worked to prepare America for the 21st century with a strategy of opportunity for all, responsibility from all, and an American community of all our citizens. To succeed in each of these areas, we must deal with the realties and the perceptions affecting all racial groups in America.

First, we must continue to expand opportunity. Full participation in our strong and growing economy is the best antidote to envy, despair, and racism. We must press forward to move millions more from poverty and welfare to work, to bring the spark of enterprise to inner cities, to redouble our efforts to reach those rural communities prosperity has passed by. And most important of all, we simply must give our young people the finest education in the world.

There are no children who—because of their ethnic or racial background—who cannot meet the highest academic standards if we set them and measure our students against them, if we give them well-trained teachers and well-equipped classrooms, and if we continue to support reasoned reforms to achieve excellence, like the charter school movement. At a time when college education means stability, a good job a passport to the middle class, we must open the doors of college to all Americans, and we must make at least 2 years of college as universal at the dawn of the next century as a high school diploma is today.

In our efforts to extend economic and educational opportunity to all our citizens, we must consider the role of affirmative action. I know affirmative action has not been perfect in America—that's why 2 years ago we began an effort to fix the things that are wrong with it—but when used in the right way, it has worked. It has given us a whole generation of professionals in fields that used to be exclusive clubs, where people like me got the benefit of 100 percent affirmative action. There are now more women-owned businesses than ever before. There are more African-American, Latino, and Asian American lawyers and judges, scientists and engineers, accountants and executives than ever before.

But the best example of successful affirmative action is our military. Our Armed Forces are diverse from top to bottom, perhaps the most integrated institution in our society and certainly the most integrated military in the world. And more important, no one questions that they are the best in the world. So much for the argument that excellence and diversity do not go hand in hand.

There are those who argue that scores on standardized tests should be the whole measure of qualification for admissions to colleges and universities. But many would not apply the same standard to the children of alumni or those with athletic ability. I believe a student body that reflects the excellence and the diversity of the people we will live and work with has independent educational value. Look around this crowd today. Don't you think you have learned a lot more than you would have if everybody sitting around you looked just like you? I think you have, [Applause]

And beyond the educational value to you, it has a public interest, because you will learn to live and work in the world you will live in better. When young people sit side by side with people of many different backgrounds, they do learn something that they can take out into the world. And they will be more effective citizens.

Many affirmative action students excel. They work hard, they achieve, they go out and serve the communities that need them for their expertise and role model. If you close the door on them, we will weaken our greatest universities, and it will be more difficult to build the society we need in the 21st century.

Let me say, I know that the people of California voted to repeal affirmative action without any ill motive. The vast majority of them simply did it with a conviction that discrimination and isolation are no longer barriers to achievement. But consider the results. Minority enrollments in law school and other graduate programs are plummeting for the first time in decades. Soon, the same will likely happen in undergraduate education. We must not resegregate higher education or leave it to the private universities to do the public's work. At the very time when we need to do a better job of living and learning together, we should not stop trying to equalize economic opportunity.

To those who oppose affirmative action, I ask you to come up with an alternative. I would embrace it if I could find a better way. And to those of us who still support it, I say we should continue to stand for it, we should reach out to those who disagree or are uncertain and talk about the practical impact of these issues, and we should never be unwilling to work with those who disagree with us to find new ways to lift people up and bring people together.

Beyond opportunity, we must demand responsibility from every American. Our strength as a society depends upon both—upon people taking responsibility for themselves and their families, teaching their children good values, working hard and obeying the law, and giving back to those around us. The new economy offers fewer guarantees, more risk, and more rewards. It calls upon all of us to take even greater responsibility for our own education than ever before.

In the current economic boom, only one racial or ethnic group in America has actually experienced a decline in income: Hispanic-Americans. One big reason is that Hispanic high school dropout rates are well above—indeed, far above—those of whites and blacks. Some of the dropouts actually reflect a strong commitment to work. We admire the legendary willingness to take the hard job at long hours for low pay. In the old economy, that was a responsible thing to do. But in the new economy, where education is the key, responsibility means staying in school.

No responsibility is more fundamental than obeying the law. It is not racist to insist that every American do so. The fight against crime and drugs is a fight for the freedom of all our people, including those—perhaps especially those—minorities living in our poorest neighborhoods. But respect for the law must run both ways. The shocking difference in perceptions of the fairness of our criminal justice system grows out of the real experiences that too many minorities have had with law enforcement officers. Part of the answer is to have all our citizens respect the law, but the basic rule must be that the law must respect all our citizens.

And that applies, too, to the enforcement of our civil rights laws. For example, the Equal Employment Opportunity Commission has a huge backlog of cases with discrimination claims, though we have reduced it by 25 percent over the last 4 years. We can do not much better without more resources. It is imperative that Congress-especially those Members who say they're for civil rights but against affirmative action—at least give us the money necessary to enforce the law of the land, and do it soon.

Our third imperative is perhaps the most difficult of all. We must build one American community based on respect for one another and our shared values. We must begin with a candid conversation on the state of race relations today and the implications of Americans of so many different races living and working together as we approach a new century. We must be honest with each other. We have talked at each other and about each other for a long time. It's high time we all begin talking with each other.

Over the coming year, I want to lead the American people in a great and unprecedented conversation about race. In community efforts from Lima, Ohio, to Billings, Montana, in remarkable experiments in cross-racial communications like the uniquely named ERACISM, I have seen what Americans can do if they let down their guards and reach out their hands.

I have asked one of America's greatest scholars, Dr. John Hope Franklin, to chair an advisory panel of seven distinguished Americans to help me in this endeavor. He will be joined by former Governs Thomas Kean of New Jersey and William Winter of Mississippi, both great champions of civil rights; by Linda Chavez-Thompson, the executive vice president of the AFL-CIO; by Reverend Suzan Johnson Cook, a minister from the Bronx and former White House fellow; by Angela Oh, an attorney and Los Angeles community leader; and Robert Thompson, the CEO of Nissan U.S.A.— distinguished leaders, leaders in their community.

I want this panel to help educate Americans about the facts surrounding issues of race, to promote a dialog in every community of the land to confront and work through these issues, to recruit and encourage leadership at all levels to help breach racial divides, and to find, develop, and recommend how to implement concrete solutions to our problems, solutions that will involve all of us in Government, business, communities, and as individual citizens.

I will make periodic reports to the American

people about our findings and what actions we all have to take to move America forward. This board will seek out and listen to Americans from all races and all walks of life. They are performing a great citizen service, but in the cause of building one America, all citizens must serve. As I said at the Presidents' Summit on service in Philadelphia, in our new era such acts of service are basic acts of citizenship. Government must play its role, but much of the work must be done by the American people as citizen service. The very effort will strengthen us and bring us closer together. In short, I want America to capture the feel and the spirit that you have given to all of us today.

I'd like to ask the board to stand and be recognized. I want you to look at them, and I want you to feel free to talk to them over the next year or so. Dr. Franklin and members of the board. [*Applause*]

Honest dialog will not be easy at first. We'll all have to get past defensiveness and fear and political correctness and other barriers to honesty. Emotions may be rubbed raw, but we must begin.

What do I really hope we will achieve as a country? If we do nothing more than talk, it will be interesting, but it won't be enough. If we do nothing more than propose disconnected acts of policy, it will be helpful, but it won't be enough. But if 10 years from now people can look back and see that this year of honest dialog and concerted action helped to lift the heavy burden of race form our children's future, we will have given a precious gift to America.

I ask you all to remember just for a moment as we have come through the difficult trial on the Oklahoma City bombing, remember that terrible day when we saw and wept for Americans and forgot for a moment that there were a lot of them from different races than we are. Remember the many faces and races of the Americans who did not sleep and put their lives at risk to engage in the rescue, the helping, and the healing. Remember how you have seen things like that in the natural disasters here in California. That is the face of the real America. That is the face I have seen over and over again. That is the America somehow, some way, we have to make real in daily American life.

Members of the graduating class, you will have a greater opportunity to live your dreams than any generation in our history, if we can make of our many different strands one America, a nation at peace with itself, bound together by shared values and aspirations and opportunities and real respect for our differences.

I am a Scotch-Irish Southern Baptist, and I'm proud of it. But my life has been immeasurably enriched by the power of the Torah, the beauty of the Koran, the piercing wisdom of the religions of East and South Asia—all embraced by my fellow Americans. I have felt indescribable joy and peace in black and Pentecostal churches. I have come to love the intensity and selflessness of my Hispanic fellow Americans toward *la familia*. As a southerner, I grew up on country music and county fairs, and I still like them. [*Laughter*] But I have also reveled in the festivals and the food, the music and the art and the culture of Native Americans and Americans from every region in the world.

In each land I have visited as your President, I have felt more at home because some of their people have found a home in America. For two centuries, wave upon wave of immigrants have come to our shores to build a new life, drawn by the promise of freedom and a fair chance. Whatever else they found, even bigotry and violence, most of them never gave up on America. Even African-Americans, the first of whom we brought here in chains, never gave up on America.

It is up to you to prove that their abiding faith was well-placed. Living in islands of isolation—some splendid and some sordid—is not the American way. Basing our self-esteem on the ability to look down on others is not the American way. Being satisfied if we have what we want and heedless of others who don't even have what they need and deserve is not the American way. We have torn down the barriers in our laws. Now we must break down the barriers in our lives, our minds, and our hearts.

More than 30 years ago, at the high tide of the civil rights movement, the Kerner Commission said we were becoming two Americas: one white, one black, separate and unequal. Today, we face a different choice: Will we become not two but many Americas, separate, unequal, and isolated? Or will we draw strength from all our people and our ancient faith in the quality of human dignity to become the world's first truly multiracial democracy? That is the unfinished work of our time, to lift the burden of race and redeem the promise of America.

Class of 1997, I grew up in the shadows of a divided America, but I have seen glimpses of one America. You have shown me one today. That is the America you must make. It begins with your dreams, so dream large; live your dreams; challenge your parents; and teach your children well.

God bless you, and good luck.

NOTE: The President spoke at 10:47 a.m. at Rimac Field. In his remarks, he referred to Coleen Sabatini, associated student body president; Georgios H. Anagnostopoulos, chair, academic senate; Robert C. Dynes, chancellor; and Richard C. Atkinson, president, University of California San Diego.

Appendix B
The Advisory Board to The President's Initiative on Race

JOHN HOPE FRANKLIN, of Durham, North Carolina, Chair of the Advisory Board, is the James B. Duke Professor of History Emeritus at Duke University. President Clinton awarded Dr. Franklin the Presidential Medal of Freedom in 1995. Dr. Franklin's scholarly work has focused on the Civil War and Reconstruction era and includes the 1946 landmark study *From Slavery to Freedom*. Dr. Franklin received his A.B. degree from Fisk University in 1935, an M.A. from Harvard University in 1936, and a Ph.D. from Harvard University in 1941.

LINDA CHAVEZ-THOMPSON, of Washington, D.C., is Executive Vice President of the AFL-CIO. Ms. Chavez-Thompson has 29 years of experience in the labor movement. She joined the American Federation of State, County and Municipal Employees in 1971 and became the first person of color to be elected to one of the top officer positions at the AFL-CIO.

SUZAN D. JOHNSON COOK, of Bronx, New York, is Senior Pastor of the Bronx Christian Fellowship. She was also the first female chaplain of the New York City Police Department. In 1983, the Reverend Cook became the first African-American woman to serve as Senior Pastor at Mariner's Temple Baptist Church, the oldest American Baptist Church in New York City. From 1993 to 1994, Dr. Cook was a White House Fellow, working for the White House Domestic Policy Council. Dr. Cook received a B.S. from Emerson College in 1976, an M.A. from Columbia University Teachers College in 1978, an M.Div. from Union Theological Seminary in 1983, and a D.Min. from Union Theological Seminary in 1990.

THOMAS H. KEAN, of Madison, New Jersey, is the former Republican Governor of New Jersey. Governor Kean currently serves as President of Drew University in Madison, New Jersey. He is Chairman of President Clinton's Campaign to Reduce Teenage Pregnancy. He also served on the U.S. Delegation to the Women's Rights Conference in Beijing in 1995. Governor Kean received a B.A. from Princeton University and an M.A. from Columbia University Teachers College.

ANGELA E. OH, of Los Angeles, California, is formerly a partner in the Los Angeles law firm of Beck, De Corso, Daly, Barrera and Oh, and specialized in State and Federal criminal defense. Following the riots in Los Angeles, she served as Special Counsel to the Assembly Special Committee on the Los Angeles Crisis. She currently travels the country speaking on race and will soon be a lecturer at the University of California, Los Angeles. Ms. Oh received a B.A. and an M.P.H. in 1981 from the University of California and a J.D. in 1986 from the University of California.

BOB THOMAS, of Fort Lauderdale, Florida, is Executive Vice President for Marketing for Republic Industries. He is the former President and CEO of Nissan Motor Corporation, U.S.A. In that capacity, Mr. Thomas created a partnership with the Los Angeles Urban League to increase opportunities for women and minorities in automobile manufacturing. Also in that capacity, Mr. Thomas was former director of the Nissan Foundation, which issued grants to support communities in South Central Los Angeles. Mr. Thomas holds a B.S. in Engineering Management from the U.S. Air Force Academy.

WILLIAM F. WINTER, of Jackson, Mississippi, is the former Democratic Governor of Mississippi and is currently in private law practice with the law firm of Watkins, Ludlam & Stennis. Governor Winter serves as chairman of the National Commission on State and Local Public Service and the National Issue Forum Institute. While governor, he fought for education reform, equal opportunity for all citizens, and better relations between the races. He received a B.A. in 1943 and an LL.B. in 1949 from the University of Mississippi.

EXECUTIVE DIRECTOR:
JUDITH A. WINSTON of Washington, D.C., is the Executive Director of the President's Initiative on Race. Ms. Winston has worked for equal opportunity and civil rights under the law for more than two decades. She has served as the General Counsel and Acting Under Secretary of the U.S. Department of Education, an Associate Professor of Law at American University, Deputy Director for Public Policy of the Women's Legal Defense Fund, and Deputy Director for the Lawyers Committee for Civil Rights Under the Law. Ms. Winston received a B.A. from Howard University and J.D. from Georgetown University Law Center.

Racial Demographics, Surveys, and Attitudes on Race—September 30, 1997
Mayflower Hotel, Washington, D.C.
Panelists and Presenters:
Lawrence Bobo, Harvard University
Jack Dovidio, Colgate University
Reynolds Farley, Russell Sage Foundation
James Jones, University of Delaware
Derald Wing Sue, California State University

Race and Higher Education—November 19, 1997
University of Maryland, College Park, Maryland
Panelists and Presenters:
Ted Childs, IBM Corporation
Norman Francis, Xavier University
Nannerl Keohane, Duke University
Mari Matsuda, Georgetown University Law Center
Joseph McDonald, Salish Kootenai College
Arnold Mitchem, National Council of Educational Opportunity Associations
Daryl Smith, Claremont Graduate University
Jesús Treviño, Arizona State University
Jennifer Walper, University of Maryland

Race and K-12 Education—December 17, 1997
Annandale High School, Fairfax County, Virginia
Moderator:
Kathleen Matthews, WJLA–TV
Panelists and Presenters:
Sharifa Alkhateeb, Herndon High School
William Bennett, Empower America
Donald Clausen, Annandale High School
James Comer, Yale University
Carol Franz, Bailey's Elementary School
Harold Hodgkinson, Institute for Educational Leadership
Cindy Hook, Annandale High School
Lisa Graham Keegan, Arizona Public Schools
Fatema Kohistani, Annandale High School
Alex Kugler, Annandale High School
Diana Lam, San Antonio Public Schools
Deborah Meier, Mission Hill Charter School
Gary Orfield, Harvard University

Richard Riley, U.S. Secretary of Education
Rodney Williams, Thomas Jefferson High School
Chris Yi, Holmes Middle School

Race in the Workplace—January 14, 1998
Phoenix Preparatory Academy, Phoenix, Arizona
Moderator:
Jose Cardenas, Law Firm of Lewis & Roca
Panelists and Presenters:
Alexis Herman, U.S. Secretary of Labor
Harry Holzer, Michigan State University
Jose Roberto Juarez, St. Mary's Law School
Glenn Loury, Boston University
Paul Ong, University of California at Los Angeles
Skip Rimsza, Mayor of Phoenix
Lorenda Sanchez, California Manpower Training
James Smith, Rand Corporation
Claudia Withers, Fair Employment Council of Washington, D.C.
Janet Yellen, Chair of the White House Council of Economic Advisors

Race in the Workplace Community Forum—January 14, 1998
Phoenix Preparatory Academy, Phoenix, Arizona
Moderator:
Frank Camacho, KTVK–TV
Panelists and Presenters:
Grant Woods, Arizona Attorney General
Mary Rose Wilcox, Maricopa County Supervisor

Race And Poverty Community Forum—February 10, 1998
Independence High School, San Jose, California
Moderator:
Barbara Rogers, KPIX–TV
Panelists and Presenters:
Mike Honda, California State Assemblyman
John Vasconcellos, California State Senator

Race and Poverty—February 11, 1998
Independence High School, San Jose, California
Moderators:
Lorna Ho, KNTV–TV
Manuel Pastor, Santa Clara University

Panelists and Presenters:
Blanca Alvarado, Santa Clara County Supervisor
Aida Alvarez, U.S. Small Business Administrator
Rose A. Amador, Center for Training and Careers, Inc.
Gordon Chin, Chinatown Community Development Center
Amy B. Dean, South Bay AFL–CIO Labor Council
Denise Fairchild, Community Development Technologies Center
Susan Hammer, Mayor of San Jose
Tarry Hum, New York University
Douglas Massey, University of Pennsylvania
Jose R. Padilla, California Rural Legal Assistance, Inc.
Raquel Rivera Pinderhughes, San Francisco State University
Matthew Snipp, Stanford University
Dennis Turner, Southern California Tribal Chairmen's Association
William Julius Wilson, Harvard University
Robert L. Woodson, Sr., National Center for Neighborhood Enterprise

Race and Stereotypes Community Forum—March 23, 1998
University of Colorado, Denver, Colorado
Moderators:
Ernest Gurulé, KWGN–TV
Nadia Younes, Norwest Bank
Panelists and Presenters:
Federico Peña, U.S. Secretary of Energy
Wellington Webb, Mayor of Denver
Edward James Olmos, Actor

Race and Stereotypes—March 24, 1998
University of Colorado, Denver, Colorado
Moderator:
Phyllis Katz, University of Colorado, Boulder
Panelists and Presenters:
Richard Estrada, Dallas Morning News
Joe Feagin, University of Florida
Susan Fiske, University of Massachusetts
William Gollnick, Oneida Tribe of Indians of Wisconsin
Shanto Iyengar, University of California-Los Angeles
Lillian Kimura, formerly with the YWCA and the Japanese American Citizens League
Federico Peña, U.S. Secretary of Energy
Helen Hatab Samhan, Arab American Institute
Claude Steele, Stanford University
Roy Romer, Governor of Colorado
Wellington Webb, Mayor of Denver

Race and Housing—April 23, 1998

Rutgers University School of Law
Moderator:
Marcia Brown, Rutgers School of Law
Panelists and Presenters:
Hilda Cree Garcia, American Indian Housing Authority
Sharpe James, Mayor of Newark
Chris Kui, Asian Americans for Equality
David Listokin, Rutgers University
Joan A. Magagna, U.S. Department of Justice
Raymond O'Cassio, La Casa de Don Pedro
Eva Plaza, U.S. Department of Housing and Urban Development
Phylis Peterman, Maplewood-South Orange Racial Balance Task Force
Lee Porter, Fair Housing Council of Northern New Jersey
Fred Profeta, Maplewood-South Orange Racial Balance Task Force

Race, Crime, and Administration of Justice—May 19, 1998

George Washington University, Washington, D.C.
Moderator:
Charles Ogletree, Harvard University
Panelists and Presenters:
William J. Bratton, CARCO Group, Inc.
Zachary W. Carter, United States Attorney, Eastern District of New York
Maria de Los Angeles Jimenez, American Friends Service Committee
Randall Kennedy, Harvard Law School
Deborah A. Ramirez, Northeastern Law School
Charles Ramsey, Washington, D.C., Metropolitan Police Department
Janet Reno, U.S. Attorney General
Christopher E. Stone, Vera Institute of Justice, Inc.
Kim Taylor-Thompson, New York University School of Law
William L. Wilbanks, Florida International University
Michael F. Yamamoto, Horikawa, Ono & Yamamoto
Robert Yazzie, Chief Justice of the Navajo Nation

Discussion and Assessment of Recommendations and Report—June 18, 1998

White House Conference Center, Washington, D.C.
Board discussion without panelists and presenters

Race and Quality Health Care—July 10, 1998

Faneuil Hall, Boston, Massachusetts
Moderators:
Hortensia Amaro, Boston University
Joan Reede, Harvard Medical School
Panelists and Presenters:

Wilson Augustave, National Advisory Council on Migrant Health
Craig Cobb, Dimock Community Health Center
Zoila Torres Feldman, Great Brook Valley Health Center
Claude Earl Fox, III, Health Resources and Services Administration
Elmer Freeman, Center for Community Health Education
Marianela Garcia, Worcester Housing Authority and Economic Development and Supportive Services
Dennis Hayashi, Counselor to the Deputy Secretary, U.S. Department of Health and Human Services
Vanna Lee, Family Health and Social Service Center
Peggy Leong, South Cove Community Health Center
Thomas Menino, Mayor of Boston
Barbara Namias, Northern American Center of Boston, Inc.
David Satcher, U.S. Surgeon General and Assistant Secretary, U.S. Department of Health and Human Services
Beverly Wright, Wanpanoag Tribe of Gay-Head/Aquinnah

Race and Immigrants—July 13, 1998
Georgetown University Law Center, Washington, D.C.
Moderators:
Bill Ong Hing, University of California at Davis
Cecilia Muñoz, National Council of La Raza
Roberto Suro, *Washington Post*
T. Alex Aleinikoff, Carnegie Endowment for International Peace
Demetrios Papademetriou, Carnegie Endowment for International Peace
Panelists and Presenters:
Robert L. Bach, U.S. Immigration and Naturalization Service
Guarione M. Diaz, Cuban-American National Council
Richard M. Estrada, *Dallas Morning News*
Nathan Glazer, Harvard University
Yvonne Y. Haddad, Georgetown University
Wade Henderson, Leadership Conference on Civil Rights
Joe R. Hicks, Los Angeles Human Relations Commission and Los Angeles Multicultural Collaborative
Gerald D. Jaynes, Yale University
Glenda Joe, Great Wall Enterprises and Council of Asian-American Organizations
Charles Kamasaki, National Council of La Raza
Clara Sue Kidwell, University of Oklahoma
Douglass S. Massey, University of Pennsylvania
Jessica Tuchman Mathews, Carnegie Endowment for International Peace
Sid L. Mohn, Heartland Alliance for Human Needs and Human Rights
Milton D. Morris, MDM Office Systems, Inc.
Karen K. Narasaki, National Asian Pacific American Legal Consortium
Leo J. O'Donovan, S.J., Georgetown University
George J. Sanchez, University of Southern California
Angie O. Tang, New York Mayor's Office of Immigrant Affairs and Language Services
Susan B. Tucker, Victim Services
Mary C. Waters, Harvard University

December 1, 1997
Miami, Florida

Advisory Board Host:
Bob Thomas
Panelists and Presenters:
Rodney Slater, U.S. Secretary of Transportation
David Lawrence, *Miami Herald*
Alfred Schreiber, Graham Gregory Bozell
Roy McAllister, Bell South Cellular
Michael Kelly, First Union National Bank
Terry Fleitas, W.R. Grace Company
Gwen Marlo, CSX Transportation
Peter Dolara, American Airlines
Windell Paige, Florida Regional Minority Purchasing Council
Walden Latham, Shaw, Pittman, Potts and Trowbridge

January 14, 1998
Phoenix, Arizona

Advisory Board Hosts:
John Hope Franklin
Linda Chavez-Thompson
Angela Oh
Bob Thomas
William Winter
Panelists and Presenters:
Alexis Herman, U.S. Secretary of Labor
Skip Rimsza, Mayor of Phoenix
Curtis Artis, Lucent Technologies
Gene Blue, Opportunities Industrialization Center
Peggy Dewey, Communication Workers of America Equity Committee
Sandra Ferniza, Arizona Hispanic Chamber of Commerce
William Lucy, American Federation of State, County and Municipal Employees
Antonia Ozerhoff, U.S. West Communications
John Sena, International Brotherhood of Electrical Workers
George Russell, American Indian Chamber of Commerce
Pat Thomas, AT&T

January 30, 1998
Los Angeles, California

Advisory Board Hosts:
Angela Oh
Bob Thomas
Panelists and Presenters:
William Daley, U.S. Secretary of Commerce
Richard Riordan, Mayor of Los Angeles
Kenneth Lombard, Magic Johnson Theaters
Melvyn Davis, Rockwell International Corporation
Martha Diaz Aszkenazy, Pueblo Contracting Services
Vivian Shimoyama, Breakthru Unlimited
Mary Ann Mitchell, Computer Consulting Operations Specialists
Judy Belk, Levi Strauss
Guy Roundsaville, Wells Fargo Bank

July 23, 1998
St. Louis, Missouri

Advisory Board Host:
Bob Thomas
Panelists and Presenters:
Rodney Slater, U.S. Secretary of Transportation
Clarence Harmon, Mayor of St. Louis
Gary Berman, Market Segment Research & Consulting
Sue Bhatia, Rose International
Harold Law, Decision and Advance Technology Association
Dora Serrano, Missouri Department of Economic Development
Jacquelyn Gates, Bell Atlantic
I. Charles Mathews, Quaker Oats Company
Susan Boyle, Monsanto
Lee Pepion, The Native American Business Alliance

Thursday, May 21, 1998
New Orleans, Louisiana

Advisory Board Host:
Reverend Dr. Suzan D. Johnson Cook
Panelists and Presenters:
Edward Cohn, Temple Sinai
Carol Cotton Wynn, District Superintendent, United Methodist Church
George Duerson, United Methodist Church
Maria Echaveste, The White House
James Forbes, Riverside Church, New York City
Roy Kaplan, National Conference of Community and Justice
Barbara Major, Crossroads Ministries
Marc Morial, Mayor of New Orleans
Joel Orona, Native American Baha'i Institute
Kim Tran, Vietnamese Alliance Church
Diane Winston, Princeton University
Marshall Truehill, Jeremiah Group
Lilia Valdez, Day of Healing
Imam Wali Abdel Ra'oof, New Orleans Masjid of Al-Islam

June 1, 1998
Louisville, Kentucky

Advisory Board Host:
Reverend Dr. Suzan D. Johnson Cook
Panelists and Presenters:
Jerry Abramson, Mayor of Louisville
Aminah Assilmi, International Union of Muslim Women
Kunwar Bhatnagar, Hindu Temple of Kentucky
Tony Campolo, Evangelical Association for the Promotion of Education
Inez Torres Davis, Evangelical Lutheran Church in America
Diana Eck, Harvard University
Robert Henderson, National Spiritual Assembly of the Baha'is
Thomas Kelly, Archdiocese of Louisville
Stanley Miles, Temple Shalom
Thomas Oates, Spalding University
Rose Ochi, U.S. Department of Justice
T. Vaughn Walker, First Gethsemane Baptist Church
Beverly Watts, Kentucky Commission on Human Rights
Alfred Yazzie, Navajo Nation

Appendix C4
Meetings With American Indian Tribal Governments

During the Initiative Year, members of the Advisory Board and Initiative staff met with approximately 600 tribal leaders and tribal members around the country to discuss race and tribal sovereignty. This includes special meetings and conferences with the following tribal governments whose official tribal representatives met with Advisory Board members and staff. Listed at the end are the intertribal organizations with whom members and staff met.

Alabama-Coushatta Tribe of Texas
Catawba Indian Nation
Cherokee Nation
Chitimacha Tribe of Louisiana
Coeur d'Alene Tribe
Comanche Indian Tribe
Confed. Tribes of Colville Indians
Coushatta Tribe of Louisiana
Eastern Band of Cherokee Indians
Gila River Indian Community
Hoonah Indian Association
Houlton Band of Maliseet Indians
Hualapai Tribe
Jamestown Klallam
Jena Band of Choctaw Indians
Jicarilla Apache
Lummi Indian Nation
Mashantucket Pequot Tribe
Menominee Tribe
Miccosukee Tribe of Florida
Mississippi Band of Choctaw Indians
Mohegan Tribe of Connecticut
Narragansett Indian Tribe
Navajo Nation
Northern Arapahoe
Oglala Lakota Nation
Oneida Indian Nation (New York)
Oneida Tribe of Indians of Wisconsin
Passamaquoddy-Indian Township
Passamaquoddy-Pleasant Point
Penobscot Indian Nation
Poarch Band of Creek Indians
Pueblo of Acoma

Pueblo of Cochiti
Pueblo of Isleta
Pueblo of Laguna
Pueblo of Picuris
Pueblo of San Ildefonso
Pueblo of Santa Ana
Pueblo of Santa Clara
Pueblo of Tesuque
Puyallup Tribe
Red Lake Band of Chippewa
Robinson Rancheria Band of Pomo Indians
Rosebud Sioux Tribe
Salt River Pima-Maricopa Indian Comm.
Seminole Tribe of Florida
Seneca Nation of Indians
Southern Ute Tribe
Standing Rock Sioux Tribe
St. Regis Band of Mohawk Indians
Three Affiliated Tribes
Tunica-Biloxi Tribe of Louisiana
Upper Sioux Community
Wampanoag Tribe of Gay Head (Aquinnah)
Washoe Tribal Council
Yankton Sioux Tribe
Yavapai Apache Tribe

Intertribal Organizations

All-Indian Pueblo Council
Dakota Territories Tribal Chairmen's
    Association
Midwest Alliance of Sovereign Tribes
National Congress of American Indians
United South and Eastern Tribes

Appendix C5
Other Advisory Board Events and Activities

Date	Event	City	State
06/24/97	Southern Growth Policies Roundtable	Nashville	TN
07/14/97	Congressional Black Caucus	Washington	DC
07/22/97	Joint Session of the North Carolina Legislature	Raleigh	NC
07/29/97	HUD Conference	Washington	DC
08/05/97	South Pontotoc High School	Pontotoc	MS
08/06/97	Nissan Corporation of America	Gardena	CA
08/06/97	Raymond High School	Raymond	MS
08/13/97	Los Angeles City Human Relations Commission	Los Angeles	CA
08/16/97	American Psychiatric Association	Chicago	IL
08/21/97	Nissan Corporation Task Force	Torrance	CA
08/28/97	Madison Elementary School	Madison	MS
09/04/97	Senate Policy Caucus	Washington	DC
09/08/97	Meeting with Bishop Desmond Tutu	Washington	DC
09/12/97	Congressional Black Caucus Roundtable Discussion	Washington	DC
09/14/97	St. Richard's Catholic Church	Jackson	MS
09/17/97	Congressional Black Caucus	Washington	DC
09/18/97	Top-ranked Mississippi Schools	Jackson	MS
09/19/97	Rand Corporation	Los Angeles	CA
09/25/97	Howard University	Washington	DC
09/25/97	National Conference of Community and Justice Summit	Little Rock	AR
09/27/97	Race Relations and American Public Education System	Washington	DC
09/27/97	The Arts Council–Oakland School District Educators	Oakland	CA
10/01/97	American Association of Medical Colleges	Raleigh	NC
10/03/97	Operation Breadbasket	Chicago	IL
10/03/97	Asian Pacifics in Philanthropy	Los Angeles	CA
10/07/97	National Council of La Raza	Washington	DC
10/10/97	National Association of Urban Bankers	R.T.P.	NC
10/10/97	Hate Crimes Conference (Satellite Site)	Atlanta	GA
10/11/97	Hispanic/Asian American Leaders Meeting	Washington	DC
10/13/97	Feminist Majority	Los Angeles	CA
10/13/97	Penbrook College	Penbrook	NC
10/15/97	Carnegie Corporation	New York	NY
10/15/97	Congressional Hispanic Caucus	Washington	DC
10/16/97	American Council on Education	Miami	FL
10/20/97	California Professional Firefighters Convention	Palm Springs	CA
10/24/97	Asian Pacific American Women's Leadership Institute	Washington	DC

10/26/97	Mt. Calvary United Church of Christ	Durham	NC
10/27/97	L.A. County Board of Supervisors Meeting	Los Angeles	CA
10/27/97	Conference on Race	Chapel Hill	NC
10/28/97	Governor Hunt's Conference on Reconciliation	Charlotte	NC
10/29/97	Southern California Association of Philanthropists	San Diego	CA
10/29/97	Mars Hill College	Mars Hill	NC
10/30/97	"Let's Talk About Race" Dialogue	Durham	NC
10/30/97	California Association of Black Lawyers Conference	Los Angeles	CA
11/04/97	Mississippi Volunteer Leaders	Jackson	MS
11/04/97	Kaiser Permanente Diversity Training Conference	Los Angeles	CA
11/05/97	Fondren Presbyterian Church	Jackson	MS
11/06/97	California State College	Dominguez Hill	CA
11/06/97	"Seeking Understanding," Millsaps College	Jackson	MS
11/07/97	Asian Pacific American Democratic Club of L.A.	Los Angeles	CA
11/08/97	Reconcilers Fellowship	Jackson	MS
11/10/97	Hate Crimes Conference Satellite Site	Los Angeles	CA
11/11/97	Jackson State University	Jackson	MS
11/12/97	National Archives Event	Washington	DC
11/12/97	Grenada High School	Grenada	MS
11/13/97	Consortium on Financing Higher Education	Washington	DC
11/13/97	Southeastern Council on Foundations	Memphis	TN
11/14/97	Pew Entrepreneurial Initiative	Colorado Springs	CO
11/14/97	California Women's Law Center Annual Luncheon	Los Angeles	CA
11/15/97	University of California at Irvine	Irvine	CA
11/17/97	Church Conference	Pickens	MS
11/18/97	National American Hispanic Federal Executives	Arlington	VA
11/18/97	American University Race Initiative	Washington	DC
11/20/97	Religious Leaders Briefing	Washington	DC
11/20/97	National Congress of American Indians Annual Meeting	Sante Fe	NM
11/20/97	"America's Black Forum" Syndicated TV Program	Washington	DC
11/22/97	National Asian Pacific American Bar Association Conference	San Francisco	CA
11/24/97	Asian Pacific American Heritage Celebration	Providence	RI
12/01/97	CEO Roundtable	Miami	FL
12/08/97	Reconcilers Fellowship Meeting	Jackson	MS
12/09/97	Race Town Meeting, National Council of Negro Women	Washington	DC
12/10/97	Minority Business Opportunity: Steering Committee	Los Angeles	CA
12/10/97	Organization of Chinese Americans	San Francisco	CA
12/10/97	Speech to Congress of National Black Churches	Shreveport	LA
12/12/97	Charter High School	Carboro	NC
12/12/97	Loredo Elementary School	Los Angeles	CA
12/15/97	Bailey's Elementary School	Falls Church	VA
12/16/97	Art, Research and Curriculum Associates	San Francisco	CA
12/31/97	Divinity Episcopal Church	Durham	NC

01/04/98	Latino Leaders Initiative, Hosting Dialogue	Los Angeles	CA
01/07/98	Urban League at Broward	Ft. Lauderdale	FL
01/07/98	Crystal Lake Elementary School	Ft. Lauderdale	FL
01/07/98	League of Women Voters	Pasadena	CA
01/07/98	Webster University	Webster Groves	MO
01/07/98	Florissant Community College	St. Louis	MO
01/08/98	National Urban League	Ft. Lauderdale	FL
01/10/98	Stuwart Leadership Conference	Richmond	VA
01/10/98	Arizona Opportunity Industrialization Center	Phoenix	AZ
01/10/98	Arizona Public Service Academy for the Advancement of Minority and Women-Owned Enterprises	Phoenix	AZ
01/10/98	Chicanos Por La Causa	Phoenix	AZ
01/10/98	Phoenix Indian Center	Phoenix	AZ
01/10/98	Maricopa Health Services	Phoenix	AZ
01/12/98	University of Alabama	Tuscaloosa	AL
01/12/98	White House Leadership Forum	Washington	DC
01/13/98	American Indian Tribal Leaders and Tribal Organizations Meeting	Phoenix	AZ
01/15/98	Association of American Colleges and Universities	Washington	DC
01/15/98	National Student Medical Association	Durham	NC
01/15/98	Madison Chamber of Commerce	Madison	MS
01/17/98	Days of Dialogue	Los Angeles	CA
01/18/98	Martin Luther King, Jr., Prayer March and Breakfast	New York	NY
01/18/98	Atlanta Episcopal Cathedral	Atlanta	GA
01/19/98	Good Hope Community Center	Silver Spring	MD
01/19/98	Itawamba Summit	Fulton	MS
01/19/98	Davis Human Relations Commission Community Forum –MLK	Davis	CA
01/19/98	Amaturo Theater Celebration	Ft. Lauderdale	FL
01/19/98	Martin Luther King, Jr., Memorial	Atlanta	GA
01/20/98	Millsaps College	Jackson	MS
01/23/98	Days of Dialogue	South El Monte	CA
01/23/98	NAACP Legal Defense Fund–New York Chapter	New York	NY
01/26/98	President's Commission on Science and Technology	Washington	DC
01/27/98	Glasgow Middle School	Alexandria	VA
01/28/98	Children's Defense Fund	Washington	DC
01/29/98	Maplewood/South Orange Racial Balance Task Force	Maplewood	NJ
01/29/98	U.S. Conference of Mayors	Washington	DC
01/31/98	Asian Pacific Administrators–L.A. Unified School District	Los Angeles	CA
02/04/98	Neighborhood Associates	Jackson	MS
02/04/98	United South and Eastern Tribes Impact Week	Arlington	VA
02/06/98	White House Women's Office	Washington	DC
02/07/98	Muslim Community Group	Jackson	MS
02/10/98	Asian Neighborhood Design	Oakland	CA

02/10/98	Glide Memorial United Methodist Church	San Francisco	CA
02/10/98	Oakland Citizens Committee for Urban Renewal	Oakland	CA
02/10/98	Start-Up	East Palo Alto	CA
02/14/98	Trailblazers Award Banquet	Greensboro	NC
02/14/98	Hunter College	New York	NY
02/18/98	Eckerd College	St. Petersburg	FL
02/19/98	Equal Employment Advisory Council	Washington	DC
02/20/98	Rotary Club	St. Petersburg	FL
02/22/98	National Organization for Women–Women of Color and Allies Summit	Washington	DC
02/23/98	Eagleton Institute of Politics, Rutgers University	New Brunswick	NJ
02/23/98	John Hope Franklin Symposium	Tallahassee	FL
02/23/98	Eagleton Institute of Politics, Rutgers University	New Brunswick	NJ
02/24/98	Pasadena Senior Center	Pasadena	CA
02/24/98	Community Leaders Forum	Jackson	MS
02/24/98	Public Screening for "Race in America"	Los Angeles	CA
02/24/98	Lawrenceville High School	Lawrenceville	NJ
02/25/98	City of L.A., Arts, Health and Humanities Committee	Los Angeles	CA
02/27/98	Speech to Civic Leaders	Winona	MS
03/01/98	Asian Pacific Americans in Higher Education	Los Angeles	CA
03/02/98	Delta Emerging Leaders Forum	Jackson	MS
03/03/98	U.S. Department of Energy	Washington	DC
03/03/98	Lee County Summit	Tupelo	MS
03/04/98	French-American Foundation	Los Angeles	CA
03/04/98	NALEO–Dialogue on Race	Washington	DC
03/05/98	Tougaloo College Students	Jackson	MS
03/05/98	Council of Social Work Education	Miami	FL
03/11/98	New York Coalition of Black Women	New York	NY
03/12/98	Association of Professional Journalists	Indianapolis	IN
03/12/98	Butler University	Indianapolis	IN
03/13/98	Leadership Conference on Civil Rights	Washington	DC
03/16/98	University of Mississippi Town Hall Meeting	Oxford	MS
03/16/98	Civic Leaders	Clarksdale	MS
03/19/98	Icons of the 20th Century	Lincoln	PA
03/19/98	Foundation for Midsouth	Monroe	LA
03/20/98	Supporters of Public Education	Starkville	MS
03/23/98	Tribal Leaders and Indian Organizations Meeting	Denver	CO
03/26/98	Museum of the New South	Charlotte	NC
03/26/98	Korean Youth and Community Center	Los Angeles	CA
03/26/98	Students Talk About Race	Santa Ana	CA
03/27/98	AFL-CIO	Los Angeles	CA
03/27/98	Saint Elmo Village	Los Angeles	CA
03/28/98	Society of Black Engineers	Los Angles	CA
03/28/98	Children's Defense Fund Youth Town Hall Meeting	Los Angeles	CA
03/30/98	Jackson State University	Jackson	MS

04/02/98	Columbia University	New York	NY
04/03/98	Baptist Ministers Conference	New York	NY
04/03/98	American Society of Newspapers	Washington	DC
04/03/98	Campus Week of Dialogue–Stanford University	Palo Alto	CA
04/04/98	Campus Week of Dialogue–U.C. at Irvine	Irvine	CA
04/06/98	Charlotte Area Donor's Forum	Charlotte	NC
04/06/98	Campus Week of Dialogue–Howard University	Washington	DC
04/06/98	Campus Week of Dialogue–Yale University	New Haven	CT
04/06/98	Pine Bluff Development Council	Pine Bluff	AK
04/07/98	Campus Week of Dialogue–Princeton University	Princeton	NJ
04/08/98	Campus Week of Dialogue–Drew University	Madison	NJ
04/08/98	Campus Week of Dialogue–Mississippi University	Oxford	MS
04/08/98	Campus Week–Town Hall Meeting	Madison	NJ
04/08/98	Campus Week of Dialogue–NCCU	Durham	NC
04/09/98	YMCA Breakfast	Charlotte	NC
04/13/98	Blacks in Government	Seattle	WA
04/14/98	ESPN Meeting on Race and Sports	Houston	TX
04/15/98	Dillard University	New Orleans	LA
04/16/98	National Civic League	Washington	DC
04/19/98	Howard University	Washington	DC
04/20/98	Jackson Lions Club	Jackson	MS
04/20/98	Santa Ana College	Santa Ana	CA
04/22/98	University Medical Center	Jackson	MS
04/23/98	Thirtieth Anniversary of the Fair Housing Act	Newark	NJ
04/26/98	Democratic National Committee Race Relations Symposium	Washington	DC
04/27/98	Volunteer Civic Group	Philadelphia	MS
04/27/98	Council on Foundations	Washington	DC
04/27/98	Neighborhood Community Funders Group	Los Angeles	CA
04/28/98	Northwest Coalition Against Malicious Harassment	Seattle	WA
04/29/98	Statewide Days of Dialogue–YWCA	Annapolis	MD
04/29/98	National Issues Forum Institute	Washington	DC
04/30/98	Statewide Days of Dialogue–Emerson Middle School	Los Angeles	CA
04/30/98	Statewide Days of Dialogue–YWCA	Winston-Salem	NC
04/30/98	Statewide Days of Dialogue–Watts Senior Citizens	Los Angeles	CA
04/30/98	Statewide Days of Dialogue–District Attorney Symposium	Los Angeles	CA
04/30/98	Statewide Days of Dialogue	Winston-Salem	NC
05/01/98	Rockefeller Institute	Albany	NY
05/05/98	Asian American/Pacific Islanders in Philanthropy	Los Angeles	CA
05/07/98	California State University at Long Beach	Long Beach	CA
05/08/98	University of Texas Labor and Employment Law Conference	Houston	TX
05/09/98	Asian Pacific American Institute for Congressional Studies	Washington	DC
05/11/98	California State Board of Education	Los Angeles	CA
05/12/98	Meridian Community College	Meridian	MS
05/12/98	Synod Lutheran Leaders	Philadelphia	PA

05/12/98	Latino/Jewish Business Roundtable	Los Angeles	CA
05/14/98	Asian American Public Employees Council	Los Angeles	CA
05/14/98	Jennings High School	St. Louis	MO
05/14/98	St. Louis School Leaders	St. Louis	MO
05/16/98	Trinity Episcopal Church Prayer Breakfast	Durham	NC
05/16/98	Asian Pacific American California School Board Officials	San Diego	CA
05/18/98	Meridian Community College	Meridian	MS
05/18/98	Ecumenical Group of Clergy for D.C. Area	Washington	DC
05/20/98	Joint Center for Political and Economic Studies	Washington	DC
05/20/98	Navajo Nation	Washington	DC
05/21/98	Mississippi Religious Leadership Conference	Jackson	MS
05/23/98	Amherst College Discussion	Amherst	MA
05/27/98	Jewish Federation Urban Affairs Commission	Los Angeles	CA
05/28/98	L.A. County Asian Pacific American Employees Association	Los Angeles	CA
05/28/98	New Jersey Region Conference	Madison	NJ
05/28/98	The City Club	Los Angeles	CA
05/28/98	Multicultural Institute Forum	Washington	DC
05/30/98	National Conference on Race and Ethnicity	Denver	CO
06/01/98	Jackson Exchange Club	Jackson	MS
06/02/98	La Canada High School	Los Angeles	CA
06/03/98	United South and Eastern Tribes Meeting	Nashville	TN
06/04/98	American Bar Association	Los Angeles	CA
06/05/98	Religious Leaders Conference	Hampton	VA
06/10/98	William Day of USET	Jackson	MS
06/12/98	Tufts University	Boston	MA
06/12/98	EOP and OMB Diversity Panel	Washington	DC
06/12/98	Chinese For Affirmative Action	San Francisco	CA
06/13/98	American-Arab Anti-Discrimination Commission	Crystal City	VA
06/16/98	Southern Growth Policies Board	Louisville	KY
06/19/98	Native American Journalists Association	Tempe	AZ
06/20/98	Community Faith Leadership Program	New York	NY
06/20/98	All-American Cities Awards of the National Civic League	Jackson	MS
06/23/98	Speech to Greater Columbia Community Relations	Columbia	SC
06/23/98	Hubert Humphrey Commemoration	St. Paul	MN
06/24/98	Corporate Executives	Los Angeles	CA
06/25/98	Jackson School Principals	Jackson	MS
06/25/98	Writer's Guild	Los Angeles	CA
06/29/98	Southern Regional Education Board	Chapel Hill	NC
07/03/98	American Friends in London	London	UK
07/07/98	Orange County Woman's Lawyer's Association	Los Angeles	CA
07/08/98	Fisk University Keynote Address	Nashville	TN
07/09/98	California School Administrators	Los Angeles	CA
07/09/98	Speech on Race Relations	Mound Bayou	MS
07/10/98	Council of Environmental Equality	Los Angeles	CA
07/10/98	Santa Barbara Woman's Political Caucus	Santa Barbara	CA

07/14/98	IHRLG Meeting	Washington	DC
07/15/98	National Asian Pacific American Legal Consortium	Washington	DC
07/17/98	University of Massachusetts Summer Institute	Boston	MA
07/18/98	Organization of Chinese Americans	Washington	DC
07/22/98	National Convention of Jack & Jill, Inc.	New York	NY
07/23/98	Racial Justice March and Candlelight Vigil	Pittsburgh	PA
07/24/98	Asian Pacific Women's Leadership Institute	Lincoln	NE
07/28/98	Canada's State Sec. for Multiculturalism	Washington	DC
07/29/98	Enterprise Corporation of the Delta	Pine Bluff	AR
07/29/98	National Association of Black Journalists Convention	Washington	DC
07/31/98	University of Southern California	Los Angeles	CA
08/03/98	National Council on Disability	San Francisco	CA
08/04/98	Asian Pacific American Legal Center	Los Angeles	CA
08/06/98	Asian American Journalists Association Convention	Chicago	IL
08/12/98	Town Hall Meeting With Rep. Dooley	Fresno	CA
08/12/98	Margaret Walker Alexander Recognition Ceremony	Jackson	MS
08/14/98	U.S. Information Agency Diversity Council		Brazil
08/14/98	Native and Resident Hawaiian Community	Honolulu	HI
08/14/98	California Commission on the Status of Women	San Francisco	CA
08/15/98	Jackson 2000 Forum	Jackson	MS
08/23/98	ISIS Women's Leadership Group	Long Island	NY
08/27/98	Colorado College	Colorado Springs	CO
09/04/98	Millsaps College	Jackson	MS
09/09/98	Jackson 2000 Forum	Jackson	MS
09/15/98	Washington and Lee University	Lexington	VA
09/17/98	Congressional Black Caucus Forum on Race	Washington	DC
09/18/98	President's Initiative on Race Culminating Event	Washington	DC
09/22/98	Mississippi School Districts Association	Jackson	MS

Appendix D
One America Conversations

One America Conversations were a grassroots outreach effort to engage Americans in the President's national dialogue on race. Approximately 175 conversations were organized by Federal officials and Advisory Board members. In addition, community leaders and individuals who asked how they could become involved in the President's Initiative hosted over 1,200 conversations. These conversations primarily were small groups of friends, neighbors, and coworkers meeting to talk about race. In total, based on the information reported, more than 18,000 people in 36 States, 113 cities, and the District of Columbia have taken part in almost 1,400 dialogues on race. The States and cities in which conversations took place are listed below.

States	Cities
Alabama	Birmingham
Arizona	Phoenix, Tucson
Arkansas	Little Rock, Mayflower
California	Berkeley, Santa Barbara, Inglewood, Oakland, Los Angeles, Monterey, San Bernardino, Chico, San Diego, Sacramento, San Francisco, Englewood, Oakland, Long Beach
Colorado	Denver
Connecticut	New Haven, Hartford
District of Columbia	Washington
Florida	Cocoa Beach, Tallahassee, Miami, Rockledge, Orlando, Tampa
Georgia	Atlanta, Albany
Hawaii	Kailua-Kona
Illinois	Chicago, LaGrange, Park Forest, Champaign-Urbana
Indiana	Terre Haute
Iowa	Davenport
Kansas	Lawrence, Topeka
Kentucky	Lexington
Maryland	Chevy Chase, Baltimore, Emmitsburg, Hyattsville, Largo, Fulton, Silver Spring
Massachusetts	Boston, Martha's Vineyard, Worcester, Brewster
Michigan	Detroit, Holland
Minnesota	St. Paul, Rochester
Mississippi	Jackson
Nebraska	Chadron, Lincoln
Nevada	Las Vegas
New Jersey	Highland Park, Madison, New Brunswick
New Mexico	Albuquerque
New York	New York, South Nyack, Corning, Elmyra, Jamestown, Rochester
North Carolina	Carboro, Winston-Salem, Charlotte, Greenville, Asheville, Greensboro, Brevard, Wilmington, Durham

Ohio	Akron, Oberlin, Marion, Elyria, Cleveland, Columbus
Oregon	Portland
Pennsylvania	Philadelphia, Allentown, Pittsburgh, Lewisburg
Rhode Island	Providence
South Carolina	Charleston, Columbia
Tennessee	Chattanooga, Memphis, Nashville
Texas	Austin, Arlington, Dallas, Houston, San Antonio, Fort Worth
Utah	Salt Lake City
Virginia	Alexandria, Charlottesville, Arlington, Fredericksburg, Fairfax, Stafford
Washington	Seattle, Vancouver, Chehalis, Longview
Wisconsin	Milwaukee

Appendix E
Campus Week of Dialogue

The Advisory Board of the President's Initiative on Race worked with numerous higher education and community organizations to encourage college and university presidents, students, faculty, and administrators to actively participate and sponsor race activities on their campuses during the first week of April 1998. Advisory Board members supported this effort by visiting campuses, engaging students in discussions about race, and encouraging them to sustain dialogue on issues related to race. Nearly 600 schools participated, including community colleges, tribal colleges, and minority-serving institutions from every State, the District of Columbia, and Puerto Rico. Students, campus and community leaders, faculty, staff, and others discussed race in town hall meetings, lectures, film showings, and service events. The following colleges and universities reported race activities and supported the Campus Week of Dialogue.

School Name	City	State
Abilene Christian University	Abilene	TX
Academy of Chinese Culture and Health Sciences	Oakland	CA
Agnes Scott College	Decatur	GA
Aims Community College	Greeley	CO
Albertus Magnus College	New Haven	CT
Alderson-Broaddus College	Philippi	WV
Allegheny University of the Health Sciences	Philadelphia	PA
American Academy of Dramatic Arts	Pasadena	CA
American Institute of Business	Des Moines	IA
American International College	Springfield	MA
American University	Washington	DC
Anderson University	Anderson	IN
Anne Arundel Community College	Arnold	MD
Antioch College	Yellow Springs	OH
Antioch University, The McGregor School	Yellow Springs	OH
Appalachian State University	Boone	NC
Arizona State University West	Phoenix	AZ
Arizona State University, Intergroup Relations Center	Tempe	AZ
Armstrong Atlantic State University	Savannah	GA
Assemblies of God Theological Seminary	Springfield	MO
Auburn University	Auburn	AL
Augusta State University	Augusta	GA
Austin Peay State University	Clarksville	TN
Bank Street College of Education	New York	NY
Barnard College	New York	NY
Barry University	Miami Shores	FL
Bates College	Lewiston	ME
Baylor College of Dentistry, Texas A&M University System	Dallas	TX
Beaver College	Glenside	PA
Belhaven College	Jackson	MS
Bellarmine College	Louisville	KY
Belmont University	Nashville	TN
Benedict College	Columbia	SC

Benedictine College	Atchison	KS
Berkshire Community College	Pittsfield	MA
Bethany Lutheran College	Mankato	MN
Bethel College	McKenzie	TN
Bethune-Cookman College	Daytona Beach	FL
Bloomfield College	Bloomfield	NJ
Blue Ridge Community College	Weyers Cave	VA
Bluffton College	Bluffton	OH
Boise Bible College	Boise	ID
Boise State University	Boise	ID
Boston College	Chestnut Hill	MA
Boston University	Boston	MA
Boston University, Goldman School of Dental Medicine	Boston	MA
Bowling Green State University	Bowling Green	OH
Bowling Green State University, Medical College of Ohio	Toledo	OH
Bradford College	Bradford	MA
Bradley University	Peoria	IL
Bramson ORT Technical Institute	Forest Hills	NY
Brandeis University	Waltham	MA
Brenau University	Gainesville	GA
Brookdale Community College	Lincroft	NJ
Brown University	Providence	RI
Brown University, School of Medicine, Office of Minority Medical Affairs	Providence	RI
Bryn Mawr College	Bryn Mawr	PA
Bucknell University	Lewisburg	PA
Buena Vista University	Storm Lake	IA
Bunker Hill Community College	Boston	MA
Cabrini College	Radnor	PA
Caldwell College	Caldwell	NJ
Caldwell Community College and Technical Institute	Hudson	NC
California College of Podiatric Medicine	San Francisco	CA
California State Polytechnic University, Pomona	Pomona	CA
California State University, Dominguez Hills	Carson	CA
California State University, Humboldt	Arcata	CA
California State University, Los Angeles	Los Angeles	CA
California State University, Monterey Bay	Seaside	CA
California State University, Northridge	Northridge	CA
California State University, Sacramento	Sacramento	CA
California State University, San Bernardino	San Bernardino	CA
California State University, San Marcos	San Marcos	CA
California State University, Stanislaus	Turlock	CA
Cambria County Area Community College	Johnstown	PA
Cambridge College	Cambridge	MA
Cameron University	Lawton	OK
Campbell University School of Law	Buies Creek	NC
Campbellsville University	Campbellsville	KY
Cape Cod Community College	West Barnstable	MA
Carl Albert State College	Poteau	OK
Carlow College	Pittsburgh	PA
Carnegie Mellon University	Pittsburgh	PA
Carroll College	Helena	MT

Carson-Newman College	Jefferson City	TN
Castleton State College	Castleton	VT
Cecil Community College	North East	MD
Centenary College of Louisiana	Shreveport	LA
Center for Creative Studies	Detroit	MI
Central College	Pella	IA
Central Connecticut State University	New Britain	CT
Central Florida Community College	Ocala	FL
Central Methodist College	Fayette	MO
Central Missouri State University, Office of Community Awareness	Warrensburg	MO
Central Wyoming College	Riverton	WY
Centre College	Danville	KY
City College of San Francisco	San Francisco	CA
Clark University	Worcester	MA
Clarkson University	Potsdam	NY
Clover Park Technical College	Lakewood	WA
Clovis Community College	Clovis	NM
Coker College	Hartsville	SC
Colby College	Waterville	ME
College of Lake County	Grayslake	IL
College of New Rochelle	New Rochelle	NY
College of Notre Dame	Belmont	CA
College of Notre Dame of Maryland	Baltimore	MD
College of Oceaneering	Wilmington	CA
College of Our Lady of the Elms	Chicopee	MA
College of the Albemarle	Elizabeth City	NC
College of the Holy Cross	Worcester	MA
College of Wooster	Wooster	OH
Colorado State University	Fort Collins	CO
Columbia College	Columbia	SC
Columbia College Chicago	Chicago	IL
Columbia University	New York	NY
Columbus State Community College	Columbus	OH
Community College of Allegheny County	Pittsburgh	PA
Community College of Aurora	Aurora	CO
Community College of Philadelphia	Philadelphia	PA
Community College of Rhode Island	Providence	RI
Community Colleges of Baltimore County	Catonsville	MD
Concord College	Athens	WV
Cornell University	Ithaca	NY
Creighton University	Omaha	NE
Cuesta College	San Luis Obispo	CA
Culinary Institute of America	Hyde Park	NY
CUNY, Borough of Manhattan Community College	New York	NY
CUNY, Brooklyn College	Brooklyn	NY
CUNY, City College of New York	New York	NY
CUNY, College of Staten Island	Staten Island	NY
CUNY, Hunter College	New York	NY
CUNY, John Jay College of Criminal Justice	New York	NY
CUNY, Lehman College	Bronx	NY
CUNY, Queens College	Flushing	NY
Cypress College	Cypress	CA

Dakota State University	Madison	SD
Dakota Wesleyan University	Mitchell	SD
Dallas County Community College, Office of Education Partnership	Dallas	TX
Dartmouth College	Hanover	NH
Deep Springs College	Dyer	NV
Dekalb College	Decatur	GA
Delaware Technical and Community College	Dover	DE
Delgado Community College	New Orleans	LA
DeVry Institute of Technology, Long Beach	Long Beach	CA
DeVry Institute of Technology, Pomona	Pomona	CA
Dickinson College	Carlisle	PA
Dillard University	New Orleans	LA
Divine Word College	Epworth	IA
Donnelly College	Kansas City	KS
Douglas MacArthur State Technical College	Opp	AL
Drake University	Des Moines	IA
Drew University	Madison	NJ
Duke University	Durham	NC
Dundalk Community College	Baltimore	MD
Durham Technical Community College	Durham	NC
Dyersburg State Community College	Dyersburg	TN
East Carolina University School of Medicine	Greenville	NC
East Carolina University, Department of Minority Student Affairs	Greenville	NC
East Central University	Ada	OK
Eastern Washington University	Cheney	WA
Edgewood College	Madison	WI
Edmonds Community College	Seattle	WA
El Centro College	Dallas	TX
Elizabeth City State University	Elizabeth City	NC
Elmhurst College	Elmhurst	IL
Elon College	Elon	NC
Emory University	Atlanta	GA
Emory University School of Medicine	Atlanta	GA
Fairleigh Dickinson University	Madison	NJ
Fairleigh Dickinson University	Teaneck	NJ
Fairmont State College	Fairmont	WV
Fayetteville State University	Fayetteville	NC
Fayetteville Technical Community College	Fayetteville	NC
Fisk University	Nashville	TN
Fitchburg State College	Fitchburg	MA
Flathead Valley Community College	Kalispell	MT
Fort Hays State University	Hays	KS
Fort Lewis College	Durango	CO
Gainesville College	Gainesville	GA
Gallaudet University, Office of Diversity and Community Relations	Washington	DC
Gateway Technical College	Kenosha	WI
George Washington University	Washington	DC
George Washington University School of Medical-Health Sciences	Washington	DC
Georgetown College	Georgetown	KY
Georgetown University	Washington	DC
Georgia Institute of Technology	Atlanta	GA
Georgia State University, Office of Diversity	Atlanta	GA

Georgia State University College of Law	Atlanta	GA
Germanna Community College	Fredericksburg	VA
Glendale Community College	Glendale	AZ
Gogebic Community College	Ironwood	MI
Gonzaga University	Spokane	WA
Gonzaga University School of Law	Spokane	WA
Goshen College	Goshen	IN
Gwynedd-Mercy College	Gwynedd Valley	PA
Hagerstown Junior College/PACT Center	Hagerstown	MD
Hamline University	St. Paul	MN
Hardin Simmons University	Abilene	TX
Hartwick College	Oneonta	NY
Haskell Indian Nations University	Lawrence	KS
Haverford College	Haverford	PA
Henderson State University	Arkadelphia	AR
Highland Community College	Freeport	IL
Hillsborough Community College	Tampa	FL
Hollins College	Roanoke	VA
Holy Cross College	Notre Dame	IN
Holy Family College	Philadelphia	PA
Hood College	Frederick	MD
Hoosatonic Community Technical College	Bridgeport	CT
Hopkinsville Community College	Hopkinsville	KY
Hostos Community College, Bilingual College	Bronx	NY
Howard University School of Law	Washington	DC
Hunter College	New York	NY
Idaho State University	Pocatello	ID
Illinois State University	Normal	IL
Independence Community College	Independence	KS
Indiana State University	Terre Haute	IN
Indiana University	Bloomington	IN
Indiana University, Kokomo	Kokomo	IN
Indiana University School of Medicine	Indianapolis	IN
Indiana University School of Nursing	Indianapolis	IN
Indiana University Southeast	New Albany	IN
Interdenominational Theological Center	Atlanta	GA
Iowa State University	Ames	IA
Jackson Community College	Jackson	MI
Jackson State University	Jackson	MS
Jacksonville University	Jacksonville	FL
Jersey City State College	Jersey City	NJ
Johns Hopkins Government School	Washington	DC
Johns Hopkins University	Baltimore	MD
Johns Hopkins University School of Medicine	Baltimore	MD
Johnson and Wales University	Charleston	SC
Kalamazoo Valley Community College	Kalamazoo	MI
Kean University	Union	NJ
Keene State College	Keene	NH
Kellogg Community College	Battle Creek	MI
Kent State University	Kent	OH
Keystone College	LaPlume	PA
Kilian Community College	Sioux Falls	SD

Lackawanna Junior College	Scranton	PA
Lafayette College	Easton	PA
Lake Superior College	Duluth	MN
Lake Washington Technical College	Kirkland	WA
Landmark College	Putney	VT
LeMoyne-Owen College	Memphis	TN
Lesley College	Cambridge	MA
Lexington Community College	Lexington	KY
Lincoln Land Community College	Springfield	IL
Lincoln University, Barrier Breakers	Jefferson City	MO
Linfield College	McMinnville	OR
Little Big Horn College	Crow Agency	MT
Lock Haven University of Pennsylvania	Lock Haven	PA
Loma Linda University, School of Nursing and Graduate School	Loma Linda	CA
Longview Community College	Lee's Summit	MO
Longwood College, Office of Multicultural Affairs	Farmville	VA
Los Angeles City College	Los Angeles	CA
Los Angeles Mission College	Sylmar	CA
Louisiana State University Medical School	New Orleans	LA
Loyola Marymount University	Los Angeles	CA
Loyola University, Chicago	Chicago	IL
Macalester College	St. Paul	MN
Madonna University	Livonia	MI
Manatee Community College	Bradenton	FL
Manchester Community Technical College	Manchester	CT
Mankato State University	Mankato	MN
Marquette University	Milwaukee	WI
Marygrove College	Detroit	MI
Marymount Manhattan College	New York	NY
Marywood University	Scranton	PA
Massachusetts College of Liberal Arts	North Adams	MA
Massachusetts Institute of Technology	Cambridge	MA
McKendree College, Lebanon	Lebanon	IL
Medical University of South Carolina	Carleston	SC
Miami University	Oxford	OH
Miami-Dade Community College, Wolfson Campus	Miami	FL
Michigan State University	East Lansing	MI
Middlesex Community Technical College	Middletown	CT
Midway College	Midway	KY
Millikin University	Decatur	IL
Miramar College	San Diego	CA
Mississippi Valley State University	Itta Bena	MS
Missouri Southern State College	Joplin	MO
Moberly Area Community College	Moberly	MO
Monmouth College	Monmouth	IL
Montana State University, Northern	Havre	MT
Moravian College	Bethlehem	PA
Morehouse College	Atlanta	GA
Morris Brown College	Atlanta	GA
Morris College	Sumter	SC
Morton College	Cicero	IL
Mount Ida College	Newton Centre	MA

Mount Mary College	Milwaukee	WI
Mount Olive College	Mount Olive	NC
Mount St. Mary's College	Emmitsburg	MD
Mount St. Mary's College	Los Angeles	CA
Mount Union College	Alliance	OH
Mount Wachusett Community College	Gardner	MA
Napa Valley College	Napa	CA
Nash Community College	Rocky Mount	NC
National Defense University	Washington	DC
National-Louis University	Atlanta	GA
Nazareth College	Rochester	NY
New Mexico Highlands University	Las Vegas	NM
New York City Technical College	Brooklyn	NY
North Carolina Central University	Durham	NC
North Carolina Central University School of Law	Durham	NC
North Central Missouri College	Trenton	MO
North Hennepin Community College	Brooklyn Park	MN
Northampton Community College	Bethlehem	PA
Northeast Community College	Norfolk	NE
Northeastern Illinois University	Chicago	IL
Northeastern Junior College	Sterling	CO
Northeastern University	Boston	MA
Northeastern University School of Law	Boston	MA
Northern Essex Community College	Haverhill	MA
Northern Kentucky University	Highland Heights	KY
Northern Michigan University	Marquette	MI
Northwestern University	Evanston	IL
Northwestern University, The Graduate School	Evanston	IL
Norwalk Community Technical College	Norwalk	CT
Notre Dame College of Ohio	South Euclid	OH
Nova Southeastern University	Fort Lauderdale	FL
Oberlin College	Oberlin	OH
Occidental College	Los Angeles	CA
Oglethorpe University	Atlanta	GA
Ohio Dominican College	Columbus	OH
Ohio State University	Columbus	OH
Olivet College	Olivet	MI
Ouachita Baptist University	Arleadelphia	AR
Our Lady of the Lake University	San Antonio	TX
Pacific Lutheran University	Tacoma	WA
Pacific Oaks College	Pasadena	CA
Pacific University	Forest Grove	OR
Paducah Community College	Paducah	KY
Pasadena City College	Pasadena	CA
Pasco-Hernando Community College	New Port Fichey	FL
Patricia Stevens College	St. Louis	MO
Paul D. Camp Community College, Oliver K. Hobbs Campus	Suffolk	VA
Payne Theological Seminary	Willberforce	OH
Penn Valley Community College	Kansas City	MO
Pennsylvania State, Lehigh Valley Campus	Fogelsville	PA
Pepperdine University	Malibu	CA
Pfeiffer University	Misenheimer	NC

Philadelphia College of Textiles and Science	Philadelphia	PA
Pitt Community College	Greenville	NC
Pittsburg State University	Pittsburg	KS
Pitzer College	Claremont	CA
Plymouth State College	Plymouth	NH
Portland State University	Portland	OR
Pratt Community College	Pratt	KS
Prestonsburg Community College	Prestonsburg	KY
Princeton University	Princeton	NJ
Quinsigamond Community College	Worcester	MA
Radford University	Radford	VA
Randolph-Macon College	Ashland	VA
Reed College	Portland	OR
Regis College	Weston	MA
Rice University	Houston	TX
Ripon College	Ripon	WI
Riverland Community College	Austin	MN
Roanoke-Chowan Community College	Ahoskie	NC
Rollins College	Winter Park	FL
Rose State College	Midwest City	OK
Rowan University	Glasboro	NJ
Rowan University, Office of Multicultural/International Affairs	Glassboro	NJ
Rust College	Holly Springs	MS
Rutgers Law School, Newark	Newark	NJ
Rutgers University	Newark	NJ
Rutgers University	Camden	NJ
Sacramento City College	Sacramento	CA
Saint Augustine's College	Raleigh	NC
Saint Michael's College	Colchester	VT
Saint Peter's College	Jersey City	NJ
Salisbury State University	Salisbury	MD
Salish Kootenai College	Pablo	MT
San Diego State University	San Diego	CA
San Francisco State University	San Francisco	CA
San Joaquin Delta College	Stockton	CA
San Jose State University	San Jose	CA
Santa Fe Community College	Santa Fe	NM
Sarah Lawrence College	Bronxville	NY
Sauk Valley Community College	Dixon	IL
School for International Training	Brattleboro	VT
Scott Community College, Eastern Iowa Community College District	Bettendorf	IA
Seattle Central Community College	Seattle	WA
Seton Hall University	South Orange	NJ
Seton Hill College	Greensburg	PA
Shaw University	Raleigh	NC
Shippensburg University of Pennsylvania	Shippensburg	PA
Shoreline Community College	Seattle	WA
Sierra Community College	Rocklin	CA
Sisseton Wahpeton Community College	Sisseton	SD
Skagit Valley College	Mount Vernon	WA
Skidmore College	Saratoga Springs	NY
South Carolina State University	Orangeburg	SC

South Seattle Community College	Seattle	WA
Southeast Community College	Lincoln	NE
Southeastern Louisiana University	Hammond	LA
Southeastern University	Washington	DC
Southern Illinois University School of Dental Medicine	Alton	IL
Southern New England School of Law	North Dartmouth	MA
Southern Oregon University	Ashland	OR
Southwest State University	Marshall	MN
Southwest Texas State University	San Marcos	TX
Southwestern University	Georgetown	TX
Spalding University	Louisville	KY
Spelman College	Atlanta	GA
Spring Hill College	Mobile	AL
Springfield Technical Community College	Springfield	MA
St. John's University	Collegeville	MN
St. Joseph's College, New York	Brooklyn	NY
St. Louis Community College at Florissant Valley	St. Louis	MO
Stanford University	Stanford	CA
State University of West Georgia	Carrollton	GA
Stephen F. Austin State University	Nacogdoches	TX
Stonehill College	Easton	MA
Suffolk University	Boston	MA
Sul Ross State University	Alpine	TX
SUNY Albany	Albany	NY
SUNY Binghamton	Binghamton	NY
SUNY Brockport	Brockport	NY
SUNY Buffalo	Buffalo	NY
SUNY Buffalo School of Dental Medicine	Buffalo	NY
SUNY College of Technology at Delhi	Delhi	NY
SUNY Fredonia	Fredonia	NY
SUNY Health Science Center at Syracuse	Syracuse	NY
SUNY New Paltz	New Paltz	NY
SUNY Oswego	Oswego	NY
SUNY Potsdam	Potsdam	NY
Susquehanna University	Selingrove	PA
Sussex County Community College	Newton	NJ
Swarthmore College	Swarthmore	PA
Syracuse University College of Law	Syracuse	NY
Tacoma Community College	Tacoma	WA
Tarrant County Junior College, South Campus	Fort Worth	TX
Temple University	Philadelphia	PA
Texas A&M University	College Station	TX
Texas A&M University, Commerce	Commerce	TX
Texas A&M University Health Science Center College of Medicine	College Station	TX
Texas Wesleyan University	Fort Worth	TX
The College of West Virginia	Beckley	WV
Three Rivers Community-Technical College	Norwich	CT
Tomball College	Tomball	TX
Towson University	Towson	MD
Transylvania University	Lexington	KY
Trinity College	Washington	DC
Trinity College	Hartford	CT

Troy State University	Troy	AL
Truckee Meadows Community College	Reno	NV
Tunxis Community-Technical College	Farmington	CT
Tyler Junior College	Tyler	TX
UMDNJ, New Jersey Medical School	Newark	NJ
UMDNJ, Robert Wood Johnson Medical School	Piscataway	NJ
United States Air Force Academy	Colorado Springs	CO
Universidad Central Del Caribe	Bayamon	PR
Universidad Interamericana de Puerto Rico	Arecibo	PR
Universidad Metropolitana	Rio Piedras	PR
University of Akron	Akron	OH
University of Akron School of Law	Akron	OH
University of Akron, Wayne College	Orrville	OH
University of Alaska, Anchorage	Anchorage	AK
University of Arkansas at Little Rock School of Law	Little Rock	AR
University of Arkansas at Pine Bluff	Pine Bluff	AR
University of Arkansas for Medical Sciences	Little Rock	AR
University of Baltimore	Baltimore	MD
University of California, Berkeley	Berkeley	CA
University of California, Irvine, Cross Cultural Center	Irvine	CA
University of California, Los Angeles, Vice Chancellor's office	Los Angeles	CA
University of California, San Francisco	San Francisco	CA
University of California, Santa Barbara, Associated Students	Santa Barbara	CA
University of California, Santa Cruz	Santa Cruz	CA
University of Cincinnati College of Law	Cincinnati	OH
University of Colorado, Boulder	Boulder	CO
University of Connecticut, African-American Cultural Center	Storrs	CT
University of Connecticut, Asian American Cultural Center	Storrs	CT
University of Evansville	Evansville	IN
University of Florida, College of Medicine	Gainesville	FL
University of Florida, Office for Student Services	Gainesville	FL
University of Hartford	West Hartford	CT
University of Hawaii, Hilo	Hilo	HI
University of Hawaii, John A. Burns School of Medicine	Honolulu	HI
University of Hawaii, Manoa	Honolulu	HI
University of Illinois, Chicago	Chicago	IL
University of Illinois, Urbana-Champaign	Urbana	IL
University of Maryland, Baltimore County	Baltimore	MD
University of Maryland, College Park	College Park	MD
University of Massachusetts, Amherst	Amherst	MA
University of Massachusetts, Boston	Dorchester	MA
University of Massachusetts, Dartmouth	North Dartmouth	MA
University of Massachusetts, Lowell	Lowell	MA
University of Michigan	Ann Arbor	MI
University of Minnesota, Twin Cities	Minneapolis	MN
University of Mississippi	University	MS
University of Mississippi Medical Center	Jackson	MS
University of Missouri, Columbia	Columbia	MO
University of Montana	Missoula	MT
University of Nebraska at Kearney	Kearney	NE
University of Nevada, Las Vegas	Las Vegas	NV
University of Nevada, Reno	Reno	NV

University of Nevada School of Medicine	Reno	NV
University of New Hampshire	Durham	NH
University of New Mexico, Los Alamos	Los Alamos	NM
University of North Alabama	Florence	AL
University of North Michigan	Hancock	MI
University of North Carolina at Chapel Hill	Chapel Hill	NC
University of North Carolina at Greensboro	Greensboro	NC
University of North Dakota, Grand Forks	Grand Forks	ND
University of North Texas Health Science Center, Fort Worth	Fort Worth	TX
University of Northern Colorado	Greeley	CO
University of Oregon	Eugene	OR
University of Oregon, ASUO	Eugene	OR
University of Oregon School of Law	Eugene	OR
University of Pennsylvania	Philadelphia	PA
University of Pittsburgh	Pittsburgh	PA
University of Pittsburgh at Greensburg	Greensburg	PA
University of Rochester School of Medicine and Dentistry	Rochester	NY
University of San Diego	San Diego	CA
University of San Francisco	San Francisco	CA
University of South Alabama	Mobile	AL
University of South Florida, Tampa	Tampa	FL
University of Southern California Law School	Los Angeles	CA
University of Southern California School of Medicine	Los Angeles	CA
University of Southern Mississippi	Hattiesburg	MS
University of Southwestern Louisiana	Lafayette	LA
University of St. Thomas	St. Paul	MN
University of Tennessee at Chattanooga	Chattanooga	TN
University of Tennessee at Knoxville	Knoxville	TN
University of Tennessee at Martin, Department of Psychology and Philosophy	Martin	TN
University of Texas, Pan American	Edinburg	TX
University of Texas at Austin	Austin	TX
University of Texas at El Paso	El Paso	TX
University of Texas at San Antonio	San Antonio	TX
University of Texas Health Science Center	Houston	TX
University of Vermont	Burlington	VT
University of Virginia	Charlottesville	VA
University of Washington, Office of Minority Affairs	Seattle	WA
University of West Florida	Pensacola	FL
University of Wisconsin, La Crosse	La Crosse	WI
University of Wisconsin, Madison	Madison	WI
University of Wisconsin, Milwaukee	Brookfield	WI
University of Wisconsin, Milwaukee	Milwaukee	WI
University of Wisconsin, Platteville	Platteville	WI
University of Wisconsin, River Falls	River Falls	WI
University of Wisconsin, Stevens Point	Stevens Point	WI
University of Wisconsin, Whitewater	Whitewater	WI
Utah Valley State College	Orem	UT
Valdosta State University	Valdosta	GA
Villanova University	Villanova	PA
Virginia Polytechnic University	Blacksburg	VA
Virginia State University	Petersburg	VA

Wake Forest University School of Medicine, Department of Pathology	Winston-Salem	NC
Wallace State Community College, Selma	Selma	AL
Washington and Jefferson College	Washington	PA
Washington College	Chestertown	MD
Washington College of Law/American University	Washington	DC
Washington State University	Pullman	WA
Washington University	St. Louis	MO
Waubonsee Community College	Sugar Grove	IL
Waycross College	Waycross	GA
Wayne County Community College District	Detroit	MI
Wayne State College	Wayne	NE
Wayne State University	Detroit	MI
Wayne State University School of Medicine	Detroit	MI
Wayne State University, Law School, Dean's Office	Detroit	MI
Wesleyan College	Macon	GA
West Chester University	West Chester	PA
West Los Angeles College	Culver City	CA
West Shore Community College	Scottville	MI
West Virginia State College	Institute	WV
West Virginia University	Morgantown	WV
Western New Mexico University	Silver City	NM
Western Wisconsin Technical College	La Crosse	WI
Westmont College	Santa Barbara	CA
Wharton County Junior College	Wharton	TX
Wheaton College	Norton	MA
Wheelock College, Student Government Association	Boston	MA
Whitworth College	Spokane	WA
Widener University	Chester	PA
Widener University School of Law, The Delaware Campus	Wilmington	DE
Wiley College	Marshall	TX
Wilkes University and King's College	Wilkes-Barre	PA
William Mitchell College of Law	St. Paul	MN
William Penn College	Oskaloosa	IA
Winona State University	Winona	MN
Winston-Salem State University	Winston-Salem	NC
Worcester Polytechnic Institute	Worcester	MA
Worcester State College	Worcester	MA
Wright State University	Dayton	OH
Xavier University	Cincinnati	OH
Yale University School of Medicine, Office of Multicultural Affairs	New Haven	CT
York College of Pennsylvania	York	PA

Appendix F
Statewide Days of Dialogue

Statewide Days of Dialogue focused on getting State and community leaders to draw attention to the importance of dialogue about race. It began on April 30, 1998, in conjunction with the YWCA's National Day of Commitment to Eliminate Racism and Erase the Hate. With encouragement and support from the Advisory Board, YWCA affiliates in 110 locations collaborated with local partners to organize discussions on race. In addition, Governors in 39 States and 2 territories and mayors in 25 cities issued proclamations in support of dialogues or participated in race-related events. Listed below are the cities and States that took part in Statewide Days of Dialogue.

Governors Participating in Statewide Days of Dialogue

State	Governor
Arkansas	Huckabee
Alabama	James
California	Wilson
Colorado	Romer
Delaware	Carper
Florida	Chiles
Georgia	Miller
Guam	Gutierrez
Hawaii	Cayetano
Idaho	Batt
Illinois	Edgar
Indiana	O'Bannon
Kentucky	Patton
Louisiana	Foster
Massachusetts	Celluci
Maryland	Glendening
Michigan	Engler
Minnesota	Carlson
Mississippi	Fordice
Missouri	Carnahan
North Carolina	Hunt
Nebraska	Nelson
Nevada	Miller
New Hampshire	Shaheen
New Jersey	Whitman
New Mexico	Johnson
New York	Pataki
Ohio	Voinovich
Oklahoma	Keating
Oregon	Kitzhaber

Pennsylvania	Ridge
Puerto Rico	Rossello
Rhode Island	Almond
South Carolina	Beasley
South Dakota	Janklow
Tennessee	Sundquist
Utah	Leavitt
Vermont	Dean
Washington	Locke
West Virginia	Underwood
Wisconsin	Thompson

Mayors Participating in Statewide Days of Dialogue

State	City	Mayor
Alabama	Birmingham	Arrington, Jr.
Connecticut	New Britain	Pawlak
Delaware	Wilmington	Sills
Georgia	Atlanta	Campbell
Georgia	Macon	Marshall
Illinois	Aurora	Stover
Illinois	Chicago	Daley
Illinois	Sterling	Aggen
Indiana	Anderson	Lawler
Indiana	Elkhart	Perron
Indiana	Fort Wayne	Helmke
Indiana	Muncie	Cannan
Indiana	Richmond	Andrews
Indiana	South Bend	Luecke
Kentucky	Frankfort	May, Jr.
Louisiana	Alexandria	Randolph, Jr.
Maryland	Annapolis	Johnson
New York	Jamestown	Kimball, Jr.
North Carolina	Asheville	Sitnick
Ohio	Canton	Watkins
Pennsylvania	Allentown	Heydt
Pennsylvania	Harrisburg	Reed
Pennsylvania	Lancaster	Smithgall
South Carolina	Columbia	Coble
Utah	Salt Lake City	Corradini

The Advisory Board supported the creation of a guide to assist those who have not engaged in dialogue about race issues or who need assistance in organizing this type of dialogue. In March 1998, the Initiative and the Community Relations Service of the U.S. Department of Justice collaborated with several nonprofit organizations specializing in race (Hope In The Cities, National Multicultural Institute, YWCA, National Days of Dialogue, Study Circles Resource Center, and the National Conference on Community and Justice) to draft and publish the *One America Dialogue Guide*. The following excerpts from the *Guide* provide useful information about having conversations about race. A complete copy of the *Guide* is available on the World Wide Web on the Internet at the following address:

www.whitehouse.gov/Initiatives/OneAmerica/america.html

Characteristics of Community Dialogues on Race

What do we mean by dialogue?

A dialogue is a forum that draws participants from as many parts of the community as possible to exchange information face-to-face, share personal stories and experiences, honestly express perspectives, clarify viewpoints, and develop solutions to community concerns.

Unlike debate, dialogue emphasizes listening to deepen understanding. Dialogue invites discovery. It develops common values and allows participants to express their own interests. It expects that participants will grow in understanding and may decide to act together with common goals. In dialogue, participants can question and reevaluate their assumptions. Through this process, people are learning to work together to improve race relations.

What makes for successful interracial dialogue?

The nature of the dialogue process can motivate people to work towards change. Effective dialogues do the following:

Move towards solutions rather than continue to express or analyze the problem. An emphasis on personal responsibility moves the discussion away from finger-pointing or naming enemies and toward constructive common action.

Reach beyond the usual boundaries. When fully developed, dialogues can involve the entire community, offering opportunities for new, unexpected partnerships. New partnerships can develop when participants listen carefully and respectfully to each other. A search for solutions focuses on the common good as participants are encouraged to broaden their horizons and build relationships outside their comfort zones.

Unite divided communities through a respectful, informed sharing of local racial history and its consequences for different people in today's society. The experience of "walking through history" together can lead to healing.

Aim for a change of heart, not just a change of mind. Dialogues go beyond sharing and understanding to transforming participants. While the process begins with the individual, it eventually involves groups and institutions. Ultimately, dialogues can affect how policies are made.

Tips for a Dialogue Leader

The following tips describe what a good dialogue leader should strive to do:

Set a relaxed and open tone. Welcome everyone and create a friendly and relaxed atmosphere. Well-placed humor is usually appreciated.

Stay neutral. This may be the most important point to remember as the leader of a dialogue. You should not share your personal views or try to advance your agenda on the issue. You are there to serve the discussion, not to join it.

Stress the importance of confidentiality. Make sure participants understand that what they say during the dialogue session is to be kept completely confidential. Define for them what confidential means. For instance, it is not all right to speak outside of the dialogue about what someone else said or did. It is all right to share one's own personal insights about the issue of race and racism as a result of the process.

Encourage openness about language. Dialogue leaders should encourage participants to offer preferred terms if a biased or offensive word or phrase should come up during the dialogue.

Provide bilingual translation, if necessary. Also, ensure that provided material is translated into the participant's first language, or recruit bilingual discussion leaders.

Keep track of who is contributing and who is not. Always use your "third eye." You are not only helping to keep the group focused on the content of the discussion, but you are monitoring how well participants are communicating with each other— who has spoken, who has not, and whose points have not yet received a fair hearing. A dialogue leader must constantly weigh group needs against the requirements of individual members.

Follow and focus the conversation flow. A dialogue leader who listens carefully will select topics raised in the initial sharing. To help keep the group on the topic, it is helpful to occasionally restate the key question or insight under discussion. It is important to guide gently, yet persistently. You might ask, "How does your point relate to the topic?" Or state, "That's an interesting point, but let's return to the central issue." Keep careful track of time.

Do not fear silence. It is all right if people are quiet for a while. When deciding when to intervene, err on the side of nonintervention. The group will work its way out of a difficult situation. Sometimes group members only need more time to think through alternatives or to consider what has just been said.

Accept and summarize expressed opinions. "Accepting" shows respect for each participant in the group. It is important for the dialogue leader to make it clear that dialogue discussions involve no right or wrong responses. One way to show acceptance and respect is to briefly summarize what is heard and to convey the feeling with which it was shared. Reflecting both the content and the feeling lets the person know that she or he has been heard. For example, you might say: "*It sounds like you felt hurt when you were slighted by someone of a different race.*" Once in a while, ask participants to sum up the most important points that have come out in the discussion. This gives the group a sense of accomplishment and a point of reference for more sharing.

Anticipate conflict and tend to the ground rules. When conflict arises, explain that disagreement over ideas is to be expected. Remind participants that conflict must stay on the issue. Do not allow it to become personal. Appeal to the group to help resolve the conflict and abide by the ground rules. You may have to stop and reference the ground rules several times throughout the discussion.

Close the dialogue. Give participants a chance to talk about the most important thing they gained from the discussion. You may ask them to share any new ideas or thoughts they've had as a result of the discussion. Ask them to think about what worked and what didn't. You may want to encourage the group to design a closing activity for use at each session. Provide some time for the group to evaluate the process in writing. A brief evaluation allows participants the chance to comment on the process and to give feedback to the dialogue leader. Remember to thank everyone for their participation.

A Sample Small Group Dialogue

The following is an overview of a generic small group dialogue. This format is based on a group of 8 to 15 participants, guided by an impartial leader using discussion materials or questions. As a rule, adults meet for two hours at a time; young people for an hour to an hour and a half.

1. **Introductions, roles, and intentions of the dialogue.** The session begins with group members briefly introducing themselves after the dialogue leader has welcomed everyone. The dialogue leader explains his or her role as "neutral," one of guiding the discussion without adding personal opinions. It is important to include an overview of the dialogue effort, the number of meetings planned, the organizers, the goals of the program, and any other relevant information.

2. **Ground rules.** Central to the opening dialogue is establishing ground rules for the group's behavior and discussion. Start with a basic list and add any others the group wants to include. The dialogue leader posts the ground rules where everyone can see them and adds more to the list as needed. The group should be sure to discuss how to handle conflict and disagreement, as well as the need for confidentiality.

3. **Discussion.** The dialogue leader begins by asking participants what attracted them to this dialogue, perhaps asking, "Why are you concerned about issues of race?" or "How have your experiences or concerns influenced your opinions about race?" The heart of the discussion follows. Members can answer a series of questions, use prepared discussion materials with various viewpoints, read newspaper articles or editorials, look at television clips, or review information on the state of race relations in their community. Whatever method is selected, it is important to structure the discussion so that it goes somewhere, is grounded in concrete examples, and offers participants a chance to take action on the issues. Dialogue participants may get frustrated if they feel the conversation is too abstract, too vague, or "going around in circles."

The dialogue leader keeps track of how the discussion is going. Is it time for a clarifying question or a summary of key points? Are all members fully engaged, or are some people dominating? Is the discussion wandering and calling for a change in direction? The participants can summarize the most important results of their discussion and consider what action they might take individually or together.

4. **Evaluation and conclusion.** In the final minutes, participants can offer their thoughts on the experience. If meeting again, this is the time to look ahead to the next meeting. If this the last dialogue, the dialogue leaders thanks the participants and ask for any final thoughts for staying involved in the effort. Participant evaluations of the dialogue can be expressed verbally and/or in writing. It may also be helpful for dialogues to be loosely recorded, if possible. Such documentation could help to measure the success of the dialogue and identify any needed improvements.

Suggested Basic Ground Rules for Dialogues

Some basic ground rules for dialogues might include the following:

We will respect confidentiality.

We will share time equitably to ensure the participation of all.

We will listen carefully and not interrupt.

We will keep an open mind and be open to learning.

We will not be disrespectful of the speaker even when we do not respect the views.

Appendix H*
Promising Practices

Communities, organizations and individuals are working together to build greater understanding across racial lines and overcome racial disparities by expanding opportunities in critical areas such as health care, education, and community and economic development. Since the beginning of the President's Initiative on Race, hundreds of organizations pursuing these goals have come to the attention of the Advisory Board, but this list of programs is by no means exhaustive.

These programs reflect a wide diversity of types, sizes, regions, and sectors of society. They attempt to make a difference in one or more of the following areas: reasonably reflecting the diversity of the local area; incorporating race consciousness in design and operation; educating about facts relating to race and culture; encouraging reflection and sharing feelings about race; encouraging civic engagement; fostering institutional change; or having a measurable impact on the participants or community. We are not making any judgments about the relative success of these programs. Rather, we hope that listing these promising practices will inspire others to become involved in programs like them and replace those that are working.

More information about these promising practices is available on the World Wide Web at the following address: http://clinton3.nara.gov/Initiatives/OneAmerica/pirsummary.html

*Appendices H-1 and H-2, listing all of the programs, their brief descriptions, personnel, and contact information, have been deleted since so much of the information has changed since 1998.

NOTES TO THE REPORT

The following notes are provided by the editor to explain or update material in the report.

[p. 37, "From the abolitionists":] The Leadership Conference on Civil Rights was founded in 1950 and consists of more than 192 national organizations. Its objective is to lobby for civil rights legislation and its enforcement.

[p. 50, "Today, as of the 1990 Census":] According to government figures from the 2004 Census, Hispanics constituted 14.2 percent of the U.S. population, African Americans 12.2 percent, Asians 4.2 percent, and American Indians and Alaska Natives 0.8 percent.

[p. 51, "The percentage of whites":] Figures for 2003 show 5.7 percent of married couples living in households with partners of different races, and 12.2 percent of unmarried, opposite sex partners living in such households. The figures for Hispanic households were 3.1 percent and 6.4 percent, respectively (http://www.census.gov/prod/2003pubs/censr-5/.pdf). Black men tend to marry non-blacks more often than black women do. Whereas 10 percent of married black men had a spouse of a different race or ethnicity, only 5 percent of married black women did.

[p. 58, "The goal would be":] For FY 1999, Clinton requested 10.6 percent more funding than was appropriated for the Office of Civil Rights in FY 1998. Congress did not accede to the president's request and instead appropriated an increase of 7.3 percent.

[p. 61, "Such efforts could include":] Head Start, Early Head Start, and Even Start are comprehensive child development programs, which serve children from birth to age five, as well as pregnant women and their families. They attempt to prepare low-income children for school. Head Start, the oldest of the three, was created under the administration of Lyndon Johnson as part of the War on Poverty.

[p. 62, "A larger, more comprehensive effort":] In 1998, Clinton signed into law the Higher Education Amendments, which extended low interest rates for student loans. It also created the "High Hopes" initiative, where colleges provided support for middle-school students in high poverty areas to help ready them for higher education. The measure included the Initiative to Get Good Teachers to Underserved Areas, which the report highlighted.

[p. 66, "What is not clear":] As of 2003, the percentage of the population on welfare remained around 3.3 percent. Department of Health and Human Services, "Indicators of Welfare Dependence: Annual Report to Congress, 2005," http://aspe.hhs.gov/hsp/indictors05/execsum.htm.

[p. 69, "A higher minimum wage":] In 2007 the minimum wage increased from $5.15 to $5.85, the first increase since the report was written. The minimum wage is scheduled to rise to $6.55 in 2008 and $7.25 in 2009.

[p. 78, "Such actions would send":] On June 17, 2003, the U.S. Department of Justice put out a "Fact Sheet" on racial profiling, which defined the problem and provided methods of dealing with it. See www.UDDOJ.gov.

[p. 78, "We strongly support":] Disparities in sentencing for crack versus powder cocaine remain.

[p. 82, "For example, a similarly targeted effort":] The number of American children without health coverage has declined largely as a result of CHIP. In 2005 there were 350,000 fewer uninsured children than in 2000. Twelve percent of youngsters under eighteen years of age were still without coverage, compared to 16 percent for adults. Overall, 46 million Americans, up from previous years, did not have health insurance. See *New York Times*, December 4, 2005, 1. In 2005, Congress did expand coverage of Medicare for prescription drugs, but a universal health insurance program still does not exist for all Americans.

[p. 85, "A mediation and community building function":] The 1964 Civil Rights Act created the Community Relations Service. It assists state and local governments, preventing and resolving racial and ethnic disputes.

[p. 89, "The White House monograph":] The monograph series did not materialize.

Suggestions for Further Reading

Anderson, Terry. *The Pursuit of Fairness: A History of Affirmative Action.* New York, Oxford University Press, 2004.

Clinton, Bill. *My Life.* New York, Alfred A. Knopf, 2004.

Dulles, Foster Rhea. *The Civil Rights Commission, 1957–1965.* Ann Arbor, University of Michigan Press, 1968.

Franklin, John Hope. *Mirror to America.* New York, Farrar, Straus, and Giroux, 2005.

Lawson, Steven F. *In Pursuit of Power: Southern Blacks and Electoral Politics, 1965–1982,* New York, Columbia University Press, 1985.

Lawson, Steven F., ed. *To Secure These Rights: The Report of President Harry S Truman's Committee on Civil Rights,* Boston: Bedford/St. Martin's, 2004.

Rainwater, Lee, and William L. Yancey. *The Moynihan Report and the Politics of Controversy.* Cambridge, M.I.T. Press, 1967.

Singh, Nikhil Pal. *Black Is a Country: Race and the Unfinished Struggle for Democracy.* Cambridge, Harvard University Press, 2005.

Report of the National Advisory Commission on Civil Disorders. New York, Bantam Books, 1968.

Wickham, DeWayne. *Bill Clinton and Black America.* New York, Ballantine, 2002.

Walters, Ronald W. *Freedom Is Not Enough: Black Voters, Black Candidates, and American Presidential Politics.* Lanham, MD, Rowman and Littlefield, 2005.

Questions for Further Study*

1. Why did President Clinton appoint the Race Initiative Advisory Board? How do you explain his timing?

2. What are the assumptions behind the report?

3. Why does the report place so much emphasis on dialogue?

4. What is the most important recommendation made in the report?

5. If you were writing the report today, would you reach the same conclusion?

6. Who is the primary audience for this report? Is it merely "preaching to the choir"?

7. How did conservatives react to the report? What do you think of their response?

8. The writing in the report is sometimes repetitive. Do you think that this is a matter of carelessness, or is it deliberate? If so, why?

9. How does the membership of the committee affect its findings?

10. Why was it important that John Hope Franklin was appointed to chair the board?

11. Why do you think more was not done to carry out the report's recommendations? Was it simply a matter of President Clinton being distracted by the impeachment process?

12. Do you think that the problems of African Americans should still be emphasized in the twenty-first century, when they are no longer the nation's largest minority group? How relevant are the issues of African Americans to other minority groups? Do racial differences cause the same problems as ethnic differences? Explain.

13. Has the United States become a "color-blind society" in the twenty-first century?

14. This government advisory board made recommendations that involved government action. How much of the solution to problems should come from government; how much from private corporations; and how much from the minority groups themselves?

*Added for classroom use by Steven Lawson (not part of original report).